CHANGING TO THRIVE

Using the Stages of Change to Overcome
the Top Threats to Your Health and Happiness

JAMES O. PROCHASKA, PHD, AND
JANICE M. PROCHASKA, PHD

Hazelden
Publishing

Hazelden Publishing
Center City, Minnesota 55012
hazelden.org/bookstore

ISBN: 978-1-61649-629-6

Library of Congress Cataloging-in-Publication Data
is on file with the Library of Congress.

Editor's note

The names, details, and circumstances may have been changed to protect the
privacy of those mentioned in this publication.

This publication is not intended as a substitute for the advice of health care
professionals.

Readers should be aware that websites listed in this work may have changed
or disappeared between when this work was written and when it is read.

Alcoholics Anonymous and AA are registered trademarks of Alcoholics
Anonymous World Services, Inc.

27 26 25 24 23   5 6 7 8 9

Cover and interior design: Terri Kinne
Developmental editor: Sid Farrar
Contributing editor: Cynthia Orange
Production editor: Heather Silsbee

To our grandchildren, who have helped us
to thrive in so many ways.
Xavier, Bailey, Zakary, Lila, and Andrew

CONTENTS

Introduction

More than thirty-five years ago, Carlo DiClemente and I (James Prochaska) developed the Transtheoretical Model of Behavior Change, more commonly called "TTM" or "Stages of Change," to describe how, for most people, behavior change occurs gradually as they move (sometimes cycling back and forth) through a process of identifiable stages. Imagine a deep canyon carved by a wild river. Now think of one side of the canyon as "need for change" and the other side as "change." To get from one side to the other, we need to build a bridge. That's where the Stages of Change and this book, *Changing to Thrive*, come in.

The six Stages of Change, which will be discussed more thoroughly throughout the book, are

1. **Precontemplation**—
   not ready; not intending to take action in the next six months

2. **Contemplation**—
   getting ready; intending to take action in the next six months

3. **Preparation**—
   ready; ready to take action in the next thirty days

4. **Action**—
   have made the behavior change but for less than six months

5. **Maintenance**—
   doing the new healthy behavior for more than six months

6. **Termination**—
   confident with the change; not tempted to relapse

This model revolutionized the addiction, mental health, and wellness fields because professionals who embraced the concept now understood how to approach the great majority of people who wouldn't automatically leap into action once they identified a behavior problem. This realization allowed helping professionals to better support their patients and clients by guiding them through the change process to achieve desired goals.

In 1994, John Norcross, Carlo, and I wrote *Changing for Good.* This important book presented the Stages of Change in an accessible way that gave both professionals and general readers valuable tools and strategies to change unhealthy behaviors and integrate healthier behaviors into daily life. Now, in *Changing to Thrive,* Jan and I incorporate major breakthroughs that have occurred since the publication of the first book to help people make even more changes with less effort, guiding them to live not only healthier lives but happier ones as well.

Behavior change isn't easy. Despite their best efforts, without expert guidance, a great number of people repeatedly fail to change high-risk behaviors that prevent them from living healthier and happier lives. Why do they fail? We wanted to know what most people thought about this, so at a workshop in Appalachia, one of the highest risk and most disadvantaged regions in the United States, we asked 300 people that very question: "Why do most people fail when they attempt to change?" Here is how they answered:

1. Not enough motivation
2. Not enough willpower
3. Not the right genes
4. Not the right personality
5. Not enough confidence

Our research has shown that all these answers were wrong, that the number one reason is, *Most people don't know how to change.*

Despite the proven success of the Stages of Change model over the last three and a half decades and the strong sales of *Changing for Good,* after hearing these answers and then talking to both professionals and everyday people about this model, we became convinced that we needed to write this book. But first we posed the following questions to the same audience:

- "Do you know about the Stages of Change?" About 10 percent of our audience members raised their hands.

- "Think of a behavior you want or need to change. Do you know what Stage of Change you are in for that behavior?" Five percent raised their hands.

- "Do you know what you need to do to progress to the next Stage of Change?" Just one percent raised their hands.

The Stages of Change model was groundbreaking when it was introduced in the late 1970s, and it is more relevant than ever today as society continues to move at lightning speed, with all the pressures, challenges, and choices that confront us. When people are faced with too little time and too much pressure, they are more vulnerable to engaging in high-risk behaviors. Fortunately, recent research on applying the Stages of Change model demonstrates how busy people can make more changes in less time.

The Top High-Risk Behaviors

When we asked 150 substance abuse counselors what behaviors account for the majority of chronic diseases and premature deaths, they immediately shouted out the correct answers: "Smoking! Alcohol abuse! Unhealthy diet! Not enough exercise!" But when we asked why these four behaviors were so critical to our health and well-being, they were less sure in their responses.

The correct answer is that these four behaviors are fundamental processes of life: breathing, drinking, eating, and moving. If we breathe toxins, we poison our bodies. If we drink alcohol to toxic levels, we do damage to both our minds and bodies. If we eat toxins, we seriously compromise our general well-being. And, if we don't move it, move it, move it enough, we don't push enough toxins out of our bodies. More than 90 percent of adults in the United States engage in two or more of those high-risk and high-cost behaviors.[1] Yet our health care systems generally fail to treat those threats effectively.

We once asked thirty-five medical directors of the largest U.S. health plans about the quantity and quality of behavior medicine that their primary care practices provided to help patients make behavior changes that would prevent or manage chronic diseases. Their answer? The quantity is typically zero, and the quality is typically awful. With this book, we hope to fill that void by offering the most effective, least time-consuming approaches to behavior change. Our goal is to take away the threats to health and happiness and replace them with thriving.

It's important to note that to our list of four toxic behaviors, professionals will typically add a fifth top threat: stress. Stress is the most common factor that drives people to breathe, drink, or eat at toxic levels. We prefer to think of this factor as "distress." Times of anxiety, depression, anger, and boredom stress our abilities to cope. These times are like fevers: They signal that something is wrong with our emotional, mental, or physical well-being. So, how do average Americans cope with different types of distress? We smoke more cigarettes, drink more alcohol, eat more comfort and junk foods, and collapse on the couch. Why is this fifth threat so critical to our health and happiness? This behavior risk factor is fundamental to another domain of well-being necessary for a happy life: our feelings.

We need to make clear that what we list as the "top five" are not the only behaviors that threaten health and happiness. Not enough sleep, too much sun exposure, and discontinuing prescribed medications are other examples of a seemingly endless list of behaviors that can endanger our physical and emotional health. The principles for changing behavior that you will learn in this book have proven effective in changing more than fifty different behaviors. So, don't worry if the behavior you're trying to change is not on our top five list—you can still use the strategies outlined in this book to help you make that change.

We have found that many people are trying to change two or more interrelated high-risk behaviors simultaneously. And one of the reasons these behaviors are so difficult to change is that by the time we recognize them as problems, they have often become deep habits. No need to worry: The practices that help you progress through the Stages of Change in order to change a single behavior and remove one bad habit work with multiple behaviors and habits as well. We will teach you how to use innovative strategies to produce the synergy that allows you to make more positive change and produce even more benefits with about the same amount of time and effort.

By removing unhealthy habits—the great deadeners of life—you can live a longer, fuller, and better life. You don't have to wait for a crisis, and you certainly don't have to wait until you have "hit bottom" before making a change.

Before we did the research that made this book possible, all we could promise was that we could provide guidance on doing the right thing at the right time to maximize your chances of changing a significant risky behavior. Such a change could enhance your health, and that was good. That is one of the reasons the book that evolved from the Stages of Change model was called *Changing for Good*. At that time, we were working from a model of health that was defined as the absence of disease and the absence of risks for disease. With new research, we now know that this is an incomplete model of health and human need, because it tells us only what should be *absent* from our lives, not what needs to be *present*.

Well-Being and Happiness

Today, we can offer you much more—we can actually help you gain greater happiness. "Happiness" is the single best word that captures the construct, or concept, of well-being. Just as there are a small number of behaviors that account for high percentages of chronic disease and premature death, there are a small number of elements that account for much of the happiness in our lives. These include

- physical well-being
- emotional well-being
- financial well-being
- social well-being
- purpose, which reflects your most valued passions

These elements, or domains of well-being, are discussed in more detail in chapter 12. What we want to highlight here is that in the process of helping you remove the biggest threats to your health, we can also help you fill and fulfill more of your life with what matters most to you.

Twenty years ago, we could not imagine making such claims. We also could not imagine that we would be blessed with a continuing series of breakthroughs in the science and practice of behavior change. We feel fortunate to have the opportunity to share these innovations with you and to help you break out of chronic, high-risk behavior patterns, or bad or unhealthy habits that might be getting in the way of your happiness and well-being.

In order to change your behavior, the first thing you need to change is your mind. You need to change your mental model of behavior change. The vast majority of people have an *action* model of behavior change. In other words, they think behavior change equals action. People see themselves as changing when they *stop* doing something: when they quit smoking, stop abusing alcohol, stop eating poorly, or stop living a sedentary life. Of course being able to stop unhealthy behaviors is important; however it takes more than just stopping something that's causing distress to achieve happiness and well-being. Dan's story helps explain what we mean.

Dan, a forty-eight-year-old owner of an antique store, was once athletic but he had let his body age much faster than it should have. He was stressed out and smoked, drank, and ate too much and exercised too little. It was not surprising that his doctor diagnosed him as having type 2 diabetes. It also wasn't surprising that his doctor delivered this news: "You have to quit smoking, cut down on your drinking, improve your diet, start exercising, lose weight, test your blood glucose, take your medication, and lower your stress."

Good luck with that.

What's wrong with this picture and this prescription? What is the doctor's mental model of change? And how about Dan's model? If you said an action model, you'd be right. One of the top reasons that most physicians in the United States do not include behavioral medicine in their practice is that more than two-thirds of them believe that the majority of patients either cannot or will not change their behavior. They have become demoralized by their action model. Dan's doctor became demoralized quickly. Out of frustration, he blurted out, "Why are you so intent on killing yourself?" Then he referred Dan to me, calling me "Dr. Change."

I met with Dan and our session seemed to boost his morale, especially when he recognized that his biggest barrier to change was in his head. Not that he was mentally ill—he was just mistaken. Like so many others, he had tried to apply an action model to behaviors that he was not ready to change.

When Dan was able to identify what stage he was at in his readiness for changing his various risky behaviors, I was able to help him move through those stages for multiple behaviors, meeting him where he was at, rather than where he was "supposed" to be. You can count on one hand and a finger the Stages of Change that Dan needed to advance through to remove his risky behaviors. Here they are again:

1. Precontemplation
2. Contemplation
3. Preparation
4. Action
5. Maintenance
6. Termination

This book will help you understand each of these stages in depth, how to identify what stage you're at in your desire to change your own risky behaviors, and how to move through the remaining stages at your own pace so you can increase your happiness and thrive.

Most programs that claim to enhance health and well-being are action-oriented and end up excluding most people. The leading free smoking "quit lines" screen people to determine whether they are prepared to take immediate action. One of them spends forty-five minutes assessing smokers, and if the callers are not ready to quit in the next week or two, they are told to call back when they are ready. As a result, states that offer such programs budget for less than 1 percent of smokers to use the service each year. These are not really public health programs that are supposed to serve entire populations. They are more like public relations programs that promise something they don't actually deliver.

Most alcohol treatment programs, including those that use a Twelve Step recovery management model, are also action-oriented, and like the smokers' quit lines, reach relatively small percentages of at-risk populations. Even when individuals show up for their Twelve Step meetings, the majority drop out quickly (and inappropriately, as judged by their counselors or sponsors). A highly prestigious medical school provides a twelve-week evidence-based alcohol treatment program. Historically, the school has reported that 75 percent to 80 percent of those who start the program don't finish it.[2] And the best known weight-loss programs are reaching and retaining fewer and fewer people. Some of these pro-grams are in serious financial jeopardy. Most weight-loss programs con-tinue to have drop-out rates in the 70 to 80 percent range.[3] Most health clubs that emphasize exercise also serve very small and select segments of their communities. Some of the lowest-cost programs count on new members who sign up at New Year's or other times to stop showing up after a month or so. These clubs can be profitable precisely because they do not need very many staff for the number of members they enroll, because so many members quit going.

Lest we be seen as too critical, we want to be clear that most of those organizations can effectively serve select segments of their com-munities. When people have reached the preparation or action Stage of Change, they are more likely to benefit from these kind of action-oriented programs. It should be noted, too, that the Stages of Change model has been adopted by many behavioral health programs and used in conjunction with other evidence-based treatment models that are helping people progress through the stages.

For decades, our mission has been to help as many people as possible enhance their health and well-being. Our goals for this book are just as grand—to take you on a journey in which you learn how to change the behaviors that most threaten your health and happiness, to help you change to thrive so that you can live healthier lives, longer lives, better lives, and fuller lives.

Chapter Summaries

Chapter 1 uses the "three Ds" of precontemplation to explain why some people seem stuck when it comes to moving toward change: They Don't know how; they are Demoralized; or they have a tendency to Defend their bad habits. It discusses how "self-changers" can address those roadblocks and transform defending into coping, which helps them move from precontemplation to contemplation.

Chapter 2 takes readers from the contemplation Stage of Change through preparation to the action stage, by using real-life examples of how some people prepared for and then took action as they dealt with the doubts, delays, fears, and excitement that come with the prospect of changing a high-risk behavior.

Chapter 3 takes readers from the maintenance to the termination stage and tackles the tough question "Is maintenance a long time or a lifetime?" It also honestly addresses the issue of relapse by explaining how change is a spiral in which it is normal to "recycle"—to revisit certain behaviors as self-changers get stronger and more comfortable with incorporating a new lifestyle change into their everyday activities. The chapter ends by defining what we mean by "termination" when we describe the last Stage of Change.

Chapters 4 and 5 introduce the Principles of Progress. Chapter 4 covers the first seven principles, taking readers from precontemplation to action as they work on helpful exercises that—among other things—teach them how to deal with stress and distress, how to relax, and how to open themselves to a fuller and happier sense of self. The final five Principles of Progress are discussed in chapter 5 as readers move from action to maintenance and beyond. Here again, practical exercises help self-changers evaluate and strengthen their commitment to change as they learn how to deal with unhealthy habits, lessen and prevent stress, foster helping relationships and social networks, and practice stimulus control so healthy habits become more automatic.

Chapter 6 is where things come together and readers discover how the Principles of Progress link with the Stages of Change and the behavior controls that have been introduced and practiced. In this chapter, readers learn about the four effects that can predict long-term success when it comes to changing a behavior: the treatment effect, the stage effect, the effort effect, and the severity effect. Later chapters include exercises that help readers apply each of these four effects to increase their progress and achieve greater success.

The chapters that follow offer specific guidance for using the Stages of Change and change principles to address the major health threats of smoking, alcohol dependence, unhealthy eating, and too little exercise.

Chapter 7 deals with the tough task of quitting smoking in a realistic and nonjudgmental way that takes environment, cravings, withdrawal symptoms, fear of weight gain, and other emotions into account.

Chapter 8 uses a similar, practical approach regarding the many issues surrounding current or potential problems with alcohol and high-risk drinking.

Chapter 9, "Healthy Eating for Well-Being and Weight," doesn't just deal with losing weight or preventing weight gain. It shows self-changers how healthy and mindful eating can positively (and permanently) affect all areas of life.

Chapter 10 focuses on how to begin or maintain regular exercise that can help self-changers manage and maintain a healthy weight while living a happier life.

Chapter 11 discusses how the Stages of Change can successfully be applied to multiple behaviors and how changing one behavior increases the odds for changing another.

Chapter 12 describes how addressing and reducing multiple risky behaviors increases multiple areas of well-being, making it even more possible for self-changers to enjoy a full, balanced, and healthy life.

The book concludes with an **Epilogue,** in which self-changers are taught to chart their individual trajectory of change so they can continue to progress long after they finish this book.

. . .

Most of us will encounter occasional bumps on the road to change that may cause us to backtrack, get stuck, or detour once in a while. We encourage you to think of this book as your expert guide to change. Our motto is "Wherever you are at, we can work with that."™ Whether you are ready, getting ready, or not yet ready to take action, we can be of help. So ready or not, here we go on an exciting and sometimes challenging adventure in change. Use this guide throughout your journey and return to it if and when you face an unexpected challenge, knowing roadblocks can temporarily throw you off course, but getting back on track can lead to healthy change that can be life altering and permanent.

Finally, this book has a number of exercises to help you evaluate yourself regarding the five risky behaviors and your progression through the Stages of Change. We recommend that you keep a paper or digital journal to document your responses to these exercises so that you have a personal record of your emerging behavior profile to amend as you progress.

We wish you a healthful and fulfilling journey.

1

Precontemplation
(Not Ready)

"Precontemplation" is the stage in which individuals do not intend to take action in the near future—usually defined as the next six months, which is about as far ahead as most people plan when it comes to making changes. Many people misunderstand precontemplation, believing it means these individuals don't want to change, but there is a big difference between *wanting* and *intending*.

We used to live in Rhode Island, the "Ocean State." Many of us *wanted* to buy a home near the water, but not many of us *intended* to actually do so. Once we shift to intending, we need to ask ourselves whether we are prepared to pay the price involved with such a change. There is no free change. Change costs us time and effort. Sometimes, as in our example, this means money, but significant change also poses a risk of failure.

People in precontemplation are often labeled as being uncooperative, resistant, unmotivated, or not ready for behavior change programs. However, our research showed us that it was health professionals who were not ready for precontemplators. It was health professionals who were not motivated to match their action programs to the needs of their patients or clients who were in the precontemplation stage. And it was professionals who resisted changing their programs to meet the needs of the majority of their at-risk populations. It was these professionals—not their patients or clients—who were not prepared to take action. Sadly, three decades later, many health professionals are still not adequately prepared to help the many people who face the biggest risks to their health and happiness.

The Three Ds of Precontemplation:
Don't Know How, Demoralized, Defensive

Since most people seeking to make change have multiple behaviors that risk their health and happiness, they are probably in the precontemplation stage for at least one of those behaviors. That's why understanding the dynamics of this stage and what keeps them from moving forward is the first step in progressing toward the desired change.

Don't Know How

As we've discovered, many people in the precontemplation stage never move beyond it because they not only *Don't know how,* they may not even realize the serious harm of their behavior and so aren't yet convinced that they even need to change. Here's an example of what we mean: The head of the Rhode Island Department of Health was asked to do a ten-second television spot that would make viewers want to learn more about getting healthier. Drawing on our TTM model, she came up with "Woman killed by couch. Details on the six o'clock news." Who could resist tuning into *that* story? It was a creative way to drive home the point that there are millions of "couch potatoes" who cannot imagine that their couch can kill them. Yet we know that inactivity can lead to serious health consequences and, yes, even death.

Take Elena, a pharmacy clerk in her early fifties, who can't wait to get home to turn on the TV, flop on the couch, and have an alcoholic drink after a hard day at work. It wouldn't be risky if Elena spent just a short time on the couch. But she devotes most of her evening to watching her favorite shows or surfing through dozens of cable stations while spending no time doing regular exercise. At this point, her couch is the only stress reducer and place of relaxation that Elena knows well. She's probably heard that "exercise is good for you," but she hasn't yet learned about the large number of benefits that can come from regular physical activity. She hasn't seen how the idea that "exercise is good for you" applies to her life and therefore doesn't realize how her couch could kill her. Elena doesn't yet intend to make changes, wouldn't know *how* to change if she did, and is a good example of someone in the precontemplation stage.

Demoralization

The second D that keeps people in precontemplation is _Demoralization_. For instance, millions of people have tried to lose weight so many times in so many ways. Their history clearly shows that they _want_ to change, but after repeated failures, they are feeling demoralized and uncertain about their abilities to change. Perhaps it is their fear of failure or what they link their failure to that is the cause of their demoralization. In their failure to change, they make what psychologists call "causal attributions."

When it comes to weight loss, here are the most common causes people give for not losing weight:

- not having enough willpower—"_If that is the cause, what can I do about it?_"
- not having the right genes—"_Good luck with genetic engineering._"
- having an externally focused personality controlled by the environment rather than an internally focused personality with plenty of internal self-controls—"_What, you expect me to get a personality transplant?_"
- not enough self-confidence—"_How can I have confidence when I have a history of failure?_"

The problem with each of these causal attributions is that they are basically personality characteristics, or what psychologists call "dispositions." Unfortunately, psychology has a long history of attributing problem behaviors to personality, psychopathology (mental health problems), biology, or society. Although these are all major forces that may certainly contribute to the original behavior, they are not _solutions_ that individuals can control to change their behavior.

Take smoking, for example. The forces that may have caused adolescents to become smokers are not necessarily the same forces that can free them to become nonsmokers. More than fifty million people in the United States have successfully quit smoking, most of them without changing their personality, psychopathology, biology, or society. The majority quit before there were nicotine replacement treatments or widespread social controls on smoking.[4]

Let's look at one more common causal attribution: not enough motivation. Here is a question we often ask our audiences: "What do you think recovery movements have taught multiple generations about what must happen before individuals with addictions will be motivated enough to overcome their addictions?" The audience usually shouts out: "They have to have a crisis. They have to hit bottom."

Then we present an example of a crisis and how it affects change. A fifty-eight-year-old teacher is hospitalized after suffering a life-threatening heart attack. Her physician prescribes free cardiac rehabilitation as part of her recovery. We ask those present what percentage of patients they think show up for this life-saving service? "50 percent," someone says. "Lower," we say. Then they guess 40 percent, 30 percent, and finally 20 percent. But the fact is that less than 20 percent of heart attack survivors in the United States do follow-up therapy for cardiac rehabilitation.[5]

"Who shows up more, men or women?" we then ask the audience. "Women!" they respond with confidence. Wrong again, although it was a good guess, because women do show up about twice as often as men for other health problems. But, out of the big five threats to health and happiness mentioned in the introduction—smoking, alcohol misuse, overeating, lack of exercise, and stress (distress)—there is only one for which men are able to move further along in the Stages of Change more easily than women. And that is *exercise.* And what is cardiac rehab seen as? Exercise. For whom? Those who are prepared to take immediate action. So what is seen as an irrational response by most heart attack patients turns out to be much more rational when you really think about it. *"Why should I go to cardiac rehab when I am not ready to exercise? I will only fail and waste my time, the therapist's time, and the health insurance company's money."*

This attitude applies to the other factors in weight loss as well. We cannot expect overweight people in precontemplation to overcome their demoralization if all our society offers are weight management programs for people who are prepared to take immediate action.

What is the best way to deal with demoralization? Hope. Providing innovative and more effective solutions for old problems is the best way to generate hope that can lead to the right type of help. That's where the Stages of Change model comes in—a model that can provide an innovative approach that brings evidence-based hope.

All too often when we talk to people in precontemplation about weight loss, we hear them say, "I've tried everything. I've tried all the leading diets and none of them worked. The only thing left is gastric bypass surgery." Unlike dieters, smokers can often honestly claim that they have tried almost everything: "I tried those nicotine patches, telephone quit lines, group counseling, hypnosis . . ."

In both cases, the problem is that all of these solutions are *action-oriented* treatments. They are not designed for precontemplators who are demoralized.

Defending

The third D that keeps people in precontemplation is the tendency to *Defend* one's risky behavior, especially if it has become an ingrained habit or addiction. Consider the sixty-year-old doctor who comes home late and pours himself a drink. His adult daughter is concerned about her father's slurred language and how he staggers after his drink. After many months of passively watching him drink himself into a stupor every night, she finally finds the courage to confront her father. The doctor is indignant. "Listen, young lady," he says, "I have only one drink a day and I know medically that one drink a day is actually healthier than no drinks." She is ready for this and responds, "But, Dad, do you realize how much alcohol you are actually drinking? It's one glass, but the way you fill it up, you are actually consuming the equivalent of four to five drinks a day." This is an example of why for decades alcoholism has been called the disease of denial, when people deny how much they are drinking or the consequences of their consumption.

However, there are many ways of defending oneself other than denial. Classic defense mechanisms were first identified by Sigmund Freud—that famous Austrian neurologist in the early 1900s who came to be known as the father of psychoanalysis. Technically, defenses were perceived by many as "intra-psychic" in nature, meaning they occur in the mind. They were developed to control internal impulses, such as taboo sexual desires (such as having sexual feelings about a parent or child), or hostile impulses directed at one's father or sibling. In TTM, we view defenses as more "interpersonal" in nature and look at what goes on between people when defenses become obvious. For example, when do defenses in children become apparent to their parents? In the "terrible twos," a time often called the "first adolescence." Children who have been relatively cooperative seem to suddenly become very stubborn, as these typical exchanges illustrate:

"Bailey, it's time to come in now!"
"No thanks."
"Alice, you need to get dressed now."
"No, I don't want to. I hate that dress!"

When we look at defenses interpersonally, we see that they emerge to protect our independence—like the ones we use when we want to keep from being controlled by our parents, people in an authority role who act like or remind us of our parents, or people who are trying to persuade us to buy their products. On a professional level, we try to teach counselors that they can make clients defensive when they try to get them to take action when the clients are not ready. Often, they react to our observations or suggestions by blaming their clients for being defensive, resistant, or noncompliant.

Here are some of the most common defenses people use when faced with someone who is trying to move them to take action before they are ready or willing to act:

Turning Inward

There are a number of ways that people defend themselves by retreating inward, including withdrawing, going silent, disattending, and internalizing.

WITHDRAWING

At a young age, children learn to distance themselves when parents are trying to pressure them into immediate action. In the "first adolescence," the distancing is mainly psychological; in the teen years, the distance may be also physical. Here's a common scenario: "Joey, get in here; it's time for dinner. Joey, can you hear me? Get in here now!" Joey has learned to tune out this controlling communication channel. Today, youth withdraw more and more into electronic games and media on their smartphones or tablets, with teens spending an average of nine hours per day with media for enjoyment.[6]

A major challenge for professional counseling programs is that clients withdraw by dropping out of treatment quickly (and inappropriately, as judged by their counselors). On average, about 50 percent of clients withdraw quickly.[7] For alcohol treatments, the withdrawal rate is more like 75 to 85 percent.[8] We shall soon see that the people who are most likely to withdraw from these action-oriented treatments are people in precontemplation. When they find themselves feeling pressured to take action before they are ready, they tend to defend themselves by withdrawing. We encourage those who feel in need of professional help to look for a counselor trained to help individuals at each Stage of Change, including precontemplation.

GOING SILENT

Louise is married to Ed, a former athlete who insists his wife needs to exercise much more. Ed likes to dominate Louise the way her dad once did, but always in "her best interest." Louise has learned to stay silent, lest her words be used against her. She also learned that the silent partner actually is much more in control. Louise could see Ed's frustration when she wouldn't talk and he couldn't control her.

DISATTENDING

Dwayne is a thirty-eight-year-old train engineer who was demoralized about his inability to lose weight, while at the same time feeling unfairly discriminated against because of his obesity. When the topic of losing weight came up in conversations, he would talk about something else. When there was a discussion about obesity on television, he would change the channel. When there was an article in the newspaper on the subject, he would turn the page. Disattending and "tuning out" may well be the most common defense that keeps individuals stuck in precontemplation. Through such selective attention, they can keep themselves from progressing to the contemplation stage of change, where they would be much freer to be influenced by conversations and information in the media that may include new evidence and new options that can bring new hope to remove their demoralization.

INTERNALIZING

When we internalize, we tend to blame all of our problems on ourselves. Such self-blame can lead to lowered self-esteem, which only adds to our demoralization. I was out golfing one day and joined up with a stranger named Frank, who had had a heart attack three months before. His physician had prescribed golf for physical activity to help heal his heart.

On the second tee, I sliced my drive into trees and said, "I'm going to have to scramble to get out of there." Frank followed with a drive into the woods and sputtered under his breath to himself, "You stupid jerk!" A little later I duffed another drive into trouble and said, "This should be fun." When Frank made a mistake, he angrily said to himself, "You never can do anything right!" I intervened and said, "Frank, this is your lucky day. You're golfing with a psychologist!" He chuckled. I went on, "Your doctor taught you correctly that lack of exercise is bad for your heart, but he may not have taught you that chronic hostility directed toward yourself can also hurt your heart. I wonder, how did your father treat you?" "Oh, he was terrible to me. He would always say I could never do anything right." I suggested to Frank that he might want to recall the most positive teacher or coach he ever had. He may want to contemplate how he could re-parent himself with a more caring and careful role model. Hopefully that helped—at least it helped to have a more relaxing walk through the woods to retrieve our golf balls.

Turning Outward

There are also several ways that people defend themselves by redirecting attention to their outward behavior, such as projecting and displacing.

PROJECTING

Projection is the opposite of internalization. Instead of blaming ourselves, we blame others for our problems. "The best defense is a good offense" is a game that we can play when we project. This was Joanna's philosophy.

Joanna was a middle-age attorney who was having repeated problems with her career. She wasn't living a healthy lifestyle—physically or emotionally. Like my golf partner Frank, she had too much anger in her life, but Joanna's anger was aimed outward rather than inward. She would blow up at whomever she was blaming and, in the process, often burned bridges by ending the relationship. Joanna was pressured into meeting with me, so I was pretty sure she was stuck in precontemplation and protecting herself through projection.

After getting a better sense of her world, I risked asserting, "Joanna, your biggest strength may be the source of your biggest weakness. You are such a good attorney, including being the attorney for defending yourself. You may be so effective at finding others guilty that you have difficulty learning from your mistakes." Joanna wanted me to give examples to back up my argument. But I said, "Joanna, my intention is not to argue a case. You are too good of an attorney; I will lose the case. I just want to help you consider what you might contribute to your chronic career conflicts, because you can have more control over your contributions than you can have over others."

Joanna still wanted to defend herself, but I asked her to take some time to think about what I said. The next day, I was so pleased when she called and said, "Jim, I just want you to know I heard what you said yesterday."

DISPLACING

Displacement is another form of turning outward, but here we redirect our distress to a substitute object or person who is safe to attack. It's the old proverbial kicking the cat because you're upset with your bullying boss. In the case of Ken, however, he was the stressed, bullying boss who directed most of his frustration at Martha, his "safe" office assistant. It was as if his assistant's job description included taking the blame and the heat for his actions. Others in the office would hear him yelling and swearing at her. They tried to support Martha by listening to her distress, but they didn't want to risk confronting Ken, fearing they would become his new "cat to kick." After many months, someone at the company finally reported Ken's abusive behavior to a company contracted to investigate employee claims of abuse. This anonymous colleague was hoping to bring social controls where there was a lack of self-controls. Ken was ordered to participate in an employee assistance program (EAP) whose counselors were trained to work with people in precontemplation.

Explaining Away Risky Behaviors

If all else fails, people may try to rationalize or intellectualize their risky behaviors or harmful habits to avoid facing the consequences.

RATIONALIZATION

This is when we defend ourselves by relying on plausible explanations for our behavior. Here's an example: About 50 percent of the doctors in China smoke, even though they are supposed to be rational empirical role models and there are campaigns to persuade and pressure them—and the entire population—to quit. So, how do they ignore the campaigns and other efforts to change their behavior? Some will say, "I have so many patients who smoke, and I just don't see that much damage or disease." Others will say, "Beijing is filled with so much smoke and so many smokers that I can't avoid breathing smoke." If even their country's doctors resort to such rationalization, it should not be surprising that more than 70 percent of smokers in China were found to be in the precontemplation stage.[9]

INTELLECTUALIZATION

When we intellectualize, we analyze or use facts to distance ourselves from our bad habits. Here is a thirty-five-year-old doctor in China, a heavy smoker, who protects his bad habit by saying he has studied the evidence: "The data demonstrate that as long as I quit smoking before I am fifty, there is minimal risk to my health." How is that different from adolescents who ignore their health by arguing they are too young to worry about things like cancer and heart disease?

Transforming Defending into Coping

Fortunately, sometimes accidentally and other times intentionally, defenses like those just described can be transformed into positive behaviors with awareness and practice. As a child, I had to cope with a dad who at times struggled with the demons of manic depression, drunkenness, and aggression. Then there were stretches of relative peace, patience, and positive parenting. But, during troubled times, to keep from being dominated by my dad's demons, I defended myself by withdrawing. Even at age six, I sought permission to stay at the Boys Club until 9 p.m., instead of 6 p.m.

By withdrawing to this second home, I was able to spend time with more consistent father figures. With my younger and older friends, I was freer to have fun and to develop skills, like playing basketball, wrestling, shooting pool, and playing Ping-Pong. Later, as a psychologist, I learned that children who distanced themselves the most from a family's dysfunction were those who went on to have the healthiest and happiest lives. Compared to my three wonderful sisters (who spoiled me rotten), I was affected the least by my father's depression. As an adult, I have to be free to withdraw into my mind: I never know what new and interesting ideas I'll discover there. The only times I feel self-conscious about being more introverted than extroverted is when I am expected to socialize longer than I like. When I am ready to distance myself from my surroundings, my mind is always open for exploration.

Our son and daughter discovered at a young age that I had unlimited abilities to "disattend." When they decided I had spent enough time in the labyrinth of my thoughts, they would start chanting, "Attention must be paid! Attention must be paid!" Then they pulled me off the couch and yelled, "Knee drops!" as they jumped on my chest with their knees. Then the wrestling match would begin, and I would always have more fun wrestling with our kids than with complicated, abstract ideas.

Jan has always had the ability to escape into a deep book. She has such appreciation of gifted authors who make writing a fine art. She discovers in her favorite novels lifelike characters who struggle with common yet profound issues in life. When Jan returns from her fictional travels, she always has good stories to share.

As we travel with you through this journey of change, we will ask you to reflect on the defenses that you or your clients developed to keep from being controlled by others. We encourage you to become aware of the defenses that prevent you from moving ahead. If you want some help, just ask a good friend, spouse, or partner to assist you. When I worked with couples, I would ask each individual to identify defenses of their partner. How quickly they could respond. This is a reminder of how our defenses are designed to fool ourselves, but they rarely fool others.

Here's one of our own examples: Early in our marriage, I took the Minnesota Multiphasic Personality Inventory (MMPI). To the statement

"I get angry sometimes," I answered false. I should not have been surprised that my score on depression was higher than normal. I asked Jan, who is a clinical social worker, to help me better understand how I express my anger. She said, "That's easy. When you start to get angry, you pucker your lips. If I push you some, you start to whistle. If I push you enough, you explode." Here I was behaving like a teapot, whistling, steaming, and with the risk of exploding! So Jan helped free me to blow my top.

Moving from Precontemplation to Contemplation (Getting Ready)

Consider that of the people alive today, 500 million will die from smoking ten years before their time.[10] That is five billion years of life lost to a single behavior. And most of those people will have spent most of their lives in precontemplation, demoralized and defensive against efforts to help them change.

Managers at Kaiser Permanente, an innovative health care system, were disappointed that only 1 percent of their patients who smoked participated in their free, action-oriented cessation clinics. To increase participation, they had their primary care physicians take time to encourage patients who smoked to sign up for the clinics. If that didn't work, their nurses took up to ten minutes to persuade the smokers to sign up. If that didn't work, they had health educators spend fifteen minutes, including sharing videos that detailed the horrors of smoking and the glories of quitting. Finally, they followed up with telephone counselor calls pressuring smokers to sign up.

This was the most intensive effort to recruit patients to a free proven program that can prevent multiple chronic diseases, disability, and premature death. At first, the efforts seemed to be successful—35 percent of the smokers in precontemplation signed up. But only 3 percent *showed* up, and only 2 percent finished the six-week program. None of the participants ended up quitting.[11]

So, as you progress from precontemplation to contemplation, appreciate how much you have accomplished. In an action model, such progress would not be viewed as any change at all. You would be seen as having failed to take action, and in such models, action is all that counts.

But look at the key benefits of such progress using the Stages of Change model. If after you progress beyond precontemplation, you decide to sign up for wellness programs at work, like Weight Watchers, or call for an appointment for alcohol counseling, studies show that you will be five times more likely to show up, seven times more likely to finish up, and much more likely to end up taking successful action.[12] No wonder in our Stages model we consider progressing to contemplation the biggest leap of all—a leap of faith in your ability to change. So let's *contemplate* together in the next chapter!

2

Moving Forward

FROM CONTEMPLATION [GETTING READY] TO PREPARATION TO ACTION

People who are at the stage of "contemplation" in their change process generally intend to take action within the next six months. As you move from precontemplation to contemplation, you become more aware of and excited about the "pros," or benefits, of changing—a sure sign of progress. But the "cons," or drawbacks, of changing become more evident as well, causing confusion. This is a source of the first two Ds of contemplation (Doubt and Delay) that can keep you from moving forward on the path to happiness and well-being.

Those in contemplation can be plagued by profound Doubt, wondering, *"Is change really worth it?"* The rule of thumb for contemplators is: *When in doubt, don't act.* This is the same rule for Wall Street: When in doubt, don't invest. Why invest your precious time, effort, and even money if you have doubts that the benefits will outweigh the costs of investing? Like a wise investor, you want to be sure that the returns on investing in change—and in yourself—will be substantial.

Doubt leads to the second D—Delay. It's not that individuals in contemplation will not do anything related to changing. Compared to precontemplators, those in contemplation are more willing and able to face the biggest threats to their health and happiness. They are certainly more likely to talk about their risky behaviors. Often it seems like they'll talk about nothing else and won't change the topic. Or they'll read about them, but they won't turn the page. Or they'll search online and in their communities for programs that address their issues, but they stay stuck—they won't change the channel. They won't actually take action toward making change.

In our studies of smokers who seek to change on their own, we were surprised how few people took any action. Although they intended to quit smoking in the next six months, without our help less than 50 percent quit for even twenty-four hours over the next twelve months. So, what are the forces that keep contemplators from moving ahead?

The first force is "chronic contemplation." In the past, when health insurance policies allowed people to be in psychotherapy for an unlimited number of sessions, there were people who spent years in treatment. If patients who were comfortable contemplating were connected with therapists who were confident with contemplating, the result was nonstop therapy. It might never end. Why are both clinician and client so tempted to continue to contemplate? One of the reasons is that it is hard to fail when you are only talking or thinking about a problem. Prior to developing the Transtheoretical Model (TTM), I included talk therapy as part of my practice. I was very comfortable and confident with talking and contemplating. It was when it came time for *action* that anxiety went up—for both my client and myself.

A second force that keeps change seekers stuck is their search and need for certainty. Friedrich Nietzsche, a famous nineteenth-century German philosopher, once suggested that we are sometimes willing to even sacrifice truth for certainty. This search for certainty can keep people stuck in contemplation because they keep struggling to remove all doubts and risks for failure. They think they need to fully understand all the causes of their problems. Others want to be certain they have the perfect solution, such as the counseling program or strategy that is guaranteed to address their problem. Truth in science, on the other hand, is "probabilistic." It's based on what's probable—not on what is absolutely certain. When it comes to change, the best we can do is to increase the probability that our action solution will be successful. That is why we emphasize results like doubling the chances that you will be taking effective action in the next few months if you progress by one stage and tripling the probability if you progress by two stages.

Yet another force that gets in the way of successful change is a rush to action before you are adequately prepared. But, in cultures like ours that are still dominated by an action model of change, there are plenty of pressures to charge into action. On New Year's Eve, we are pressured to make some resolutions—with either taking action or doing nothing as the only choices. At medical visits we might be given a prescription with a "quit date" for smokers. Quit smoking in the next thirty days—ready or not.

From Contemplation to Preparation (Ready)

When people reach the preparation Stage of Change, they generally intend to take action within the next month. They are excited about the possibility of getting free from a major threat to their health and well-being. But they might also be afraid, feeling the weight of the big "D" of preparation that keeps them from moving: the Dread of failing—again. Take Tony for instance.

Tony was a thirty-six-year-old restaurant manager who had started drinking when he was fifteen. Because his parents also began drinking in high school, they weren't too concerned about their son and, like Tony, they rationalized his drinking as being "normal." It wasn't until Tony was arrested for driving drunk that someone took his drinking seriously. He was sentenced to attend court-ordered treatment. Although he was physically present at the treatment, he withdrew emotionally and mentally; he was disattending mentally—just as Dwayne, the train engineer from the previous chapter, did when he tuned out about weight loss.

Tony's parents did insist that when he went to a party he have a designated driver available, which he did do—most of the time. When he didn't, he would sleep at a friend's house or in his car until he was at least somewhat sober. Tony was very smart intellectually, if not emotionally. He was accepted into a good college, where he joined the fraternity known for its "hardy parties." Tony felt right at home in this environment until he crossed a line. As a sophomore, he had sex with a first-semester student who was drunk. She brought charges against Tony, who was mandated to alcohol abuse therapy.

At least this time, Tony was engaged in treatment—at least enough to break the barrier of denial. He admitted he didn't have control when he was drinking. He progressed to contemplation, but his profound ambivalence and doubt kept him from taking serious action. He now saw that there were significant benefits to stopping drinking. But he also realized quitting would come with significant costs, especially since his social life largely revolved around his fraternity's drinking parties. Tony intellectualized that he would soon follow the norm of other college students who stopped drinking or reducing their alcohol abuse enough to progress through college and begin preparing for their careers.

Tony's career, however, was restaurant management, which involved being around—and eventually engaging in—a lot of drinking. He made numerous attempts to quit drinking, and he was able to do so for short periods. But each time he ultimately failed. He became more and more demoralized until he read about TTM and the Stages of Change.

Tony started therapy in the contemplation stage and progressed quite quickly to preparation. He had already learned from life about chronic contemplation, where he said he would control his drinking when he finished school and began his career. However, he also learned that there was no certainty when it came time to take action on a behavior, even one that had threatened his future for the past two decades. And his exposure to TTM helped him understand that rushing to action in the face of a crisis would last only until the crisis ended.

Now Tony faced his <u>D</u>read of failing yet again. But this time, applying the Stages of Change helped to transform his view of past failures into learning experiences. His past experiences had taught him about denial and demoralization, intellectualization, and rationalization. The challenge was that this type of "learning" relies on trial and error, in which he would try a certain approach and learn from his errors. Then he would try that same approach again and learn some more. The problem with trial-and-error learning is that it can be highly inefficient and often ineffective—it takes too many trials and too many errors before the desired change can be achieved. This can sometimes increase feelings of demoralization to the point that the person hits bottom. The average smoker and drinker experiences too many trials over too many decades, while inflicting too much damage on their minds and bodies and on the lives of others. In TTM, Tony was becoming familiar with "guided learning," which is much more efficient and effective than trial and error. He was learning how to be guided—like we were by ordinary people who taught us from their successes and their failures at each Stage of Change. Tony was getting ready to take action.

From Preparation to Action

Action is defined as making a change during the past six months that, according to public health criteria, removes one or more of the highest risk behaviors. With smoking, the action called for is clear—total abstinence. The smoker quits lighting up. With drinking, the criteria can be different for different people. For people who have been diagnosed as alcoholics—that is, with having a severe alcohol use disorder—the criterion has been total abstinence. For those with problem drinking, alcohol abuse, or binge drinking (a mild to moderate alcohol use disorder), the public health criteria in the United States have been (1) no more than two drinks a day for men and one for women, and (2) no more than four drinks on any occasion for men and three for women. The criteria are even more complex for diet, exercise, and stress, which we'll discuss later.

TTM has been criticized for using six months as the criterion for staying in action because some argue that six months is an arbitrary time period. It is arbitrary to an extent, as are most public health criteria—such as the goal of the total cholesterol level now being below 200 mg/dL, when it used to be 250. But there is solid evidence that led us to adopt a six-month criterion. For example, we compared how hard ordinary people were working not to relapse at different intervals: between zero and three months, three and six months, and six and nine months. We found no differences in efforts between zero and three and three and six months. But those who were in the six- to nine-month range were having far less difficulty maintaining their behavior change, which meant they had less risk of relapse.[13]

Other research shows that the relapse curves across different behaviors (such as smoking, problem drinking, and heroin addiction) are steepest in the early months of action. The relapse curve does not level off until around six months. These findings convince us that those seeking change should be prepared for six months of concerted action.[14]

Since action is the most demanding of the Stages of Change, you need to be prepared to increase your resources to help prevent relapse. We encourage individuals to think of the action stage as the behavioral equivalent of life-saving surgery. With life-saving surgery, most folks understand the importance of prioritizing their recovery—of putting in the time and effort needed to efficiently and effectively recover from the acute effects of surgery. If you were facing such surgery, would you let your friends and family know that recovery from surgery will be your top priority? Would it be best to explain that you will not be at your best so they might make fewer demands on you? And should you tell them you will need more support during a time when you are facing greater demands? The huge D of "too many Demands" can lead to regressing rather than progressing during the action stage.

The Myth of Twenty-One Days

The most common question we are asked by the media is, "Is it true that people can develop new healthy habits in twenty-one days?" We have tried to track down the origin of this myth, but with no success. Resolutions are discussed in most media outlets around New Year's Day. One of the facts often highlighted in these discussions is how many people relapse to old behaviors in the first twenty-one days: between 40 percent and 50 percent.[15] Unfortunately, some members of the press seem to interpret this to mean that *all* of the people who stick to their resolution goals for twenty-one days are successful. But remember that steep relapse curve that doesn't level off until about six months? Clearly many individuals continue to relapse after twenty-one days of trying a behavior change they resolved to make as their New Year's goal.

The myth is particularly appealing to those attracted to fast foods, fast cars, and fast company. Those who believe this myth expect that the worst is over after twenty-one days, and they begin to let up on their efforts to change way too early. For example, although the worst is over biologically in just three days for nicotine addiction—because nicotine leaves the body in that brief period—behaviorally and psychologically, the temptations to smoke continue far longer and only gradually decrease over time.

Being Adequately Prepared

People who seek change usually intend to quit an unhealthy habit for good. But are the preparations good enough? Have they planned for months of effort? Have they prepared for other demands that will emerge while they are making difficult changes? For example, if drinking has been a key part of how they cope with difficult days, will staying sober remain their priority when other challenges arise? Have they let others know they will need more support during these demanding days? Or will they turn to the bottle for comfort?

The problem in the past was that people had no good guides for assessing whether they were prepared enough. One of the surprising parts of our TTM programs is that we may tell people not to take action. We may say, for example, "Don't quit smoking; you're not ready." Sometimes this can be difficult to accept. For example, we worked closely with Johnson & Johnson managers when they were bringing their nicotine patch over the counter. We created an assessment that smokers could take to help them decide whether they should start on the nicotine patches. A common answer was no, since they weren't ready. One of the senior leaders at Johnson & Johnson became very upset when he learned about this guidance. "What do you mean you are telling our potential customers not to buy our product?" However, others viewed such advice as ethical because it would help keep people who weren't yet ready to take action from failing. This didn't mean they wouldn't ever be prepared to take action toward change; they just weren't ready to do it at that time.

When prescription patches and other nicotine products came out, the market soared because many demoralized smokers suddenly had a new hope available. But too many of them thought that the nicotine replacement alone would solve the problem. They weren't prepared to make the other efforts needed, so the majority relapsed. And the nicotine replacement market crashed.

One of the many things you will learn in the chapters ahead is how to assess whether you are prepared enough to keep from crashing soon after you have launched your action plan.

From Maintenance
to Termination

Maintenance is one of the most controversial of the Stages of Change. When we maintain something, we strive to keep it in good condition—that goes for our physical and emotional health and well-being as well as our homes and automobiles.

Maintenance: A Long Time or a Lifetime?

When it comes to our minds and bodies, many professionals and many ordinary people believe that to be effective, maintenance must last a lifetime because recovery is not a sure thing. They believe you are always at risk for relapse. Others believe that maintenance lasts a long time. In our Stages of Change model, maintenance is measured in part by time: maintaining a behavior change for five years without relapse.

This time line is similar to the one doctors use for cancer. They usually consider patients "cured" if they are in remission from cancer symptoms for five years. It may well be that being cured or free from some of the most common *causes* of cancer—namely each of the five biggest threats to health (smoking, alcohol abuse, unhealthy diet, lack of activity, and stress)—also takes five years. This doesn't mean that for five years you will have to continue to work as hard as you initially did to keep from relapsing. (Remember, the relapse curve levels off at around six months.) But you will need to be prepared to deal with a big "D"—Distress—if you want to maintain your desired behavior change.

Distress is the biggest barrier to continued progress in the maintenance stage. Three of the most harmful ways people commonly cope with distress are by smoking, drinking too much, and eating too much unhealthy food. These are all "oral consumptive" methods of coping. Maybe Freud was on to something when he came up with his idea of oral fixations—an idea that led some to theorize that infants who get distressed by not having enough oral gratification might grow up to become fixated on cigarettes, bottles, and comfort foods. When our kids and grandkids were infants, we responded to their wails of distress by either having their mother breast-feed them or by running for their bottle or pacifier. And what else would we do? Comfort them! We're guessing we aren't the only parents and grandparents who can become fixated on feeding and comforting as a way to deal with the threat of the baby's distress getting out of control.

When we ask our audiences, "What is a healthy form of oral behavior that people can use to cope with distress?" some yell out, "Kissing," which is sweet. In San Francisco, someone yelled out, "Oral sex," which is sexy. But many counselors yell out, "Talking," which is true. The number one reason people go to primary care is because of their distress, but they only get to talk for about thirty seconds before their doctor interrupts them and starts looking for a medical cause to their problems. Too often patients report that they don't ever get to talk about what is most distressing in their lives.

A good friend who is very outspoken told me how the day before he had gone to his doctor and hardly had a chance to talk. His doctor gave him a prescription on the way out the door. When he was driving home, he said out loud, "Wait a minute! I paid for that appointment, and I didn't get to talk about what was worrying me most!" So he turned around, drove back to the doctor's office, and told the nurse, "Listen, the doctor may have been done with this appointment, but tell him the patient wasn't!" My friend drove home with less distress.

When we ask an audience of professionals, "What are the three best methods for reducing distress?" again the counselors yell out, "Talking." Many kinesiologists (exercise experts) yell out, "Walking," and many preachers yell out, "Praying." In this case they are all right! As many of you have no doubt experienced, talking, walking, or praying, especially with family or friends, are great tension relievers. It's only relatively recently that research has begun to demonstrate how effective each of these can be in reducing stress and distress. For example, a Duke

University study found exercise to be as effective in reducing depression as the leading antidepressant.[16]

In a survey asking people whether they would prefer psychotherapy or antidepressants for depression, what do you think the majority chose? Most professionals guess the antidepressants, but two-thirds of the people questioned actually said they would prefer psychotherapy.[17] So why do so many people still get prescribed a pill when they really want and need to talk to someone qualified to help with their problems? Sometimes, of course, it is the most appropriate course of treatment. But other times it is the easier option because it's a quicker fix from the doctor's perspective and a more available remedy for most patients.

We wonder what the result would be if people were asked if they preferred medication, psychotherapy, or exercise to deal with depression. We think it would be an interesting and useful study. Until such research is done, we do know that the three best ways for preparing for and coping with distress are talking, walking, or relaxing—letting the distress leave our bodies and minds by doing things like praying, practicing mindfulness or other meditation techniques, doing yoga, or getting a massage.

Relapse or Recycling: The Spiral of Change

In an exclusively action model of change (as opposed to the Stages of Change model), the biggest barrier is relapse. For example, a six-week group smoking cessation program may spend the first five sessions developing an action plan. Participants are encouraged to put their houses in order, such as purchasing nicotine replacement patches and removing all cigarettes and ashtrays from their homes. The fifth week is the targeted quit date, and the sixth week is for celebrating their successes. The plan is to have everyone quit at the same time and then gather to share their experiences. There is pressure to quit in this "ready or not" approach. As a result, some participants who were not ready choose not to come back, so for research purposes, those folks have to be counted as failures. Some choose to lie, so everyone who claims to have quit has to be given biochemical tests to validate that they really have quit. Others may quit for the last session and then return to smoking after the pressure is off.

Our TTM programs are markedly different. There is no pressure to quit a behavior at any time. If anything, as we've already explained, participants are persuaded not to take action until they are ready. Often participants in TTM smoking cessation programs quit months after the intervention ends, but at significantly higher rates than those in the control groups. In our studies, the "lie rates," or what we prefer to call "misreporting" in our type of program, were only 2 percent, compared to action programs with rates fifteen to twenty times higher.[18]

When we were asked to join other authors to draft a Surgeon General's report on smoking, we reviewed 125 studies on lie rates in smoking cessation programs and confirmed that lie rates are much lower under conditions when there were no pressures or incentives to lie. At first, the other authors who were action-oriented said our "2 percent" findings couldn't be true and that there was no way our claim would be included in the Surgeon General's report. But our results did prove to be valid and are in that Surgeon General's report.[19] Our findings were later accepted by the National Cancer Institute so they could fund research proposals on smoking cessation programs like ours for entire populations.

The same "lie rate" problem exists with weight management programs. Under some conditions, when people are pressured to take action whether they are ready or not, lying can be a big barrier to getting valid research findings. So, program participants must weigh in to verify their results, just as biochemical testing is used in some smoking cessation programs. But in our approach, under conditions that really respect the motto of "Wherever you are at, we can work with that,"™ people feel free to be honest about their progress. The misreporting of weight in our TTM studies is only 1 percent. There is no need to rush to action or pretend that action is the only measure of success when the goal is to move forward at your own rate. Success is a process that unfolds over time and involves progressing through the Stages of Change.

The Stages of Change are often illustrated as a straight line, as in the following chart.

FIGURE 1

Stages of Change

PRECONTEMPLATION ▶ CONTEMPLATION ▶ PREPARATION ▶ ACTION ▶ MAINTENANCE ▶ TERMINATION

This suggests that individuals should follow a linear pattern, progressing straight through from one stage to the next. Some do. But many follow a spiral pattern, as illustrated in figure 2. They may progress from one stage to the next, but then return to an earlier stage. This spiral pattern is similar to what happens in the stages of child development. Young children may progress to a more independent stage, such as moving from sleeping with their parents to sleeping in their own bed. But when they encounter distress from certain events, such as their parents going away for a weekend and leaving them with a babysitter, they may return to their parents' bed. After their parents reassure them that they will still be there when needed, the children progress back to their own bed.

FIGURE 2

Stages of Change Spiral

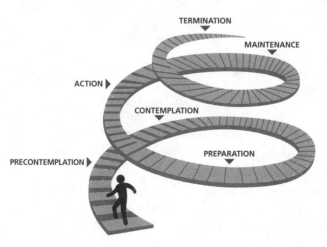

With TTM, relapse is seen as just one type of regression (usually from the action stage back to an earlier stage). But in a model focused *only* on action, relapse is treated as if it is the same as regression. Judy's story demonstrates what we mean.

Judy, a fifty-four-year-old secretary in Nebraska, finally felt prepared to lose weight again after being demoralized for about a decade. She had learned how demanding the action stage is, so she was setting it as her top priority. But then bad news arrived—her husband was diagnosed with prostate cancer. Understandably, Judy decided *his* recovery needed to be *her* top priority at that time. So, she returned to the contemplation stage, quite confident that in the next six months, her husband's cancer would be under control and she would again be ready to move forward toward her goal. She also thought that inviting her husband to join her in losing weight when he was feeling recovered might be good for his health and happiness as well—so she purposely put her own weight-loss plans on hold.

Unlike Judy and others who use the Stages of Change model, individuals starting an *action*-oriented weight management program who are faced with an unexpected stressor may be among the majority who end up withdrawing and dropping out. They may recognize early how demanding the action-focused plans will be and decide, like Judy, that this is not the best of times to take action. They may feel like failures for dropping out, and their counselors may view them as failures. But the real failure may be that the program wasn't flexible enough to match their help to the participant's Stage of Change.

Relapsing or Recycling?

In TTM, instead of "relapsing," we think "recycling," and we view this as a normal part of the change process. And while most research on relapse has focused on experiences that trigger relapse, we have focused heavily on stress and distress. But in addition to examining the causes, we've also studied the *consequences* of relapse. We know that perhaps the biggest barrier to successful change is demoralization and that this can be a consequence of relapse. In TTM, we often find that people who regress from action or maintenance all the way back to precontemplation are the most likely to feel demoralized. Fortunately, with the folks we have worked with, more than 80 percent get back on the path of change. They return to contemplating, then move on to preparing for their next action attempt. This is especially true with behaviors like smoking cessation or exercise.*

We've learned that there is only one major mistake self-changers make when they relapse—they become demoralized and give up all hope that they can change. We let our clients know that we won't give up on them and that we'll do our darndest to keep them from giving up on themselves. We want our readers to know this too.

Termination

Is it better to be "in recovery" or "recovered"? This is the most controversial question raised by TTM. This question asks whether the maintenance stage can be terminated and whether people can successfully exit from the change process altogether. We use three criteria to determine whether someone has solved a problem and is done with the change process. The first is that they have *zero* temptation to return to their previous problem behavior. With addictive behaviors, for example, to be considered "done" with the Stages of Change process, individuals have to experience no temptations to return to a behavior such as smoking or drinking regardless of any risky situations they may find themselves in. Whether they are anxious, angry, bored, depressed, distressed, lonely, or stressed, they need to have no temptation to go back to the bottle or to nicotine. The second criterion is that they have full confidence, or self-efficacy, that they will not relapse back to old behaviors—no matter how challenging the situation. The third criterion is that they are so comfortable with the change that they no longer have to make any efforts to keep from relapsing.

Given how controversial this issue is, we need to make clear that these individuals aren't saying they *can* smoke or drink and have no risk to relapse. They are saying *that with zero temptation and total confidence, there is no risk of returning to their addictive behavior.* This is not a decision they are making. This is the stage they have reached after years of effort and after having already mastered tempting situations and building their self-confidence.

---

* We have, however, found that when it comes to patients who stop taking a medication for their condition, more than 80 percent regressed all the way back to precontemplation. Further research is needed. These results suggest the importance of providers accurately assessing their patients' readiness to take their medication as prescribed, since with some meds, they may only have one chance before the patients give up on the medication.

When I train substance abuse counselors and I reach this stage of teaching, there is strong and immediate pushback. Hands go up and voices call out in protest, since many of the counselors have been or are in recovery. Since the advent of Alcoholics Anonymous's abstinence-based Twelve Step model, most treatment programs and addiction experts have supported the idea that alcoholism and other addictions are chronic diseases that require lifelong recovery maintenance, including going to peer support meetings and practicing the Twelve Steps each day. Strong arguments are made that being in recovery (as opposed to being "recovered") is best, such as this addict's dramatic testimonial:

> Each day in recovery I remind myself of the hell I had to live through and the efforts I have made to make sure alcohol doesn't retake control of my life. Being in recovery has been the majority of my life; it is such a part of who I am and who I intend to be.

Frankly, we noticed that it seems harder for some of those who see themselves as recovered to speak out publically. Sometimes they talk to us privately and say things like this:

> I have been sober for twenty-five years. I haven't gone to a recovery meeting for years. I really love knowing that alcohol is no longer a part of my present, though it was an important part of my past. I feel so free to put my time, energy, and efforts into enhancing other parts of my life.

Unfortunately, there has been all too little research on the termination stage. In part, this is because we usually follow people for only two or three years after they reach the maintenance stage. When it comes to gathering information regarding the termination of unhealthy habits, there seems to be a difference between people's perceptions and their reality. Informal surveys of individuals with long-term abstinence from multiple substances like nicotine and alcohol, show that most people believe they can "recover" from a nicotine addiction, but they cannot be "recovered" alcoholics. However, we found that in the first five years of recovery, the results were almost the same for nicotine addicts and alcoholics regarding their temptation and confidence levels. About 20 percent of both groups reached the criteria of zero temptation and total confidence. In addition, despite the belief that it's harder to quit drinking than smoking, research by others has found that individuals with multiple addictions typically report that the hardest habit to break free from was tobacco—harder than heroin, alcohol, marijuana, or cocaine.[20]

One guess for this discrepancy is that historically, unlike alcoholics, few smokers counted on recovery communities, like Nicotine Anonymous, to get free from their nicotine addiction. There is no question that being a part of a recovery community has been an incredibly powerful and helpful experience for millions of people. For many, those communities have been like second families, often healthier and more helpful families. For many folks, being in recovery is a proud part of their identity and offers them a sense of community. Others have found sufficient support in their families, friends, non–Twelve Step support groups, religious congregations, and communities and they want to take pride in being recovered.

Without a doubt, *all* of these individuals have reason to take pride in their many accomplishments. Our hope is that we can continue to learn from these extraordinary people and that, regardless of the terminology, we can draw upon those lessons and upon TTM to help dramatically reduce years of suffering and struggling and increase the years of thriving for all who change.

Although much of this chapter has focused on smoking and alcohol addiction, we want to stress that this book is for *all* self-changers on the continuum of change. No matter what Stage of Change you are in, you will find ongoing help in the coming chapters for moving through the Stages of Change and using the Principles of Progress to meet your particular goals, whether your goal might be eating more healthily, cutting back on drinking (if you aren't an alcoholic and need to stop drinking altogether), or developing an exercise program that contributes to physical well-being while reducing stress. Of course, those who *are* addicted to nicotine and/or alcohol, and who do view abstinence as their ultimate goal, will also find help in these pages.

Now that you know the Stages of Change represent a map for your important journey of change, you will learn a series of practical principles and procedures for progressing from one stage to the next. Your first journey will focus on moving through the Stages of Change for managing stress and distress with healthy and effective habits. Since stress and distress drive so much of the four biggest threats to your health and happiness (smoking, alcohol abuse, unhealthy eating, and lack of exercise) and are the biggest reasons for relapse, this journey will provide a solid base for bringing down the biggest risky behaviors for your health and building the multiple domains for happiness and well-being.

4

The Principles of Progress, Part I

PRACTICAL TOOLS FOR MOVING FROM
PRECONTEMPLATION TO ACTION

In the last chapter, we described some similarities between the Trans-theorectical Model (TTM) stages of *intentional* change and the stages of *developmental* change in children. We focused on how in both cases individuals can regress to an earlier stage. While these types of change patterns have things in common, there are also serious differences. In the case of the stages of developmental change in children, there appears to be built-in motivation to progress from one stage to the next. For example, Jan and I personally watched each of our five grandchildren learn how to become freer by moving about and mastering crawling. But even though they became skilled at flying across the floor on their hands and knees, they still were driven to learn to walk. They were determined to master gravity—even in the face of big barriers, like having some painful falls and embarrassing missteps.

Precontemplation, Motivation, and Change

We have not found the same internal, built-in motivation for people in the precontemplation stage of behavior change. They can remain stuck in this stage for decades, doing much damage to their bodies, their minds, and their relationships with others. Over many years of working with change seekers, we have identified some developmental events that produce progress. For example, we have found that after numerous trials and errors, self-changers who wanted to quit smoking reached maintenance at a mean age of thirty-nine. Of course, when we use "mean" in this context, we're talking about averages, although those of us who have made it past age thirty-nine know that it is indeed a "mean" age!

It is a middle age when we stop to evaluate how we have been living so far and whether our harmful habits will keep us from reaching a ripe and happy old age.

We also found that individuals who faced a crisis like a heart attack were more likely to be motivated enough to break out of precontemplation. Other people were motivated to reach maintenance because of other life circumstances. One couple, for example, told us that they offered their son whatever special gift he might want for his twenty-first birthday. He said, "Mom and Dad, what I would most love is if you would stop smoking together." His wish motivated them to change. Another couple—also longtime smokers—had a beloved dog die from lung cancer. That sad event caused the wife to progress through the Stages of Change until she finally quit smoking. (The husband wasn't as successful; although he was driven to buy a new dog!)

Staging Yourself for Healthy Stress Management

To apply the change principles most effectively, you need to assess what stage of change you are in. We will start by applying the change principles to healthy stress management, since stress is so closely linked to the causes of relapse for the other four high-risk behaviors—smoking, alcohol abuse, unhealthy eating, and inactivity.

The criteria for healthy stress management includes spending at least twenty minutes every day on intentionally relaxing, walking, or talking (seeking support) to let the stress leave your body and your mind. To assess what Stage of Change you are in, check the statement that best reflects where you are in the process of healthy stress management:

☐ I don't intend to spend at least 20 minutes a day on healthy stress management.

☐ I intend to adopt healthy stress management in the next six months.

☐ I intend to adopt healthy stress management in the next month.

☐ I have been practicing healthy stress management for less than six months.

☐ I have been practicing healthy stress management for more than six months.

☐ I don't experience stress in my life.

Next we will explore how the pros and cons of changing vary across each of the stages of change, with an emphasis on practicing healthy stress management.

Making Decisions: To Change or Not to Change?

When my colleagues and I developed TTM, we included decision making as one of its most important elements—a concept our research showed was missing in other leading systems of psychotherapy. Originally, we assumed decision making about health and well-being would follow more traditional lines, where people make rational, practical decisions by weighing the benefits and costs, gains and losses, or pros and cons of changing.

We started by examining the "decisional balance sheet" model created by Irving Janis and Leon Mann at Yale in the late 1970s.[21] The decisional balance sheet records the advantages and disadvantages of making a decision: the practical gains and losses for self, practical gains and losses for significant others, self-approval or disapproval, and approval or disapproval from significant others. When we came up with questions to assess the importance of Janis and Mann's theories for decisions about taking action, we found that the decision-making process was usually much simpler. After concluding that only *two* factors—the pros and cons of changing—were involved, we were able to develop brief assessments of six to eight questions to assess the pros and cons of a behavior change. Then we could determine how the pros and cons varied across the Stages of Change.

Although we didn't realize it for some time, we were also discovering that making the decision to change one's behavior for improved health was nowhere near as rational and "scientific" as we had assumed. Nor was it nearly as conscious.

Our research about decision making showed that when we plotted an individual's raw scores (the average scores for *all* responses) for the pros and cons of a behavior like quitting smoking across the Stages of Change, the pros scored higher than the cons at each stage. Then we went deeper by carefully examining responses to each Stage of Change among a broader cross section of self-changers and taking into account things like how easy or difficult it may be to respond. We discovered a remarkably different pattern. In precontemplation, the cons of quitting outweighed the pros for twelve different behaviors. In contemplation, the pros and cons were about tied, reflecting the doubt or ambivalence about the value of taking action. With preparation, the pros and cons crossed, and the pros were consistently higher. With action and maintenance, the pros and cons typically continued to separate with the pros getting increasingly higher than the cons.

In other words, TTM captured how most of us approach and think about self-change. At first (in the precontemplation stage), the idea of change doesn't seem all that appealing or doesn't seem possible. Then the more we weigh the pros, the more possible and desirable change seems. When we get to the point where the positives outweigh the negatives, we're on the road to action. And when we finally get to maintenance, we grow more certain that our decision was the right one for personal happiness and well-being.

In my previous book on the Stages of Change, *Changing for Good*, I describe the day I decided to see if I could measure how much the pros increased from precontemplation to contemplation to action and how much the cons decreased. I relied on the highest technology in my study back then: namely, a ruler. I discovered that across twelve different problem behaviors, the pros increased substantially. I won't go into all the statistical details here, but I was astounded by how much above the norm they were. A comparison would be if an individual's IQ increased 15 points. Average college students have IQs of about 115. If they could increase their IQs by 15 points, they would be geniuses! One of the goals of this book is to help you increase your behavior change IQ by just 5 points. You don't have to be a genius to change: You just need to work smarter rather than harder.

From precontemplation to action, the cons decreased by about half the amount the pros had increased. Then I applied all these findings into a new dataset and found remarkably similar and predictable results. I excitedly told Jan what an amazing discovery I had made. It was a real breakthrough to be able to predict the magnitude of change, let alone the *direction* of change. Jan tried to calm me down, since she felt I was getting a little "manic" (which I confess I am prone to do), but

I couldn't contain myself. I immediately imagined what these findings could mean when it came to all behavior change—especially things like smoking and cancer prevention. So I called my secretary, Elaine, and told her to call an immediate meeting with the Cancer Prevention Research Center. Fortunately, they were as excited as I was. This new understanding of the change process would significantly affect the way we came to help self-changers shed unhealthy habits and embrace healthier lifestyles that could extend—and even save—their lives. Since we had determined that the pros for change need to increase two times as much as cons decrease, we decided that in this book we would put at least twice as much emphasis on helping you raise your pros for a particular behavior change.

Decades later, my amazement at this discovery has increased as my findings have grown even more solid—with more studies being done on even more behaviors and with more groups of self-changers. For example, using much more advanced technology, one of our former students, Kara Hall, and her major professor and colleague, Joseph Rossi, applied advanced statistics to analyze 125 studies conducted on forty-eight different behaviors with participants from ten different countries.[22] They found that the pros increased the same as what I had discovered using my simple ruler, while the cons also mirrored my findings.

The Stages of Change are like a map that helps us identify where we are in the journey of change. But this map does not tell us how to progress from one stage to the next. When my colleagues and I developed TTM, we started with the processes of change used in leading systems of psychotherapy, counseling, and behavior change. We then discovered how different change processes were emphasized most at particular stages of change. This laid the foundations for developing what we call the "Principles of Progress," twelve practical principles that we view as effective approaches for applying the theoretical processes of behavior change. We will now look at the seven principles that you can apply as you move from stage to stage in changing one or more behaviors.

The First Principle of Progress: Increase Your Pros to Move from Precontemplation to Contemplation

To progress from precontemplation to contemplation, your pros of changing must increase. If your pros are not increasing, you are not progressing—which means you are not changing.

The following exercise is an experiment to see if you can dramatically increase your pros of changing one of the five big threats to your health and happiness: *stress.*

We continue our journey of change by helping you affirm more of your body, your mind, and your relationship with others by appreciating the importance of one fundamental process of life—feeling. Feeling better. Feeling healthier. Feeling happier. This Feeling Better exercise contains more than forty-five pros, or benefits, that can accompany healthy management of stress and distress. Your challenge is to select the pros that are important to a decision to practice healthy stress management for at least twenty minutes every day. The more benefits you accept and view as important, the greater the return will be when you are ready to commit to action.

The good news is we consistently have been able to help the majority (60 to 75 percent) of participants in our programs adopt and continue effective and healthy management strategies in just a few months. Practicing such stress management behaviors gives you a more solid and secure foundation, making it more likely that you will succeed in changing the other critical four threats to your health and happiness.

One of the weird realities and paradoxes of behavior change is that the very process of changing can be a major cause of stress and distress, which we're trying to reduce. How many changes in your life have you had in the past twelve months? Research shows that the more changes you have experienced, the more stress you have to cope with. And here we are, asking you to add more changes to your life! But keep in mind the title of this book—*Changing to Thrive*—as you do this exercise, as you read more about change throughout the book, and as you follow the suggestions we offer as we guide you through it. All we ask is that you are open to change your mind and begin to believe that the effort you make to incorporate healthy changes in your life is really worth it.

———————————————— **EXERCISE** ————————————————

Feeling Better: Benefits of Healthy Stress Management

We have grouped more than forty-five pros into different domains of well-being, such as, physical and emotional well-being. This approach can help you progress toward healthy stress management. This grouping can also help prepare you to enhance these multiple domains of well-being discussed in chapter 12.

Please select the benefits that are important to you from the lists below and write them down on a separate piece of paper or digital sheet. Then, add your own benefits for each category and rank them in order of importance.

Behavioral Well-Being. *I want to*

- ☐ Reduce cravings for smoking
- ☐ Reduce cravings for drinking too much
- ☐ Reduce cravings for unhealthy food
- ☐ Reduce excuses for lack of exercise
- ☐ Reduce cravings for other risky behaviors (add these behaviors to your list of benefits)

Physical Well-Being. *I want to*

- ☐ Reduce the risk of high blood pressure
- ☐ Reduce the risk of digestive problems
- ☐ Reduce the risk of chronic fatigue
- ☐ Reduce the risk of headaches
- ☐ Reduce the risk of heart disease
- ☐ Reduce the risk of a stroke
- ☐ Reduce the risk of colds, flus, or sore throats
- ☐ Reduce the risk of high blood sugar
- ☐ Reduce the risk of an impaired immune system
- ☐ Reduce the risk of jaw pain (temporomandibular joint disorders, or TMJ)
- ☐ Reduce the risk of irritable bowel syndrome
- ☐ Have fewer injuries
- ☐ Have fewer incidents of asthma, hives, and eczema

☐ Have fewer hot spells

☐ Have fewer backaches

☐ Have less muscle tension

☐ Have a body that will be better able to fight off illness

Purposeful Well-Being. *I want to*

☐ Have more interest in the future

☐ Have better self-esteem

☐ Have more control in my life

☐ Function better at work and home

☐ Have more resources to fulfill my passions

Emotional Well-Being. *I want to*

☐ Reduce the risk of anxiety

☐ Reduce the risk of depression

☐ Reduce nervousness

☐ Increase joy in my life

☐ Feel more relaxed

☐ Enjoy life more

☐ Have fewer psychological problems

☐ Sleep better

☐ Reduce my worries about the future

☐ Feel more centered

Social Well-Being. *I want to*

☐ Feel good about the example I am setting

☐ Help my loved ones to worry less about my health

☐ Be less grouchy around friends, family, and co-workers

☐ Improve my relationships with others

☐ Prevent sexual problems

Functioning. *I want to*

- ☐ Have more energy
- ☐ Improve my concentration
- ☐ Increase my motivation
- ☐ Reduce periods of forgetfulness
- ☐ Improve my ability to make decisions

After you've done this exercise and added more benefits of your own, look over your list of benefits. The more benefits you identify as important, the better prepared you will be to take the next step toward lasting change.

Jan has a PowerPoint presentation that illustrates how employees can react to more changes at work. It is a photo of Clint Eastwood playing his popular Dirty Harry character in the movie *Sudden Impact*. With his pistol pointing out, Clint repeats his classic line "Go ahead, make my day," with this twist: "Go ahead, make one more change!" Keep this image in mind as a dramatic reminder that positive change can help you more effectively manage the stress or distress that can occur when you make one or more changes.

The Second Principle of Progress: Increase Your Consciousness to Increase Your Behavior Change IQ

"Consciousness raising"—which, put simply, means getting the facts you need to be better informed—is an important and essential element in the change process. We first encountered this process in the work of Sigmund Freud, whose theory emphasized making unconscious processes conscious.[23] In fact, almost all major therapies begin by trying to raise your level of awareness about your problems and solutions to your problems. And that's exactly what we're trying to do with this book.

We began by sharing what we've learned about change from the remarkable self-changers we've worked with and studied over many years. In doing so, we are intentionally trying to help you change your mind—your mental model of how people change—just as our minds have been changed and opened by all that we've discovered about the Stages of Change. We believe in the old saying "Knowledge is power." When we know more about change, we can develop more willpower or control over behaviors that we may have once felt helpless or hopeless to change.

Imagine that there were no maps, and you have to find your way to Orono, a town in Maine. How long might it take you before you felt helpless and hopeless and lost? At times, we characterize the Stages of Change as a map. Instead of saying, "You can't get there from here," we try our best to guide you. We assess and respect where you are at in your journey of change.

Many professionals and programs *say* they use TTM, the Stages of Change model, or Prochaska model, but they don't really. And often they misuse it by excluding at-risk individuals who are in precontemplation or contemplation, but not yet ready to move to the preparation stage. By excluding people in precontemplation or contemplation, their "action only" success rates appear higher because they only deal with a select group of "ready for change" individuals. Yet they're leaving a large portion of at-risk people behind—they aren't helping nearly as many people as they could. Our model is an inclusive one, and our goal is to leave no travelers behind.

While the Stages of Change are like the map that shows you where you are on your journey of change, they do not tell you *how* to travel to the next stage. That is where the principles and processes come into play. Individuals in precontemplation, for example, progress by increasing their pros and their consciousness. Freud emphasized that consciousness raising works best when resistance is analyzed first. That's what you were doing when you reviewed your inward and outward defenses and took an honest look at what gets in the way of your self-change efforts. You were analyzing your resistance, as Freud advised us to do if we want to become more self-aware.

Remember that defenses are designed to help us fool ourselves, since they don't fool others very often. As long as we can fool ourselves—whether we convince ourselves that inactivity is not a risk, deny the consequences of binge drinking, withdraw from conversations or counseling because it feels like too much pressure to change, readily give good reasons for bad habits, or blame others for our distress—it is difficult to take an honest look at our problems and increase our consciousness enough to move from the precontemplation stage to contemplation. You can probably see why precontemplating clients who are pressured by a professional into moving directly to action are almost certain to fail.

Professionals who use TTM the way it is intended to be used are not impatient with their clients. Our goal is to be a positive influence without becoming a negative source of pressure. We help our clients become more conscious by offering education, information, and feedback. What follows is a consciousness-raising exercise that will help you become more aware of the many ways stress can manifest itself. Check which of these you experience, and then track how each decreases in frequency, duration, and intensity as you learn more healthy ways to manage your stress.

──────────── EXERCISE ────────────

Raising Your Consciousness about How Your Stress Shows Itself and How It Hides Behind Unhealthy Behaviors

I know I am stressed when I

- ☐ increase my smoking
- ☐ increase my drinking
- ☐ increase my eating of "comfort" foods
- ☐ decrease my exercise
- ☐ get headaches
- ☐ get backaches
- ☐ get neck aches
- ☐ get a dry mouth
- ☐ get wet palms
- ☐ have a tight chest
- ☐ have rapid breathing
- ☐ grind my teeth
- ☐ worry more than usual

- ☐ forget things
- ☐ have rashes
- ☐ have diarrhea
- ☐ have constipation
- ☐ have an upset stomach
- ☐ have more gas than usual
- ☐ have trouble sleeping
- ☐ feel fatigued
- ☐ have lower self-esteem
- ☐ feel grouchy
- ☐ avoid friends and family
- ☐ feel little joy
- ☐ others (list on a separate sheet)

Before TTM was developed, behavior science had concluded that education does not produce behavior change. Such thinking was based on "quit rates." For example, in clinics that tried to get smokers to quit by teaching them about the multiple diseases that smoking can cause, there were little or no significant improvements in quit rates compared to their control groups. The problem was that each technique or change process was tested to determine if it led to *immediate action*, like quitting right away. In TTM, education is not expected to lead to immediate action; it is expected to lead to contemplation. The following example explains this further.

While it's true that the U.S. Surgeon General's report revealing the harmful effects of tobacco use is credited with having the largest impact on smoking, this report didn't lead to immediate action. Rather, it led to deliberation and contemplation that then led to preparation and action, and this resulted in a roughly 1 percent reduction in smoking each year for the past fifty years. In the meantime, each year about 500,000 smokers still died prematurely from their addiction. The point here is that a single-stage change process, no matter how powerful, cannot carry the entire load of helping individuals and populations change efficiently and effectively. As you will see, increased consciousness is an essential element for change, but it isn't the only necessary ingredient.

The Third Principle of Progress: Use Dramatic Relief to Move from Precontemplation

"Dramatic relief" (paying attention to feelings) is one of the oldest traditions used in the change process. Ancient Greeks relied on art and dramatic theater to relieve and release strong emotions and enhance well-being—a technique called "catharsis." When we hold our feelings in, we can get distressed or depressed. However, if we can release difficult emotions like anger or guilt, we also reduce the emotional pressure they contain, and we aren't as tempted to numb them with one or more of the four high-risk behaviors. We first found this process in Fritz Perls's writings on Gestalt therapy, which focuses on how we experience our web of relationships to people and our environment in the present moment and is very effective at raising and then relieving emotional pressures.[24]

A patient suffering from alcohol abuse and gastrointestinal symptoms from his unhealthy diet found himself weeping heavily while watching an Ingmar Bergman film—a dramatic story of a husband and wife's relationship called *Scenes from a Marriage.* As he watched the movie, he began to feel how angry he was at himself for having traded the possibility of a more satisfying marriage for the security of his current unhappy situation. Because of the inspiration he felt from the Bergman classic, he felt his distress beginning to lift. In its place was a new determination to leave his hopelessly lifeless marriage. This patient's own scene from a marriage illustrates how dramatic relief can include positive emotions like inspiration, as well as the release of more troubling feelings like guilt or self-blame.

In TTM, dramatic relief is intended to move you *emotionally* from precontemplation. The techniques we suggest come from others who have been able to break out of demoralization and move toward action. Methods like journaling or keeping a diary, for example, can help you openly (and safely) express your emotions and produce considerable relief from stress and distress. They can also help with addictive behaviors like alcohol and drug misuse.

The following exercise is designed to help you determine whether you deal with your distressing feelings more directly and effectively or more indirectly and deficiently. When doing this exercise, we encourage you to think about stress and how it is often connected to having too many demands placed on you and not enough resources to cope with those demands.

EXERCISE

How I Deal with My Distressing Feelings

For each of the following examples, circle the appropriate numbers to rate how regularly you do that behavior, and how much it helps you deal with your distressing feelings.

---

1. I tell family and friends that I have too many demands on me and need more support.

NEVER				REGULARLY
1	2	3	4	5

NOT HELPFUL				VERY HELPFUL
1	2	3	4	5

---

2. I tell myself I should be able to cope with whatever comes my way.

NEVER				REGULARLY
1	2	3	4	5

NOT HELPFUL				VERY HELPFUL
1	2	3	4	5

---

3. I read blogs or watch TV shows that inspire me to think about changing an unhealthy behavior.

NEVER				REGULARLY
1	2	3	4	5

NOT HELPFUL				VERY HELPFUL
1	2	3	4	5

---

4. I get upset with myself over the number of times I have tried and failed to change.

NEVER				REGULARLY
1	2	3	4	5

NOT HELPFUL				VERY HELPFUL
1	2	3	4	5

5. I express or experience my feelings through activities like journaling, drawing, or watching movies.

NEVER				REGULARLY
1	2	3	4	5

NOT HELPFUL				VERY HELPFUL
1	2	3	4	5

6. I stuff my feelings with tobacco, alcohol, or junk food.

NEVER				REGULARLY
1	2	3	4	5

NOT HELPFUL				VERY HELPFUL
1	2	3	4	5

The good news about stress is that you can receive effective relief in healthy ways that are less dramatic (and dangerous) than smoking, drinking, and overeating. You can learn to let go of your stress by relaxing your body, your mind, and your entire being. The following exercise presents relaxation techniques that can provide immediate relief. Check the ones you will try out to see if they are effective for you.

──────── **EXERCISE** ────────

Relaxation Techniques

Relaxation and meditation are great stress management techniques that can be done anywhere, anytime. With so many different kinds of relaxation exercises to choose from, chances are you can find one that is right for you.

Relaxation Choices: Which Will You Try?

☐ **Progressive muscle.** Beginning with your head, systematically tense and relax each part of your body. Hold the tension for about thirty seconds and then release. This helps you learn the difference between how tension and relaxation feels.

☐ **Autogenics (giving suggestions to yourself).** Beginning with your head, imagine that each part of your body is feeling warm and heavy. Concentrate on the warmth and weight of each limb in turn.

☐ **Visual imagery.** Imagine a peaceful scene or location. Use your senses to focus on the sounds, sights, and feelings of the peaceful place.

☐ **Meditation.** Repeat a peaceful, single-syllable word (such as "om," "calm," "one," or "peace") to yourself over and over again.

☐ **Countdown relaxation.** If you have less time, count from one to ten as you inhale deeply; then exhale slowly counting from ten to one, feeling yourself relax as you approach one. If you'd like, imagine yourself letting go of a worry with each deep breath you take and feeling calm and relaxed when you finish.

Don't be discouraged if you find yourself getting distracted as you practice these techniques. If your mind wanders, simply bring your thoughts back to the exercise. In time, you will find yourself becoming less and less distracted.

The Fourth Principle of Progress: Decrease Your Cons to Move from Contemplation

To progress from contemplation to preparation, your cons of changing must decrease—but as noted earlier, only by half as much as your pros need to increase. That's why we put twice as much emphasis on increasing your pros as we do on decreasing your cons. For most behaviors, the number one negative against changing is the time it takes. Just one more demand you have to squeeze into your busy day. *"Is it worth it, or should I put it off?"*

The following exercise can help you identify ways to decrease the number one con—time—as well the other negatives you list. (Personally, I have two pet peeves about time. I hate being late! And I hate being early!) The more than forty-five benefits of healthy stress management can also be particularly helpful in thinking about time and the investment it takes to change an unwanted behavior. The more pros of healthy stress management you uncover as being important to you, the better you are able see how worthwhile it is to invest time in your efforts to change.

Change is a "bank" that gives great returns! When I'm considering whether a new change is worth my time, I am more likely to commit my time if I can earn thirty benefits compared with only three—that's ten times as much return on my time. So keep increasing your pros and you can also reduce the number one con—time.

EXERCISE

Decrease Your Cons with Correct Comebacks

Look over the following cons and check those that apply to you and your attitudes toward changing. Then read through the comebacks for new messages you could give yourself. Can you think of others? If so, jot them down on a separate paper or digital sheet. Take a minute to think about how it feels to have this "dialogue" with yourself. Do you feel your attitudes becoming more positive?

_____ **#1 Con: It takes too much time.**

Comebacks:

- I can get more than forty-five benefits for twenty minutes of time. What else do I do that pays off this well?

- If I don't take time to stop the aches and pains—physical, emotional, and social—everything will probably get worse. Then it will take more time to reach a point where I feel better—physically, emotionally, and socially.

- The time I invest can save me much more time than I now spend on worrying, forgetting, and avoiding.

_____ **#2 Con: It is easier to smoke, drink, or eat.**

Comebacks:

- My multiple symptoms of stress are telling me that smoking, drinking, and eating are not making me merry!
- Smoking, drinking, and eating are magnifying my symptoms of stress rather than lessening them through healthy stress management.
- If I manage my stress effectively, I can win a trifecta of managing my breathing, drinking, and unhealthy eating more effectively.

_____ **#3 Con: Stress drives me to be more productive.**

Comebacks:

- That's not what the evidence says. Unmanaged stress costs employers about $2,500 per employee per year, mostly due to lost productivity.
- Unmanaged stress drives me to the doctor, the bathroom, the bar, and the refrigerator.
- Stress is speaking loud and clear, telling me, *I have too many demands and not enough resources, so I have to invest more in resources to manage my demands.*

_____ **#4 Con: I don't know how to manage stress effectively.**

Comebacks:

- I am learning.
- I am motivated to find new methods and move ahead.

The Fifth Principle of Progress: Use Environmental Reevaluation to Move from Contemplation to Preparation

"Environmental reevaluation" (noticing your effects on others) combines both emotional and cognitive (mental) assessments of how the presence or absence of a threatening habit can affect your social environment. An example would be how someone's alcohol abuse can affect his or her family and friends. Originally this change process was identified only from our interviews with people but was not emphasized in any of the leading theories of therapy. That may be because we did not include the Twelve Step model of recovery maintenance in our initial comparative analysis. When we originally developed TTM, Alcoholics Anonymous (AA) was the predominant Twelve Step model of treatment and recovery maintenance for alcoholics (people with a moderate to severe alcohol use disorder). And at that time, AA was viewed as a self-help program managed by laypeople. Since then, studies have proven that the AA program is an excellent and effective way for people to emotionally and cognitively assess how their alcoholism affects their families, friends, companies, and communities, as well as themselves. Al Anon—the leading Twelve Step program for family and friends of alcoholics—furthers this assessment, because it acknowledges the many ways a loved one's drinking hurts relationships and confronts the social damage that can result from alcohol misuse.

To move beyond unhealthy behaviors to happiness and well-being, all self-changers, not just alcoholics, need to think about how their stress and distress can threaten the health and happiness of others as well as themselves. As part of a collaborative team, I helped create an anonymous website where soldiers could seek help for whatever behaviors were bothering them. The program was based on TTM, but also included an innovative aspect we called "behavior agnostic." By this, we meant that it doesn't matter what behavior you believe you need to change. Regardless of your problem, "Wherever you are at, we can work with that."™ Again, TTM principles have shown to be effective with more than fifty behaviors, so helping self-changers apply the principles to their priorities is part of our mission to increase behavior change. For example, in our initial pilot project for soldiers, the behaviors named as top priorities were all emotional behaviors, like stress and distress. This was not surprising given how many soldiers have served in traumatic situations that can produce post-traumatic stress disorder (PTSD). The behavior that was selected the most was anger. Clearly there were troops who struggled with how their anger affects their families, friends, and fellow soldiers, as well as themselves.

Use the following exercise to assess how your own threatening habits may negatively affect others and how changing your behaviors may enhance the health and happiness of those you care about.

---------------------------------- **EXERCISE** ----------------------------------

Environmental Reevaluation: Notice Your Effects on Others

Circle the appropriate number to rate how frequently or intensely others react to your unhealthy habits and would react to your getting free from them.

---

1. Others worry about how my smoking, drinking, eating, or moving habits affect my health.

NEVER				REGULARLY
1	2	3	4	5

---

2. Others will be happy for me when I get free from my unhealthy habits.

NOT AT ALL				INTENSELY
1	2	3	4	5

---

3. Others worry about how my unhealthy habits can affect their health and habits.

NOT AT ALL				INTENSELY
1	2	3	4	5

---

4. Others will feel better about their health when they get free from the effects of my unhealthy habits.

NOT AT ALL				INTENSELY
1	2	3	4	5

---

5. Others worry about how my unhealthy habits encourage others to live less healthy.

NOT AT ALL				INTENSELY
1	2	3	4	5

---

6. Others will feel inspired to work on their unhealthy habits when they see me progressing.

NOT AT ALL				INTENSELY
1	2	3	4	5

---

7. Others fear that if I don't change, my health will get worse.

NOT AT ALL   INTENSELY

1   2   3   4   5

8. Others will feel happy when I keep moving ahead in the face of setbacks.

NOT AT ALL   INTENSELY

1   2   3   4   5

Total your score. A score of 30 or more indicates that your changing will enhance not only your own health and happiness but also the health and happiness of people you care about.

Total score: _____

I offer the following story to demonstrate how useful the Principles of Progress can be. I was flown out overnight to Hollywood to help an ad agency use TTM in a television media campaign designed to highlight the toll smoking can take. In the thirty-second TV spot, an obviously grieving man mourns, "I always feared my smoking would cause lung cancer. I always worried my smoking would lead to an early death. But I never imagined it would happen to my wife." And then on the screen we see the message "50,000 deaths a year in the U.S. due to passive smoking."

In thirty seconds, three powerful Principles of Progress for nicotine addicts in precontemplation or contemplation are hit upon: (1) Consciousness raising: 50,000 deaths are due to passive smoking; (2) Dramatic relief: You can reduce your fear and worry if you begin progressing to stopping smoking; and (3) Environmental reevaluation: Here's how my smoking can hurt others and how my quitting could help. This brings us to the next Principle of Progress.

The Sixth Principle of Progress: Use Self-Reevaluation to Move from Preparation to Action

In developing TTM, we were first influenced by Albert Ellis, the cognitive therapist who defined self-reevaluation as the cognitive reassessment of someone's unhealthy behavior, an honest look at the kind of person someone with that behavior is likely to be, and the kind of person he or she could be by changing that particular behavior. However, further research with our self-changers taught us that self-reevaluation is both an emotional and a mental reassessment of self. *"How do I think and feel about myself as a smoker (or drinker, or non-exerciser, or unhealthy eater) and how will I think and feel about myself if I quit my unhealthy behavior?"* That is the type of question we encourage you to ask yourself.

Self-reevaluation is particularly important in making progress from preparation to action. First, the individual is looking backward. Judo, a forty-six-year-old teamster and truck driver, wrote in his journal, "Early on I saw myself as more of a man—like the Marlboro Man. I liked the image—tough truck driver doing his thing. But as I got older, I started to see myself as more like a dumb truck driver—risking my lungs and my heart." Later, in the preparation stage, he wrote, "I am looking forward to saving money and protecting my health. But I see myself as maybe more stressed, given how much I depend on cigarettes when I'm upset. I hope my work on managing my stress will make a big difference."

Judo was preparing to take action, but he first needed to learn and accept that his stress might increase for the first few months of action. He had to prepare himself for what initially would be the hardest time and take the greatest effort to keep from regressing to an earlier stage and risking relapse. It is true that the additional demands he faced can be distressing. But after the worst part of action is over, Judo is very likely to experience significantly less stress as he moves toward becoming a nonsmoker.

The following exercise is designed to help you reevaluate your own sense of self as you, like Judo, prepare to take action toward your own desired change.

─────────────── **EXERCISE** ───────────────

Self-Reevaluation: Toward a Healthier and Happier Sense of Self

For each of the following examples, circle the appropriate numbers to rate how regularly you do it and how helpful it is to you.

1. I tell myself I am developing a smarter and healthier image of myself managing stress.

NEVER				REGULARLY
1	2	3	4	5

NOT HELPFUL				VERY HELPFUL
1	2	3	4	5

2. I see exercising as one of my best ways to reduce stress.

NEVER				REGULARLY
1	2	3	4	5

NOT HELPFUL				VERY HELPFUL
1	2	3	4	5

3. I see myself progressing from struggling to thriving as I keep moving ahead in the face of stress and distress.

NEVER				REGULARLY
1	2	3	4	5

NOT HELPFUL				VERY HELPFUL
1	2	3	4	5

4. I imagine letting go of my view that I need unhealthy habits to cope with stress.

NEVER				REGULARLY
1	2	3	4	5

NOT HELPFUL				VERY HELPFUL
1	2	3	4	5

5. I look forward to becoming free from one of my unhealthy habits for managing stress.

NEVER				REGULARLY
1	2	3	4	5

NOT HELPFUL				VERY HELPFUL
1	2	3	4	5

6. I tell myself I am sure I have the strength to break this habit.

NEVER				REGULARLY
1	2	3	4	5

NOT HELPFUL				VERY HELPFUL
1	2	3	4	5

7. I think about a happier self, having removed one of my biggest threats to my health.

NEVER				REGULARLY
1	2	3	4	5

NOT HELPFUL				VERY HELPFUL
1	2	3	4	5

8. I believe I will be less stressed without one of my unhealthy ways of coping.

NEVER				REGULARLY
1	2	3	4	5

NOT HELPFUL				VERY HELPFUL
1	2	3	4	5

Total your score. If your score is 60 or higher, you are affirming an image of someone who can mange stress effectively and healthfully.

Total score: _____

The first few principles of progress included decision making. You needed to be building the benefits and decreasing the costs. As your pros begin to outweigh the cons of changing, you are in the process of deciding to take action. When you are ready to take action, you need to apply the process we call "self-liberation."

The Seventh Principle of Progress: Make a Commitment to a Better Life through Self-Liberation to Move to Action

We first identified self-liberation in Rollo May's existential therapy[25] where he defines "self-liberation" as the belief in your ability to change your own behavior and your commitment and recommitment to act on that belief. Usually people refer to this process as willpower. Many people believe that willpower alone is the secret to success, and they rely almost exclusively on *willing* their way to health and happiness. When they do this, they overtax the willpower they do have and can easily demoralize themselves by ending up feeling powerless.

We will soon see in the following chapter that besides self-liberation, there are six more Principles of Progress you need to apply if you are to transform your initial action into a lasting success. While some other theories of change that rely primarily on willpower and commitment may show significant progress at six months, by twelve months the benefits usually fade. In other words, commitment alone cannot carry the whole load of lasting changes. By applying the Stages of Change and employing the Principles of Progress, however, we have found that self-changers *can* produce better outcomes at twelve months and beyond.

Commitment can be a powerful process. But you have to know how to apply it, improve it, and appreciate it as only part of the solution. First, we need to be clear that making commitments is not the same as making decisions. Ideally, decisions are rational and practical. When we make a decision, we consciously evaluate the evidence, weigh the positive and negative factors, and make the decision that is likely to have the best outcome—confident that we are following the correct course. But commitments have to go beyond evidence or certainty.

Consider a couple that was trying to decide whether or not to have a child. They read articles and books, talked to doctors and friends, but were still left with challenging questions: *"What if our child has some significant problems? We are healthy and happy now, coping effectively with the demands in our life. But will we be able to cope with all the demands that come with having and raising a child? Will we be able to handle all the emotional demands, time demands, financial demands, or all the other demands?"*

This couple was trying to turn life-changing commitments into decisions. They thought that if they just thought enough, talked enough, or read enough, they'd find the best answer. This same pattern is often followed by chronic contemplators, which causes them to be stuck in contemplation where they put off preparation until they can be *certain* they are following the correct course of action. They are like the people Friedrich Nietzsche wrote about who are prepared to sacrifice truth for certainty. Remember what we said about science—how the best we can do is to increase the probabilities that the course we follow will be the best for us? Self-liberation is an acceptance that we need not be absolutely certain about our course of action; we can still commit and recommit to change.

While TTM and the Principles of Progress don't rely solely on will-power, it is, of course an important ingredient in the change process. Here are some simple techniques for strengthening your willpower and increasing your probabilities for lasting success. If you go public with your commitment to change, you will strengthen your willpower. If you keep it a secret, you weaken your willpower. Unfortunately, many people—probably most of us—stay silent about our determination to change an unhealthy habit because we're uncertain that we'll actually succeed in our efforts. Silence is a self-defense, a way we defend ourselves from the distress of being embarrassed or ashamed when our colleagues and family watch us fail once again.

Who do you intend to tell about your commitment to change? Imagine yourself telling others that you are committing to managing your stress. Would that increase your commitment and the efforts that follow from your commitments? Consider the courage that it takes to make such public commitments. With today's easy access to email and social media like Facebook and Twitter, you can tell most of your world (or those in your world who matter most to you) about your commitment to change one of the biggest threats to your health and happiness—an act that can strengthen your willpower and deepen that commitment.

Another relatively simple technique to deepen your commitment is to increase the *healthy* choices you have for coping with the stress and distress that may come with making a change in your lifestyle. If there were only one alternative for dealing with distress, like talking to a counselor, you would be compelled to choose this option or fail, which can seem stressful. On the other hand, research on consumer behavior tells us that if people have too many choices, they can feel overwhelmed, get extremely distressed, and delay their decisions—like people in contemplation. So, having only one choice can weaken your confidence that this is the one that will work for you. If you have two choices, you strengthen your willpower. Three choices are even better. Four choices, however, moves into that overwhelming range of "too many choices"—a place where neither your commitment nor your willpower is increased. This is why, whenever we can, we try to give you *three* good choices for applying different Principles of Progress.

Earlier, we discussed three excellent options for healthy management of stress and distress that are readily available for most people. They are relaxing, walking, or getting support by talking to an attentive listener. An important part of an effective plan for taking action on any of the other four top threats we specifically cover in this book (smoking, alcohol abuse, unhealthy diet, and not enough exercise) is to be prepared to deal with stress and distress without relapsing. With the following exercise, you can assess which techniques you will apply to strengthen your commitment.

--- **EXERCISE** ---

When I Make a Commitment

Read the following techniques that you might use to strengthen your commitment and circle the number that best applies to you. Please pay special attention to the answer choices. Sometimes a 5 is "Definitely would use" and sometimes "Definitely would *not* use."

1. I plan to go public and tell family and friends about my action plan.

DEFINITELY WOULD NOT USE			DEFINITELY WOULD USE	
1	2	3	4	5

2. I will keep my plans to myself.

DEFINITELY WOULD USE			DEFINITELY WOULD NOT USE	
1	2	3	4	5

3. I will commit and recommit to at least one healthy stress management behavior.

DEFINITELY WOULD NOT USE			DEFINITELY WOULD USE	
1	2	3	4	5

4. I will tell myself that once I am certain the pros outweigh the cons of changing, I can just follow through on my decision.

DEFINITELY WOULD USE			DEFINITELY WOULD NOT USE	
1	2	3	4	5

5. In addition to willpower, I will apply multiple Principles of Progress.

DEFINITELY WOULD NOT USE			DEFINITELY WOULD USE	
1	2	3	4	5

6. I will rely just on willpower whenever I need to.

DEFINITELY WOULD USE			DEFINITELY WOULD NOT USE	
1	2	3	4	5

Add up your total score for your six answers. If your score is 24 or higher, you will be strengthening your commitment and your willpower. If your score is less than 24, then you should decide on which of the six techniques you can try to increase your scores; for example, by definitely applying more change processes besides willpower.

Total score: _____

There are also proven methods to weaken your willpower. One common way is to try to will the un-willable by obsessing about past mistakes and not accepting that the past has passed. Here's an example of how that occurs.

Mary is a thirty-two-year-old accountant who takes pride in her perfectionism. She was trained to believe that accountants don't make mistakes. Mistakes are unintended accidents. But Mary made a serious mistake. She hit the send button and sent a confidential financial statement to the buyer in a deal when it was supposed to be sent only to the seller. Almost immediately, she recognized her mistake, and her stress went up. And up, then up some more. She tried to stop her message from going out, but of course she couldn't. She called her IT support person in hopes of finding a creative computer trick to correct her mistake. He tried to comfort Mary, but he couldn't. She said, "There must be a way to stop the message!" He said, "There is no way to reverse the past." And her stress got worse. But Mary refused to accept her past mistake. Her stomach was knotted up. Her upper back was cramping up. Her voluntary muscles were all tensed up, as she tried to will the un-willable. She knew she wasn't going to sleep that night. She told herself she wouldn't be able to sleep until she found a way to reverse her serious error.

How often do you beat up on yourself for not being able to change the past? *"I should have gone to college; I'm never going to do anything important!"* *"I should have married Jackie rather than not being able to make a commitment for life and losing her to that doctor."* Should haves, could haves, if only I would haves—all are ways to weaken your willpower.

Here is another classic example of what we mean by trying to will the un-willable: Early in my career, I received a federal grant to help an anxiety clinic in a state mental health center. I trained a couple of the staff in evidence-based treatments for anxiety-related behaviors. This was at the time when the researchers William Masters and Virginia Johnson were receiving well-deserved recognition in their breakthrough studies on sexual dysfunctions and performance anxiety. The *Providence Journal* decided to do a feature article on our anxiety clinic, which was welcome because we were ready and eager to serve more

Rhode Islanders. The story covered the range of anxiety disorders we could treat—including sexual dysfunctions. But the headline appearing on the front page of the Sunday paper focused on only one problem, reading "State Opens Sex Clinic!" The governor on vacation in Maine immediately called the Health Department director and shouted, "What the hell do you mean—the state opens a sex clinic? This is a Catholic state, and I'm up for re-election."

Well, when the *Providence Journal* portrayed our anxiety clinic as a sex clinic, we were flooded with calls. Fortunately, we received an outpouring of public support, particularly from men who were impotent. When the men told us how they tried to change what is now called erectile dysfunction (ED), they described their attempts at applying willpower—which, of course, just made their situations worse. More than one described how they would clench their fists, like they were making muscles in both biceps, and say something like, "Come on baby—get it up!" They did this because they had learned with so many other problems that the harder they willed something, the more they called on their voluntary nervous system, and the better they would feel. But in the case of ED, their willpower was backfiring. They were drawing blood flow away from their involuntary nervous system, such as their genitals, and driving it to the voluntary parts of the body, like the muscles in their arms. Instead of feeling better, they would actually feel more impotent and not have the power to will their "un-willable" erections. They needed to learn how to reduce the acute stress they placed on their love lives and how to let their love flow more involuntarily, without placing their self-esteem and their manhood on the back of their erections. Sometimes they imagined their male member saying, "I am not a muscle that you can make hard by clenching your fists and your jaw and expecting me to follow your every command. You need to go with the flow—the flow of love and desire and pleasure. When you try to hold on to it, like holding on to the past, it flows away from you."

The takeaway from the story is this: You can't will the un-willable without weakening your willpower and increasing your stress and distress. We urge you to keep this in mind as you continue to progress through your Stages of Change.

In this chapter, you learned about seven practical principles and processes for applying theoretical processes of change that were first identified in leading systems of psychotherapy, counseling, and behavior change for managing stress and distress. Here's a summary:

- First you need to increase your pros and your consciousness and experience your emotions to move from precontemplation to contemplation.

- Next, to progress to preparation, you have to lower your cons and reevaluate how your changing will affect others in your social environment.

- To move forward to action, you first need to reevaluate yourself by looking back at the major threats to your health and happiness and then imagine how you will think and feel about yourself as you get free from such threats.

In the next chapter, you will learn simple techniques from easy exercises that apply five more practical principles. These will help you move from action to maintenance and ideally to termination, where healthy ways of coping with stress and distress become automatic with minimal risk of relapse.

5

The Principles of Progress, Part II
PRACTICAL TOOLS FOR MOVING FROM ACTION TO MAINTENANCE

Now that you are ready to take action, you will apply a series of powerful principles to help you progress to maintenance.

The Eighth Principle of Progress:
Counter Conditioning to Use Substitutes for Unhealthy Habits to Move from Action to Maintenance

We first discovered the concept of counter conditioning in Joseph Wolpe's work on behavior therapy.[26] Wolpe emphasized how learning a new behavior could inhibit or block an old habit and become a healthy substitute. Let's see how this can happen.

You have been changing your mind; now it's time to change your brain. Too many people, including too many psychologists, believe that our biological brain controls our behavior. And it does—unless we know how to change our brains with new behaviors. Old behaviors that are well established, like habits, addictions, and conditioned responses, are overlearned and automatic. They are hardwired into our brains. There are networks of neurons (nerve cells) that are connected and conditioned to respond together. Though they cannot be removed, we can learn new behaviors that, over time, become stronger substitutes for the old neural pathways.

My favorite example is Tiger Woods, who many (including myself) thought was (or would become) the greatest golfer in history. Jan and I had a chance to follow Tiger when he was a teenager at the U.S. Amateur Championship in Newport, Rhode Island. We could stand right by him for every shot, since there were no ropes or staff to keep the crowds back. His father was there and told us, "Don't turn your head—you may miss something amazing!" And we did see many amazing shots on his way to winning the championship. Tiger Woods's dad, Earl, had begun to teach his son to golf at age two at a public course in California. That same year, he appeared on the *Mike Douglas Show,* hitting amazing shots. Tiger was wired to win.

As a maturing adult, Tiger was winning major championships at an unprecedented pace—a pace that would pass golf legend Jack Nicklaus's record. But for whatever reasons, maybe the wear and tear on his body with 1,000 powerful swings per day, he couldn't continue to be as great with his overlearned, automatic swing based on muscle memory. With a new coach, he began to substitute a new swing that was better suited for his more mature body and self. But even with 1,000 swings a day for twenty-one days, Tiger knew that his new habit was not strong enough to compete with the behaviors he had learned and practiced for practically his whole life and that he wasn't prepared to perform like his old self. He hadn't mastered his new behaviors, or more accurately, they weren't hardwired in strongly enough to master his old muscle memories. There were times when he would duff a shot (looking more like me when I play golf!), and he would explain that his old habits were competing with his new ones, and sometimes they would win and he would lose.

After about a year, Tiger had changed his golf behavior and his brain. And he was back on track, until other, more serious unhealthy personal behaviors began to negatively impact his career and his life.

Tiger Woods's story is a good example of why it is important to fully understand and integrate each Stage of Change as you move through the change process at your own pace. While Tiger Woods was able to rewire his brain when it came to improving his golf game, other risky behaviors interfered with his ability to maintain that significant change. Our intention in this book is to coach you on how to change your mind and change your brain so that the big threats to your health and happiness don't defeat you.

ABCDs for Preventing Stress and Distress: Cognitive Counters

A major challenge for managing stress is accepting that much of stress is caused by forces that are not under our control. A majority of employees report that they have too many demands at work and not enough resources to cope with those demands—a stress-filled situation to be certain. Now they need to cope with the stress and distress their workload caused.

As we've mentioned, relaxing, walking, talking with a supportive person, or using other healthy coping mechanisms can reduce stress, but they don't necessarily prevent it. While we might not be able to control all the outside forces of stress, there are sources of stress that we participate in creating that we can control and prevent. The most common causes of such stress are automatic and overlearned beliefs that are permanently embedded in our brains. To understand how these beliefs work, we need to learn the ABCs (and D) of changing our beliefs.

A. *Activating events.* These are the events that we are likely to perceive as the causes of our stress and distress. Jane was a talented forty-year-old office manager in a small jewelry manufacturing company. Troy, the owner of the company, was on the critical side, priding himself on seeing "what is wrong with this picture," so it could be corrected. Jane also has a father who was critical and, as a kid, she saw him as constantly correcting her. So, whenever Troy was critical, Jane become very stressed and distressed. She ended up constantly complaining to her family, friends, and colleagues about how terrible it was to have to work for Troy. Sometimes a friend or colleague would say, "If you really can't stand his criticism, you should quit." Easy to say, but in an industry and state with high unemployment, not easy to change.

B. *Beliefs.* What were Jane's beliefs and thoughts about these critical events? What would she say to herself and others about her critical encounters? We already have clues that her automatic responses would include "This is terrible. I can't stand it. I shouldn't have to put up with such severe situations."

C. *Consequences.* What are the consequences of Jane's beliefs and thoughts about her critical encounter? Stress and distress. If something is terrible, you have to feel stressed. If you can't stand a situation, you must feel distressed.

D. *Dispute.* Challenge the distressing statements you say to yourself. Here you need to call on more rational and less emotional statements to dispute and counter your less rational and more emotional self-statements.

Here's how ABCD might play out in the activating events just described.

Robert, Jane's coworker, could be very dramatic in his efforts to help her lessen her distress. *"Think of something terrible that could really cause terror—like the marathon bombers in Boston who blew away lives and legs of innocent bystanders."* With such examples, Robert could help Jane see the point: *"You're right. I am telling myself this is terrible. Well, it is irritating, but not as terrible as the Boston bombing."* That's a good start, for Jane to see that irritating can be annoying but not terrible.

When Jane tells herself she can't stand being criticized by her boss, she gets stressed by thinking she might have to consider quitting. But how long has she been able to stand such critical events? For years. So maybe she could tell herself, *"I don't like it, but I can stand it."* Jane might also be asked by Robert, *"Are there other employees who don't get upset by Troy being critical?* To which she may respond, *"Yeah, there's Rose. She just says, 'That's Troy being Troy.'"* In this way, Rose's beliefs help Jane understand that Troy being critical is a statement about Troy. She doesn't have to take it personally.

By not distressing herself, Jane can be more rational and objective. *"Is Troy criticizing a situation that I can help correct, or is it just something Troy does to help himself feel better? I don't have to feel bad about it."* Once Jane learns how she has been conditioned to automatically process criticism with less rational and more emotional beliefs, then she can begin countering her distressing beliefs with more rational and helpful thinking. Still, her old beliefs will remain embedded in her brain. She will have to practice her new way of thought processing until these beliefs build new neural pathways that lead to responses that counter rather than cause unnecessary stress and distress.

Take a few minutes to think about how you process criticism. Do you react emotionally like Jane? How might you use the ABCD method to counter and prevent your own stress and distress?

The Ninth Principle of Progress: Reinforce Your Progress by Using Rewards to Move from Action to Maintenance

In 1971, the psychologist B. F. Skinner applied two basic principles for controlling and changing behavior: reinforcement and punishment.[27] When we followed 1,000 self-changers for two years, assessing them every six months, we studied how frequently they reinforced and punished themselves in the past month. Not surprisingly, they exercised reinforcement the most when they were in the action stage. It was surprising, however, that they rarely relied on punishment to change their own behavior. We speculated that while most of us use reinforcement to change ourselves, we might rely on punishment more to change others—like our children, partners, or employees.

We were also surprised that individuals in action relied much more on "self-reinforcement" rather than social reinforcement from others. For example, Leo related how many of his family and friends told him that quitting smoking was the single most important change he could make to improve his health and maybe their happiness. However, he said that when he was in the midst of the stress of quitting smoking, his friends and acquaintances would reinforce him with praise and sometimes with prizes—but only once or twice. He said to himself, *"They told me quitting smoking was the most important change I could make in my life. But look how quickly they take it for granted!"* He could have easily become disappointed and eased up on his efforts, but he hung in there.

What is the lesson learned from Leo? You need to be prepared to rely mostly on self-reinforcement or you may be disappointed by how little reinforcement you receive from others. Leo discovered that immediate consequences control our behavior much more than delayed consequences. This is called the "law of effect." So, how do self-changers "obey" this law? Most successful self-changers rely heavily on self-statements that can immediately reinforce positive responses. After learning this, here's what Leo began telling himself: *"Nice going Leo, you handled that stress with deep breathing rather than breathing smoke."* Someone else might say, *"Way to go, girl, you countered that distress with drinking a relaxing hot cup of herbal tea rather than booze."*

Positive self-reinforcement is an important element in the Stages of Change. TTM expresses this philosophy with this slogan: "Working in harmony with how people change naturally." Like other researchers and clinicians, we find that the most natural way for people to reinforce themselves for positive responses is through immediate positive self-talk: *"Nice going!" "You're on your way" "That's it, let that worry go." "Dig deep, breathe deep." "That's hard, but it's not awful. You can stand it."*

It is natural to react to distress with anger, but here's how that re-action can backfire. Fernando had a major challenge with his temper. When he would lose it, he would be very tempted to go back to alcohol. Like many people, Fernando judged his improvement with anger by the intensity of his outbursts. If it wasn't a major explosion, he thought he was handling stress successfully. But clinical experience indicates that the first sign of progress is typically having less frequent outbursts. In Fernando's mind, the number of outbursts didn't count—in fact, he didn't even count the frequency of his outbursts.

The second thing to change is usually the length of angry outbursts. As self-changers learn to manage their distressing emotions like anger, they get better at stopping outbursts more quickly. This type of progress reminds us of research we did with a talented class of fourth-graders on sibling rivalry. These youngsters actually chose this challenging behav-ior to study, since they all experienced it. First, we reviewed some of the literature on how to treat angry outbursts connected to sibling rivalry. One leading therapist recommended that the mother lock herself in the bathroom, so her children wouldn't be reinforced by the special mater-nal attention they received when they were fighting. Our fourth-graders just laughed at this solution, believing their sibling fights were over turf or other control issues, like who goes first in a game.

The fourth-graders developed a questionnaire to study sibling rival-ry in their peers. They discovered that siblings actually played together much more frequently and for much longer than they fought. One of the conclusions from the students' research was their hope that their parents could learn to get over their arguments as quickly as their kids can. We published our fourth-graders' research to share the lesson we learned from them with other professionals and parents.

The last dimension of emotional change is typically "intensity"— the measurement Fernando used to assess his anger. However, when we focus only on how intense anxiety attacks or angry outbursts make us feel, we can fail to reinforce ourselves for the important progress we are making by first dramatically reducing the number and length of our emotional outbursts.

While reinforcement is important, there are serious limitations to relying on a single process when it comes to changing our behavior. Beginning around age five for most of us, reinforcement works primarily when individuals are aware of what behaviors are being reinforced and how they are being reinforced. This is called conditioning with awareness. Further research indicates that, in addition to awareness, individuals also have to be willing to change. As we've discussed, people who are not ready or willing to change can also consciously resist attempts to change their behavior through reinforcements. By definition, the reliance primarily on self-reinforcements calls for individuals who are ready and willing to take action to change and to maintain that action. This is another example of how relying on a single change process, no matter how powerful, is much too simple of a solution for the complex challenge of progressing through the Stages of Change.

Here's an example of how strict reinforcement can end up punishing people. Years ago, the president of the Safeway supermarket chain met with the president of the United States to brief him about a wellness program Safeway had implemented. Employees who smoked had to quit smoking as verified by saliva samples being free of cotinine (a derivative of nicotine). Overweight employees had to lose significant amounts of weight as verified by their health care provider. Employees who failed to pass such tests had to pay higher premiums on their family's health insurance, 20 percent (about $3,000) per year.

Safeway statistics supposedly showed that in 2006, this program led to decreases in the company's health care costs.[28] Safeway received support to have Congress increase the maximum paid by employees who fail from 20 percent to a maximum of 50 percent, or $7,500 per year. But an investigative reporter found out that Safeway did not implement this contingency program until 2009. And in 2009, the company's health care costs went up more than average for its industry.

In a national conference on health promotion in 2013, a professional panel discussed this type of incentive program and recommended that health researchers and professionals support it. I stood up for five minutes and delivered a rant against such simple but serious misuse of negative reinforcement. First, I cited the reporter's article. Then, I said that behavioral coercion is when one party (the company) receives a positive reinforcement (such as smokers quitting) and the other party (the employee) receives a negative reinforcement (such as not losing a major amount of money). When people feel coerced, they are likely to feel justified in "gaming" the program. For example, smokers can quit for seventy-two hours and pass the cotinine test. I added that when I consulted with the U.S. Army's health promotion program, the officer in charge told me their history with their fitness program. Once a year, all personnel had to pass a fitness test or they would lose their jobs. The result was that most everyone worked out intensively for the month before the test. And the U.S. Army was truly fit one month a year!

Jan and I just learned from a friend, who volunteers at The Henry Ford Museum in our hometown of Dearborn, Michigan, about Henry Ford's policy. His famous increase in pay to five dollars a day for factory workers was not just because much better pay would result in more sales of Model Ts. He was also having trouble retaining employees who worked on the boring, hot, and relentless production lines. But with such increase in pay came serious contingencies. Ford had a sociological department that would make home visits. If employees were found to be abusing alcohol or their salaries, they could face significant reductions in their incomes or even be fired.[29] During that same era, teachers could be fired if they were too overweight or even if they got pregnant. The consequence was a rapid increase in unions to protect the rights of workers.

The lessons learned in these examples are that effective and lasting change is more likely to occur when self-changers are

- willing and ready to change on their own
- not pressured or forced to change out of fear of punishment
- practicing positive and genuine self-reinforcement and receiving ongoing encouragement from others

Which brings us to our next Principle of Progress.

The Tenth Principle of Progress: Foster Helping Relationships and Find Someone You Can Count On for Support to Move from Action to Maintenance

While successful self-changers teach us to count on self-reinforcement much more than social reinforcement, they also teach us about the need for social support, or what TTM calls helping relationships. We found this change process beautifully described in the work of the American psychologist Carl Rogers.[30] At times, Rogers called his therapy "client-centered" therapy and at other times "non-directive" therapy. Both of these labels reflect Rogers's basic assumption that it is the *client* who is at the center of the change process and the *client* who directs the change process. The therapist relies on the client's internal and external ability to apply self-reinforcements when the client feels such reinforcement is warranted.

So, what can a "client-centered coach" provide? A helping relationship that includes *unconditional positive regard* that is present whether the client is progressing or regressing. Such unconditional acceptance helps clients accept that in struggling to change their brains and their behaviors, they will have both successes that they can celebrate and setbacks that they can learn from.

Helping relationships also include *empathy,* which allows helpers to feel what the self-changer is feeling, such as anger toward one's self for eating away too much of health and happiness. This compassionate understanding also communicates a deep caring that provides social support when the self-changer is feeling weakened by distress and tempted to regress to eating comfort foods or resorting to some other unhealthy habit as a way of coping. The comfort of caring from a coach or a friend can provide support and strength so self-changers don't give up on themselves. The unconditional positive regard communicates that the coach, friend, or family member will not give up on you.

Being genuine is the third part of helping relationships that Rogers recommends. The most effective caregivers communicate the message, "I don't pretend to be your parent who knows what is best for you. I am limited in the help that I can provide, but the help I provide can help you grow in the direction that you decide is best for you." It's like the line from the old Beatles song: "I get by with a little help from my friends."

I am reminded of Ralph, an engineer, who had the most intense inferiority complex that I have ever witnessed. He was a successful software architect, but he was very socially isolated. He was convinced that he was ugly and saw his nose as huge, and he was convinced that movies, restaurants, and clubs were places only fit for attractive people. It was easy to empathize with the profound distress that Ralph felt from his sense of inferiority and social isolation. Given such isolation, Ralph seemed to be seeking, first and foremost, someone who could care about him and accept him as he was, so he might better accept himself. I knew he was progressing when he started a session by saying, "You know, Doc, I think I *am* getting better. Now I feel inferior to everybody but you," which warmed my heart and reinforced the need for unconditional and non-judgmental support when it comes to working with change and self-changers.

The importance of the helping relationship in therapy is reflected by the fact that the best predictor of success across a broad range of therapies is what is called the "therapeutic relationship" or the "working alliance." But the best predictor of the therapeutic relationship is the client's Stage of Change before therapy begins. As emphasized earlier, it is critical for counselors and coaches to be able to understand what it feels like for people to be in precontemplation—demoralized, defensive, and expecting counselors to pressure them in a rush to action.

The client-centered tradition has been continued and enhanced by William Miller with his wonderful work on "motivational interviewing."[31] Like Rogers, Miller and his colleagues emphasize empathy and positive regard, taking care not to increase clients' resistance by directing them to take action before they are ready. Counselors learn to roll with the resistance and to help clients work through their profound ambivalence; for example, the love-hate relationship abusers and addicts have with their favorite substance. If and when you feel the need to add counseling to your plans for change and you are in precontemplation or contemplation, a counselor who uses motivational interviewing is an outstanding choice to help you get started on the change process.

By definition, successful self-changers don't call on counselors or coaches or others to help them change. As we have seen, however, many individuals could save considerable time and effort with the guidance of counselors, if they are relying on trial-and-error learning. But successful self-changers do seek *social support,* especially when facing the demands and stresses of taking action. So, key questions we ask are, "Who is your intimate or confidant? Who can you be open with when you are feeling at your emotional and psychological weakest?" This question is especially critical at a time when 25 percent of adults in the United States report that they have no close confidant.[32] In our mobile society that requires too many people to work too many hours, close, caring relationships are spread all too thin. If you are one of the 25 percent who has no one to confide in, working with a caring counselor or coach can be a critical choice. Such counselors and coaches are prepared to help you through the darker and more distressing times of life, without relapsing to one or more of the major threats to healthier and happier lives.

The Eleventh Principle of Progress: Increase Personal Freedom through Social Liberation by Noticing Social Trends to Move to Maintenance

"Social liberation" is the process by which changes in society increase the options and opportunities for individuals to live healthier and happier lives. This process was first identified in feminist therapies that recognized that people were held back from change more by social barriers than by barriers they had constructed as individuals. Barriers to equal education, employment opportunities, pay, and health care are some of the forces that have stood in the way for not only women, but for entire populations—keeping them from living healthier, longer, and fuller lives. When professionals seek to remove or reduce such social barriers, they function as advocates more than therapists.

As a therapist, I have at times personally taken on the role of advocate for my clients. Tina, age twenty-eight, was a Hispanic American who worked as a court clerk. She functioned very effectively until one of the judges began to make suggestive comments and inappropriate advances. Tina felt increasingly anxious, in part from feeling powerless to change her work environment without losing her job. She was in the preparation stage for increasing her assertiveness to counter her anxiety. But she was in precontemplation when it came to increasing her ability to counter her powerlessness. So, we spent time on each behavior, including discussing the pros of becoming a more assertive self-advocate. These included benefits to herself and her colleagues in the court. The pros included increasing her self-esteem and social esteem by generating more respect from colleagues, including leaders in the court. We worked on reducing the cons, such as risks of being fired, by calling on helping relationships from attorneys in legal services. Tina progressed rapidly, becoming prepared to call on the process of social liberation that included rights for her to be free from sexual harassment at work. Tina ended up taking effective action and experiencing the multiple benefits we had discussed, including increases in self-esteem and social esteem.

Positive and Negative Social Networks

Since the time I worked with Tina, social networks have seen tremendous growth, with more than one billion people on Facebook alone. Individuals now have increasing options for applying a variety of change processes. They can join a social network for cancer survivors where they can learn about new strategies to cope with the distress that comes with cancer. The inspiration from others who have progressed from suffering to struggling to thriving can provide them with dramatic relief as they reevaluate how they have been living and consider ways to enhance the longevity and quality of their lives. I always like asking audiences, "And who else are you going to tell about your commitment to take action?" People who are on Facebook can go public with their commitments to hundreds of their online "friends."

Of course, social networks are not new—only digital networks are—so we should be aware of lessons learned from research on social networks. The creative research reported in the book *Connected,* by Nicholas Christakis and James Fowler, reveals how members of social networks can influence behavior changes even when the individuals are a continent apart.[33] What is striking is that such changes occurred decades before Facebook, since the data came from the famous Framingham Study on behaviors critical for heart disease, like smoking, unhealthy diet, and inactivity.[34] The study found that individuals who quit smoking in California could influence connected smokers in New

England to also quit. These were clearly positively connected networks. Unfortunately, negatively connected networks also exist, as exemplified by family and friends who gain weight in New England affecting the weight gain of family or friends in the Midwest.

One of the concerns we have about how social networks are positively or negatively connected may be closely related to trends in a larger social network, like the United States. For at least the past three decades, our country has experienced a trend of weight gain in children and adults. Large percentages of these populations have gone from having a healthy weight to becoming overweight or even obese. In this scenario the probability is that individuals gaining weight in New England will be negatively connected to individuals gaining weight in the Midwest. With smoking, on the other hand, the trend has moved in the opposite direction for even longer. The percentage of the U.S. adult population who smokes has dropped from about 50 percent to less than 20 percent. In this scenario, individuals who quit smoking in California will likely be positively connected to individuals who quit smoking in New England. The point here is that our changes can be influenced not only by the individuals we are connected to, but also by the trends in the society we are connected to.

What are the implications for you when you are trying to reverse your personal trends from smoking to nonsmoking or from being overweight to achieving and maintaining a healthy weight? You need to assess your social networks, like those at home, at work, in the community, or at a distance to see which are likely to be positively connected and which are negatively connected. If you are a smoker, there is about a 50 percent chance that you live with a smoker and an even greater chance that you have friends who smoke. If you have a problem with drinking, the same prediction holds—you are highly likely to be connected with others who have a problem with drinking.

With weight, I discovered something intriguing when I consulted with one of the world's largest producers of pet foods. The number one problem for family pets—namely, cats and dogs—is being overweight and obese. What was found was that the percentage of overweight and obese pets was almost identical to the percentage of overweight and obese children. We need to reevaluate ourselves and our environments and reframe the challenge as overweight households rather than just over-weight individuals.

Here is a further fact when it comes to changing one of these risky behaviors. We know that if individuals who smoke are married to smokers and only one of them works on progressing to quitting smoking, one of two outcomes is predictable. Either they fail or they end up having marital problems. Jan and I have a special relationship with Don, a man who shines shoes at the Providence Airport. Don does much more than that as he advocates with politicians who stop for a shine, trying to get them to support legislations like increasing the minimum wage. Don had been delaying some health care for himself and his wife until he was able to afford insurance from the Affordable Care Act. His smoking and his wife's, however, would make his premiums beyond his reach. So, he was contemplating quitting. Besides consulting with Don, Jan gave him a copy of Pro-Change's successful Smoking Cessation stage-matched manual, and I gave him a copy of *Changing for Good*. He was relieved to discover that he and his wife could both work on quitting, even though they were in different Stages of Change. In the past, one or the other would be a barrier to changing because one was prepared to try to quit and the other was not. You will learn more about the progress of Don and his wife later. The lesson learned so far is that if we are in a social network that is likely to be negatively connected and hold each other back, then one strategy is to work on progressing together even if you work at different paces or are in different stages.

A second strategy is to dramatically increase the time we spend in networks that are positively linked, like friends from church, a hobby group, or a book club, and decrease time with those who are negatively linked, like drinking companions at the neighborhood bar. My eighty-year-old Aunt Helen was a wonderful role model in this regard. She was struggling with depression over her memory problems. She said to me, "Jim, I get depressed about my memory. You're a psychologist, what should I do about it?" "Oh just forget it, Aunt Helen," I joked. She had a good laugh. But she also had a good idea. Besides going to her traditional Catholic church, she joined a Baptist church and a Bible study group. Now she had three positive social networks with three times more services, social events, and social support to counter and reverse her depressing trend. Aunt Helen teaches us another strategy—become a member of a social network designed to help people be positively connected. While church attendance in the United States has declined considerably, research on well-being shows that people who are members of such communities have significantly higher levels of happiness and well-being.

One of the wonders of the world is a free social network dedicated to helping people be in recovery. Bill W. cofounded this movement many decades ago to aid his own recovery from alcoholism and, in turn, to help others. Alcoholics Anonymous (AA) is by far the best known and largest social network that makes the Twelve Step approach to recovery available to an unlimited number of people. This, and other Twelve Step organizations such as Narcotics Anonymous and Gamblers Anonymous, is a community or network of communities that seek to create positive connections between the new and old members. One limitation of AA and other Twelve Step recovery groups is that they are designed much more for people who are prepared to take action, in part, because of a crisis or feeling they hit bottom. This book can help readers in earlier Stages of Change become ready for recovery, so that they will have an excellent chance of becoming positively connected if they choose to join a recovery community. (More about this is in chapter 8, which is about drinking.)

The Twelfth Principle of Progress: Practice Stimulus Control to Manage Your Environment to Make Healthy Habits Automatic and Move to Maintenance and Beyond

It is not clear who first identified "stimulus control." Nevertheless, unhealthy habits fall under the category of stimulus control when the presence or absence of something causes an action or behavior. A stimulus occurs and it triggers an unhealthy behavior. For example, Victor was a 300-pound barber in his mid-sixties who watched a lot of television. When particular commercials came on, and he heard something like the old McDonald's jingle "You deserve a break today," Victor would slowly rise from his couch, walk to the refrigerator, and take out a "pop" (the term used for soda in the Midwest). When he was having a particularly stressful day, he would consume way too many ounces of sugary soda. When he wanted to change this habit, the first action step he took was to remove all the pop from his house, just as a smoker would remove all cigarettes and ashtrays from the house and car. This step would obviously break up the automatic link between commercials and consuming soda. Although Victor might still be tempted to rise and walk to the refrigerator, he followed our recommendation to be more mindful and to ask himself, "Why do I want to be controlled by commercials?"

Our son avoids stimulus control by automatically turning off the sound as soon as a commercial comes on. His three sons now model the same habit—turning off the sound of the commercial rather than be influenced by it. Sometimes I think they all have inherited my unlimited ability to disattend. What is striking, however, is that *I* am still conditioned to hearing the sounds of commercials and can become uncomfortable with the silence, as if I might miss something. The lesson here is that we can be controlled by our automatic, overlearned responses to stimuli. Or, we can develop new and stronger automatic responses to the stimuli over time, such as Victor did by learning to rely on healthy cold drinks instead of sugary sodas when feeling a need to take a break from stress and distress.

In this chapter you likely recognized that progressing through the action stage may be the most challenging and demanding time in your journey to a healthier and happier life. Here's a quick summary:

- First, you need to work on substituting healthier behaviors and thoughts in order to counter the unhealthy habits ingrained in your brain and your life.
- Then, reinforcing your progress helps you to keep moving ahead.
- Next, a little help from your friends and family can provide support to keep from slipping back, especially when distressed.
- The more you can connect to social networks that are moving in the same direction as you are, the freer you will be to reach your goals.

- And finally, the more you change your environment to remove tempting triggers and add positive cues, the more self-control you will gain from stimulus control.

In the next chapter, you will see how each piece of the puzzle of change fits together in your journey from precontemplation to maintenance and beyond.

6

Integrating the Stages with the Principles of Progress and the Processes of Change

As you have been learning, in precontemplation you need to be increasing your appreciation of the pros of changing. Raising your consciousness—becoming more aware—of how you defend yourself against, or resist, change and how you can begin changing without being pressured to take immediate action, is another key component to removing barriers to change. Dramatic relief—paying attention to feelings—helps you release emotions and thereby find the motivation to move ahead. And environmental reevaluation—noticing your effects on others— helps you to be moved by how your current problems can hurt others and how your changing can help them. These powerful principles and processes happen primarily inside of you. We often refer to them as "experiential" processes that you experience but others might not see. As you have been learning, sharing such experiences with others can be helpful to you *and* to them.

Seeing How It All Fits Together

Throughout the years, our successful self-changers have taught us which principles and processes they found most useful at each Stage of Change. Figure 3 provides the big picture on the logical relationships between the Stages of Change, the principles, and the processes of change.

FIGURE 3

Stages by Principles and Processes of Change

As figure 3 shows, the principles and processes you experience in precontemplation continue in contemplation as you work to decrease the cons of changing. As you do this, you also begin to reevaluate how you feel and think about yourself—how your unhealthy behavior threatens your (and others') health and happiness, and how your self-image could be enhanced as you move closer to getting free from such threats. So, in the early Stages of Change, you are relying on thinking, feeling, evaluating, and deciding, and the exercises we provide for each threat are designed to activate experiences to apply those processes.

During preparation, you become more confident and convinced that the pros of changing outweigh the cons. With self-liberation, you are encouraged to go public with your commitments to take action. In action, your changes are external as well as internal. People can see you stopping smoking or drinking, eating healthy, and exercising more. So, while they are likely to reinforce you for the changes they notice you making, you have also learned to count more on self-reinforcement as others start to take your actions for granted. However, you still need to reach out for the type of support that comes from helping relationships.

Then comes perhaps the hardest work when you are applying "counter conditioning" to change your brain as well as your behavior. You've learned that you can't recondition your brain in twenty-one days. So, you prepare yourself (and others) for the six months or more of concerted effort that is needed to make such significant changes. This plan includes stimulus control where you make changes in your environment to increase your self-controls, and social liberation where you notice social trends that support your change. Keep in mind that you don't do all of this at once: You make big progress by making change happen one stage—one step—at a time. The good news is that you'll follow the same pattern with each of the five biggest threats to your health and happiness. And the same pattern can be applied to any other behavior you may need or want to change.

Next, we will look at how applying different principles and processes at every stage will help you transform your unhealthy breathing, drinking, eating, moving, and feeling from being more automatic and under stimulus control into new *healthy* habits of breathing, drinking, eating, moving, and feeling that with time and effort become more automatic.

From Precontemplation to Termination—from Unhealthy Stimulus Control to Healthy Stimulus Control

FIGURE 4

Behavior Controls and Stages of Change

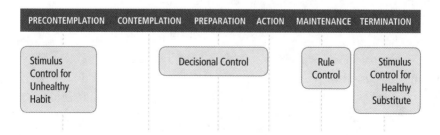

Figure 4 presents behavior control principles that can affect behaviors at different Stages of Change. As you have learned, in precontemplation, high-risk habits, like addictions, are overlearned, hardwired in, and heavily under stimulus control. Here's an example that explains this further.

When I spoke to an audience of four thousand nurse practitioners, I challenged them to guess what has historically been the most common stimulus that triggered a smoker to light up. Members of the audience yelled out, "Stress." Common, but not the most common trigger for wanting to smoke. The second guess was, "Another smoker smoking." Again, common but not the most common. Then some guessed, "Drinking alcohol." Important, since individuals with alcohol problems are much more likely to smoke, but not the most common. Digging deeper, someone shouted, "Waking up." Some of my students wake up several times in class, but it isn't the most common stimulus for wanting to smoke. Still another shouted, "Drinking coffee." Important because caffeine and nicotine are antagonists—the more you drink coffee, the more you break down nicotine, and the more you are likely to smoke—but still not the most common stimulus. Fewer hands went up in the air as the group's overall confidence declined. Then a brave soul yelled, "After sex!" Not that common a stimulus for wanting a cigarette, although this response did get a good laugh. "After eating?" someone ventured to guess. Not that common. "At work breaks?" another asked. Common, but still not the most common.

Often the audience gives up on guessing, frustrated that their best hypotheses haven't held up. You may share their frustration by now if you've been guessing along. Here's what I told the exasperated nurse practitioners, "Here is the trick behind this question. I asked historically what was the most common stimulus. You were guessing for today's smokers."

Historically, the average smoker would light up about every thirty minutes. By this time, about 35 percent of the nurses would have been lighting up their second cigarette in the auditorium. Why? Because the half-life of nicotine is thirty minutes. So, historically, what was the most common stimulus? Then the nurses knew the answer: "Nicotine blood level." Smokers would claim they were having a "nicotine fit" after thirty minutes without a cigarette and felt a physical need to light up immediately to reduce their distress. So, *historically,* smoking was linked to a biological stimulus control. Then with changes in public health policies designed to protect others from passive smoking, public smoking bans brought smoking under social or environmental control. The amazing fact is that almost all smokers complied almost immediately with new social controls.

This natural experiment raises serious questions about the power of biological controls. Common knowledge has it that addictions are so difficult to overcome because addicts are physically dependent on the substance to which they are addicted. But, with smoking at least, that is because society allowed that to happen. Perhaps addictions are more like the other major threats to health and happiness. Perhaps they are all under biological controls in the brain, once these habits are overlearned and hardwired in the brain. As we have learned, the solution is to condition new healthy alternatives by "rewiring" our brains.

The debate about whether a behavior is due to nature or nurture has been going on since before Jan and I were undergraduates in psychology—which was a long time ago! And still it continues when people wonder if behavior is under biological controls or social controls. But what is missing from this critical question? *What about self-controls?*

Self-Change Requires Self-Control

With this book as your guide, we are trying to help you build and maintain your self-controls. Take another look at figure 4. Do you see where in contemplation and preparation behavior change is too often under decisional control? As we pointed out in chapter 2, in contemplation you are likely trying to decide, "*Is changing worth the effort or not? Do the pros outweigh the cons? Should I keep progressing or should I put change off?*" Even in preparation you can be faced with the question, "*Will I succeed or will I fail?*" And that doubt can cause you to regress to more contemplation. If you keep thinking instead of doing, you can't actually fail because you haven't made any action attempts.

Our ideal goal is to have you apply self-change processes effectively so that you recondition your brain and body to deal with each of your biggest threats. By reinforcing your new habits and getting support from helping relationships and positive social networks, you can develop positive neural (nerve) networks that are more powerful than your old unhealthy habits. Take skim milk for instance, which Jan and I now both drink automatically. We don't decide to do it; we just do it. Jan looks in the refrigerator and says, "two skim," and I write that down on the shopping list. When I go to the milk cooler at the store, I automatically pick out the blue half gallon of skim. The only *decision* I make is which is the freshest half gallon available. Contrast that with me in front of the ice cream section, where decisions definitely come into play. *"Should I get the low-fat ice cream, or premium frozen yogurt, or the ice cream bar that limits the portion size?"* Clearly such decisional control is not nearly as strong as the automatic blue signal that controls my milk-buying actions.

But exercise isn't as automatic. When we ask audiences how many of them have their exercise routine under stimulus control, typically only about 10 percent of both professional and public audiences say that exercise is automatic for them.

For decades I had exercise under "rule" control. My rule was that I would exercise vigorously at least three times a week for 45 minutes, plus resistance or weight lifting. I would also average 150 minutes of walking a week. Most of my vigorous exercise was under stimulus control. I would follow the rule for where, what, and for how long I would exercise: at the health club, including the lifecycle (so I could multitask, such as reading or listening to podcasts), for 45 minutes. What wasn't at all automatic is *when* I would make time. When to exercise was under decisional control, and when I was faced with too many demands and too few resources—like time—I would feel compelled to forgo the vigorous exercise. Fortunately, I continued with the moderate to fast walking with Jan or playing nine holes of golf on a hilly course in 72 minutes. Also, fortunately, I regressed only from maintenance back to preparation and am planning to recommit to three days a week at the health club for that type of workout.

Those rules served me well for decades, and I am sure they will again. Sometimes I think of my rules as my own "private health policies"— similar to the public health policies designed to help us live longer and better. You may also want to think of your rules for changing as your personal health policies. Think about how policies like no smoking in public places immediately transformed so much of smoking from being under biological controls to becoming under social controls. Developing our personal health policies and rules can help transform our biggest threats from being under physical (biological) and social controls to being under self-control.

When I return to having my exercise under rule control, I intend to try to take the next step and bring exercise under stimulus control, like the 10 percent of our audiences who say they have done this successfully. Our friend Enoch, a professor at Princeton, had a good idea for how Jan and I could do this. He said the first thing we needed to do was book our tennis time, golf time, or time for exercise into our calendar. All the work and other demands of living have no problem finding their way onto our calendars—so why not exercise? I had what, where, and how much I would exercise under stimulus control. By booking a regular time into my calendar, I can bring when I exercise under stimulus control too, instilling the cues in my calendar that trigger what I do at particular times.

The journey of progressing through the Stages of Change involves applying powerful processes of change at particular stages. This includes transforming unhealthy habits that are already under stimulus control and hardwired into our brains to being freer and more flexible as they come under decisional controls. Then, we advance to the more powerful rule controls that represent our personal health and happiness policies. Here we are even freer from the old habits that have dominated so many of our days, months, and years. Usually we don't think of rules making us freer, because we typically think of rules that are made by others, like schools, employers, governments, or churches. But who rules our lives? Those who *make* the rules for our lives. With the Stages of Change and Principles of Progress, we have been freeing ourselves to make and remake our *own* rules for being and behaving. When we adopt rules for ourselves that lead to healthier and happier lives, we are constructing the type of *self*-controls that can rule our lives.

Ideally, we want our healthier and happier habits, decisions, and rules to become automatic, with little if any effort needed. We want to recondition our lives so the positive new neural networks are strong enough to automatically control our brains and behaviors.

Four Effects That Predict Long-Term Success

Across each of the five biggest threats to your health and happiness, we have discovered four effects that predict progress to long-term success.[35] The first effect comes from participating in programs based on expert guidance. We often call this "the treatment effect," since in research we often call our computerized, tailored intervention programs "treatment." The treatment effect has shown that participants randomly assigned to treatments are significantly more successful than those in no-treatment or control groups. One major reason is that our Stages of Change treatments include expert guided learning, which, as we have mentioned, is much more efficient or effective than the trial-and-error learning common among individuals not receiving treatment. The lesson here is that the more you read this book and the more you apply the principles and processes of change, the greater your success is likely to be.

The second effect, the "stage effect," reflects the finding that the further people are in the Stages of Change at the start of treatment, the more success they are likely to have overall. This finding shows us that helping you progress sooner to the next Stage of Change is likely to bring you earlier success.

The third effect is the "effort effect," which reflects the fact that individuals who are making the best efforts are likely to have greater success. That is why the exercises we provide in this book involve expert guidance designed to help you progress to the next stage by putting your time and efforts into the change processes that produce the most progress.

The fourth and final effect, the "severity effect," reflects the fact that individuals who have less severe unhealthy habits are usually able to achieve greater long-term success. That is why we also include exercises that can help you take evidence-based, stage-matched small steps that immediately reduce the severity of your unhealthy habit. Reducing your smoking by a single cigarette a day, for example, can help you progress in precontemplation. In contemplation, we recommend that you reduce your cigarettes by about four, since that is the difference in severity between preparation and contemplation.

The one exception to the severity effect regards stress. Here, the more severe the stress, the more likely individuals are to attain long-term success. This exception is probably due to those with more stress having more immediate motivation to progress to action in order to get more immediate relief from negative, severe emotions. This assumption is also supported by the fact that our treatments have the greatest success with stress in the shortest amount of time. And, with our approach, this more rapid success is maintained over long-term follow-ups.

As you have no doubt discovered by this point in the book, stress and distress are threats woven into the other four high-risk behaviors we address in these pages. Hopefully, if you have followed our suggestions and guidance for adopting healthy substitutes for managing your stress—like relaxing, walking, or talking with a trusted friend or relative—you will have given yourself a much greater chance of changing any other major threats to your health and happiness.

The following chapters will address the four other major threats to your health and happiness and offer even more specific guidance on how to use the Stages of Change and Principles of Progress to deal with them, so you can indeed change to thrive.

We will begin with the threat of smoking. This was the first high-risk behavior we examined in discovering the Stages of Change and how different principles and processes produced progress at each stage. Even if you don't smoke, you may benefit from the wisdom that was shared with us by the 1,000 self-changers who struggled with their smoking and who taught us how to change. As you'll continue to learn, these same principles and practices can be applied to other risky behaviors that can compromise your well-being.

7

The Breath of Life

USING THE STAGES OF CHANGE AND PRINCIPLES OF PROGRESS TO FREE YOURSELF FROM SMOKING

Of the people alive in the world as of this writing, 500 million will die from smoking. They will lose an average of ten years of their lives. This means that five billion years of life will be lost to a single unhealthy behavior. Ironically, five billion years is about as long as the earth has been in existence.

In the United States, in 2014 there were still about 40 million smokers, and an estimated 450,000 people in the country die from smoking each year.[36] This is the equivalent of about ten airplane crashes per day. In spite of such disasters, too many of the cessation programs in this country do not treat smoking seriously enough to be effective. As we saw earlier, most treatments for smoking are limited to the relatively small minority of 20 percent of smokers who are in the preparation stage of quitting. This chapter treats smoking seriously. It is for all smokers, whether you are ready, getting ready, or even not yet ready to quit.

We take smoking seriously because it's one of the most difficult habits to break. Studies on individuals who successfully changed multiple addictions, such as smoking and heroin, smoking and cocaine, or smoking and alcohol, found that smoking was typically the toughest behavior to change.[37]

For more than a decade our toughest challenge was to do better than our best TTM results for smoking cessation that produced about 25 percent abstinence at long-term follow-up. Our goal was to just reach 30 percent abstinence. The good news is that not that long ago, we finally had a major breakthrough. Instead of our 30 percent goal, we broke through to a 40 percent level of success by adding tailored texting (text messages individualized by stage and principles and processes of change for smoking cessation).[38] That included when we were treating a population in which the vast majority of smokers were not prepared or motivated to quit. When we take into account the percentage of populations we were reaching, we about doubled the previous impacts of our program. And when we compared our results against the average impacts of smoking cessation treatments in the typical employer's wellness programs, our impacts were four times as great.

Given how hard it has been for people to quit smoking, and taking into consideration the success we've had with our approach, we urge you to participate in each exercise in this chapter, each of which is designed to give you your best chance of success. We start by helping you appreciate just how many pros, or benefits, you can gain from working smarter and harder. For example, if you are focused on a new benefit each week, you could go two years before you repeat a benefit. Making significant, positive changes means making a huge investment in yourself.

To get started, assess what Stage of Change you are in by checking the statement that best reflects where you are in the process of quitting:

☐ 1. I don't intend to quit in the next six months.

☐ 2. I intend to quit in the next six months.

☐ 3. I intend to quit in the next month.

☐ 4. I quit in the past six months.

☐ 5. I quit more than six months ago.

If you checked 1, you are in precontemplation; if you checked 2, you are in contemplation; if you checked 3, you are in preparation; if you checked 4, you are in action; and if you checked 5, you are in maintenance.

We asked you to assess your stage so you can track your progress over time. Also, you are free to progress right to the section (for instance, contemplation) that addresses your current stage. We recommend, however, that you review the guidelines in each stage to better prepare yourself to quit or stay quit, such as making sure your pros are plenty high and your cons and defenses are low.

After completing the first exercise, you should be able to see what a terrific return on investment you can realize by getting free from this huge threat to your health and well-being.

Precontemplation: Raising Your Awareness

The first Principle of Progress (increasing your pros) is one of the most important and most powerful of the principles. Not only does it help you to break out of precontemplation, it also helps you dramatically increase your motivation as you discover the benefits, or pros, that are important to you. This first exercise will also build a more solid foundation for moving forward. This is like building a new house. First you need a solid foundation in order to stand the tests of time. This exercise will serve as a base or basis for building new behaviors strong enough to counter what many experts believe is the toughest behavior to change—smoking cigarettes. Given how hard it is to quit smoking, it is important that you appreciate how you are affirming so much of your body, your mind (or self), your health, and your happiness. Later you will call on this exercise when you are ready to take action.

Following is a list of more than one hundred benefits you can realize when you quit smoking. Check each pro, or benefit, that is important to you. Remember that the ultimate aim of this book is not only to help you remove the biggest threats to your health, but also to increase your happiness and well-being. We have organized the pros of quitting smoking around different domains of well-being to help you to become more conscious of how quitting smoking can increase your overall well-being.

———————————————— **EXERCISE** ————————————————

Benefits of Quitting

From the lists that follow, select the benefits that are most important to you and check them off or write them down on a separate digital or paper sheet. Try to choose at least one from each category. Then, add your own personal benefits to the list. The more good reasons you have, the easier it will be to take the next step—when you are ready.

Physical Well-Being

- ☐ You will live longer.
- ☐ Your heart will be healthier.
- ☐ Your brain will be healthier.
- ☐ There will be less secondhand smoke in your environment.
- ☐ You will be less likely to have irregular periods and early menopause.
- ☐ You will reduce risks associated with oral contraceptives, which are unsafe for smokers.
- ☐ Sinuses will be clearer.
- ☐ Wounds will heal faster.
- ☐ Blood pressure will be lower.
- ☐ You will have fewer colds and recover more quickly.
- ☐ You will be able control your allergies better.
- ☐ You will have less bronchitis and pneumonia.
- ☐ You will have healthier gums.
- ☐ You will eliminate smoker's cough.
- ☐ You will prevent gum disease.
- ☐ You will decrease the complications of diabetes.
- ☐ You will reduce reproductive health problems.

Reduce your risk of

- ☐ Lung cancer
- ☐ Breast cancer
- ☐ Cervical cancer
- ☐ Mouth cancer
- ☐ Stomach cancer
- ☐ Cancer of the kidneys
- ☐ Pancreatic cancer
- ☐ Bladder cancer
- ☐ Lip and throat cancer
- ☐ Stroke
- ☐ Coronary heart disease

- [ ] Chronic bronchitis
- [ ] Emphysema
- [ ] Hearing loss
- [ ] Peptic ulcer
- [ ] Osteoporosis
- [ ] Cataracts
- [ ] Acute myeloid leukemia
- [ ] Ectopic pregnancy, miscarriage, still birth, and having a baby with low birth weight
- [ ] Obstructive lung disease
- [ ] Abdominal aortic aneurysm
- [ ] Macular degeneration

Appealing Well-Being

- [ ] Your teeth will be whiter.
- [ ] Quitting smoking slows the aging process.
- [ ] You will get fewer wrinkles under your eyes.
- [ ] Your fingernails won't be yellow.
- [ ] You won't have burns on your clothes.
- [ ] Your clothes will smell better.
- [ ] Your breath will smell better.
- [ ] Your hair won't have that smoky odor.
- [ ] You may prevent premature balding.
- [ ] Your house will smell better.
- [ ] Your car will smell better.
- [ ] You won't have any more smelly, unsightly ashtrays.

Financial Well-Being

- [ ] You will save lots of money by not buying cigarettes.
- [ ] You will save lots of money on health insurance.
- [ ] You will save lots of money on life insurance.
- [ ] You will decrease the chances of household fires.
- [ ] You will be more likely to get hired or promoted.

Functional Well-Being

- ☐ Sense of smell will improve.
- ☐ Taste buds will work better, so food will taste better.
- ☐ Eyes will be healthier.
- ☐ Peripheral and night vision will improve.
- ☐ Your body will be able to deliver more oxygen to your muscles.
- ☐ Your risk of macular degeneration will decrease.
- ☐ Your risk of erectile dysfunction will decrease.
- ☐ Your blood flow in the penis will increase, improving your sex life.
- ☐ You will improve your fertility.
- ☐ You will feel more independent.
- ☐ You will feel more in control.
- ☐ Your concentration will improve.
- ☐ You will breathe easier.
- ☐ You will have more energy.
- ☐ You will not get as winded.
- ☐ Your likelihood of developing dementia will decrease.
- ☐ You won't have to leave your office or work station to smoke.
- ☐ You won't have to stop and buy cigarettes.
- ☐ You will miss fewer days of work.
- ☐ You won't have to hunt for ashtrays.

Social Well-Being

- ☐ You will be more kissable!
- ☐ You will feel good about the example you are setting for others.
- ☐ You will know that you are no longer supporting the tobacco companies.
- ☐ Your children and grandchildren will have fewer colds, flus, and ear infections.
- ☐ Your family will breathe more easily.
- ☐ Quitting can reduce others' allergies and asthma.
- ☐ You will reduce others risk of smoking-related diseases.
- ☐ You won't expose friends to secondhand smoke.

- ☐ Your pets, who can be affected by secondhand smoke, will be healthier.
- ☐ Your children won't be at risk of nicotine poisoning from picking up and eating cigarette butts.
- ☐ Your children and grandchildren will be less likely to suffer lasting health effects like high blood pressure and faster heart rates.
- ☐ Your partner will be relieved because you can likely share a longer and healthier life together.
- ☐ Your family members will be relieved.
- ☐ Your health care provider will be pleased.
- ☐ Quitting may make you more attractive to the larger population of nonsmokers.
- ☐ You won't have to worry about places having a smoking area.
- ☐ You will not be adding secondhand smoke to the environment.
- ☐ You will help prevent deforestation.

Purposeful Well-Being

- ☐ You will spend less time and energy defending your habit.
- ☐ You won't get judged by others.
- ☐ You won't be criticized for secondhand smoke.
- ☐ You won't have to put up with critical looks from nonsmokers.
- ☐ Quitting smoking will set an example about making healthy choices.
- ☐ You will be a healthy role model for kids.
- ☐ As you move through the stages, you will set a great example for other smokers.

Emotional Well-Being

- ☐ Your body will be less stressed.
- ☐ You will reduce your risk of depression.
- ☐ You will be more relaxed.
- ☐ You won't have to stand outside in the cold or rain to smoke.
- ☐ You won't have to feel embarrassed.
- ☐ You won't have to sneak cigarettes.

Add your own benefits on a separate sheet and rank them in importance.

Raising Your Awareness to Raise Your Behavior Change IQ

You now have the opportunity to apply your increased knowledge about how to change from being a smoker to a nonsmoker. Remember, one of the goals of this book is to increase your "Behavior Change IQ." The following quiz helps assess what you've already learned about changing unhealthy behaviors. Circle what you think is the right answer; then look after the quiz to see if you are correct.

1. **If you are in the precontemplation stage, what should be your first goal?**

   a. Set a quit date

   b. Progress to contemplation

   c. Increase your willpower

   d. Tell people about your commitment to quit

2. **To progress from precontemplation, the first principle of progress says you need to do what?**

   a. Increase your pros

   b. Decrease your cons

   c. Have your pros higher than your cons

   d. Use trial-and-error learning

Correct answers: 1. b, 2. a

Almost 80 percent of smokers in the United States *want* to quit smoking. But 80 percent of those people are not ready or prepared to quit. If your stage assessment showed that you are in the precontemplation stage, chances are you still want to quit. So, we will help you build on that motivation. As you move through this section on precontemplation, we will try to help you start to change your mind and increase your motivation by applying the Principles of Progress and processes of change.

Decrease Defenses

As you've already learned, while increasing your pros helps you to progress, you also have to decrease your defenses that can keep you stuck in precontemplation. Here are some of the common defenses, or barriers, we discussed earlier that you may need to reduce.

Check the defenses you use to protect your smoking and then read some thoughts on how you can reduce them.

Defense	Example
☐ Withdrawal from others	You go silent or change the topic when you feel someone is pressuring you to quit smoking.

Non-defensive response: *I know you want to help me quit smoking, so I need to share with you what I've learned about how to quit. I'm in the first stage of quitting and am not ready to take action. When I feel someone is pressuring me to take action, I get defensive, like withdrawing from the person by going silent or changing the topic away from smoking. What would help at this stage would be if you ask how I am doing with progressing to the next stage of change. Then, we could talk about all the benefits of quitting that I am learning about.*

    ☐ Like this idea   ☐ Dislike this idea

Defense	Example
☐ Internalizing	I blame myself for being so dumb for not quitting a long time ago.

Non-defensive response: *I can tell myself that I didn't know how to change; for example, I didn't know about how to determine what stage I'm in and how to progress. I can feel smarter as I am learning about changing at each stage of quitting.*

    ☐ Like this idea   ☐ Dislike this idea

Defense	Example
☐ Projection	I blame others I am close to who smoke and tempt me to smoke.

Non-defensive response: *I can share this book with them and let them know I will respect where they are in the Stages of Change. They don't need to be ready to quit, just like I don't need to be ready. If we are both doing some work to progress, we can help pull each other forward rather than hold each other back.*

☐ Like this idea   ☐ Dislike this idea

Defense	Example
☐ Rationalizing	I can quit anytime I want.

Non-defensive response: *I have wanted to quit smoking in the past and know wanting to quit doesn't mean I know how to quit. Now I am being more reasonable and can apply lessons learned to help me progress.*

☐ Like this idea   ☐ Dislike this idea

Express Your Emotions (Dramatic Relief)

I am learning that being reasonable is not enough. I also need to be emotional and express feelings that can hold me back.

Chances are you have been attached to your cigarettes—they seem like a friend who gets you through tough times of distress. Who else can you call on when you are feeling anxious, angry, or depressed? Who else can calm you down so quickly or give you a lift when you are feeling drained? You may need to mourn the loss of something in your life that has functioned like a friend in so many situations. To let go of your smoking, you may need to let go of feelings of sadness, regret, and even anger. These feelings are the same emotions linked to the grieving process. In 1969, Swiss psychiatrist Elisabeth Kübler-Ross wrote the now classic book *On Death and Dying* in which she categorized the stages of grieving.

It isn't easy to let go of an unhealthy behavior we have clung to for comfort or escape. We mourn what we are losing—even when, deep down, we know we will be better off without it. Viewing your change through the lens of Kübler-Ross's stages of grief might help you better understand the emotions that can well up as you change from being a smoker to becoming a nonsmoker:

1. *Denial.* Just like you may deny that your smoking *can* hurt you, you also might deny that letting go of it won't hurt.

2. *Anger.* When you say something to yourself like, "I really resent that I have to lose something that has been such a part of my life in order to enhance my life. What kind of deal is that?"

3. *Bargaining.* When you may say to yourself something like, "Maybe I can hold on to my favorite brand that makes me feel like more of a man or woman, if I cut back a little."

4. *Depression.* Where you begin to realize and can admit, "I am sad and resign myself that in order to welcome more health and happiness into my life, I have to let go of something that has been such an important part of my life."

5. *Acceptance.* When you reach a point where you can say, "I need to accept and mourn the fact that I am losing something I have really liked in my life. But I accept that I will pay this price to earn more than one hundred benefits that can enhance my health and happiness."

Historically, the stages of grieving have been applied to losses *imposed* on us, such as the loss of a loved one or a job. But grieving and mourning can also be powerful ways of letting go of attachments that we intentionally choose to lose—like our attachment to cigarettes.

Contemplation Stage: Decreasing Key Cons to Progress to Preparation

If you are in contemplation, you have plenty of company. Four out of ten smokers are in contemplation and are working to get ready to quit.

Fortunately, you have already been learning how to make *smarter* efforts to decrease key cons that can get you stuck in contemplation. Here's an exercise to help you progress.

––––––––––––––––––––––––––– **EXERCISE** ––––––––––––––––––––––––––

Decreasing Your Cons for Quitting Smoking

Check which cons concern you, and then read how you can decrease them.

KEY CONS	SMARTER EFFORT
☐ I may feel anxiety, irritability, or stress, or be depressed as part of withdrawal.	You have already been preparing in earlier chapters how to manage such emotions without relying on smoking.
☐ I have to leave behind packs of cigarettes that have been like packs of friends.	You have just learned how to grieve the loss of your packs.
☐ I will have cravings for a cigarette.	Tell yourself such urges last just a few minutes, like a wave in the sea that you can dive through.
☐ All the withdrawal symptoms, such as trouble concentrating or sleeping, mild headache, and fatigue, may be too strong for my self-controls.	Tell yourself most of these will pass in a few days or a couple of weeks. But we will discuss how you can strengthen your self-controls by temporarily using biological controls, like nicotine replacement therapy.
☐ I am concerned about craving sweets and other comfort foods.	Prepare for your sense of taste to increase after it stops being smothered by smoke. Taste for sugar can be a strong temptation. For now, have healthy snacks available (such as carrot sticks and sugarless gum) that can gratify oral cravings. In the healthy eating chapter, you will see how sugar is a big dietary threat to your health and well-being and how you can control that.
☐ I am concerned about gaining weight.	Tell yourself many smokers do not gain weight but most who do gain five to ten pounds. If you do gain weight, you can work to lose it in a month or two while gaining freedom from the most deadly threat of smoking.

Environmental Reevaluation: How Quitting Smoking Affects Others

Remember that thirty-second television spot we talked about earlier in which the grieving man talked about his wife's death? He said, "I always worried that my smoking would cause lung cancer. I always feared my smoking would lead to an early death. But I never imagined it would happen to my wife." Messages like this were designed to elicit the process of "environmental reevaluation"—which means taking an honest and emotional look at how your behavior may affect those around you.

Here is a quiz to help you reevaluate how your quitting smoking can increase the health and happiness of others who care about you.

—— **EXERCISE** ——

Caring for Others by Quitting

Circle whether each statement is true or false for you.

1.	I will help protect someone else's health if I quit.	T	F
2.	I can help someone else to quit if I share my progress with them.	T	F
3.	I can help others to not worry as much about my health if I quit.	T	F
4.	I can help kids to not start smoking if I quit.	T	F
5.	Others will feel proud if I quit.	T	F
6.	Others can appreciate the extra money we will have if I quit smoking.	T	F
7.	I can inspire others to change a threat if I tackle smoking, which is perhaps the toughest threat.	T	F

8. Others can have a more pleasant environment, one free from tobacco smoke, if I quit.	T	F
9. Others won't have to feel sensitive about expressing their negative opinions about smoking if I quit.	T	F
10. Others will be happier if I quit.	T	F

Tally how many "trues" you have circled. Seven is a good score, but the more you have, the more motivated you will be to move on from contemplation.

Preparation: Using Self-Reevaluation to Prepare to Quit

By progressing into the preparation stage, you have about tripled your chances of successfully quitting smoking in the near future. Now you need to emphasize self-reevaluation to change your image of yourself as a smoker and how you imagine you will view yourself as a nonsmoker. Here's my story.

I started smoking in the seventh grade. I smoked several times a week for a year and smoked well more than the one hundred cigarettes that would lead the Centers for Disease Control and Prevention to label me a smoker. But I never labeled myself as a smoker. If I had stayed a smoker, it is clear I would have smoked Marlboros. At that age, I was obsessed with my image. I would look in the mirror and imagine seeing a tough, stoic image, like a cowboy. Besides, my dad grew up on a cattle ranch and was impressive on horseback. And he smoked, just like the Marlboro Man in the commercials. Yet for some reason, regardless of seeing myself as a tough cowboy, I never considered myself a smoker. It did not become part of my identity, even though riding horses and spending two summers rounding up cattle in South Dakota with my dad at his best friend's ranch did become a lasting part of my history and my identity.

This differs from those who remained smokers well into their adulthood—those for whom smoking has become part of their identity. This identification as a smoker is reinforced when you are asked about smoking habits on the health history forms you have to fill out for insurance or at a doctor's or dentist's office.

The following exercise will help you reevaluate your self-image.

EXERCISE

Viewing Yourself as a Smoker vs. a Nonsmoker

First, check off the adjectives that describe how you think the tobacco industry wants you to view yourself as a smoker. In the second group of words, check how you currently view yourself as a smoker. Finally, in the third set of words, select how you imagine you will view yourself as a nonsmoker once you quit.

How would the tobacco industry like you to view yourself as a smoker?

☐ Cool   ☐ Independent   ☐ Risk taker   ☐ Nonconformist   ☐ Fun loving

☐ Attractive   ☐ Sexy   ☐ In control

How do you view yourself as a smoker?

☐ Look older   ☐ Dependent on nicotine   ☐ Not so smart   ☐ Irresponsible

☐ Insensitive to others   ☐ Stigmatized   ☐ Strong willed   ☐ In control

---

How would you view yourself as a nonsmoker?

☐ Freer   ☐ Healthier   ☐ Conformist   ☐ In control   ☐ Responsible

☐ Sensitive to others   ☐ A quitter   ☐ A winner

How are these three views different? Thinking about how being a nonsmoker can improve your self-image can help you take steps toward quitting.

Using Self-Liberation as a Way to Commit to Quit Smoking

With smoking cessation, there are several excellent evidence-based options when you are ready to take action. Here we will describe the most widely used options among people who quit smoking, but we will also talk about a couple of alternatives for smokers with special needs.

Going "Cold Turkey" or Reducing Your Nicotine Intake

Historically, it was thought the best way to stop smoking was to go "cold turkey" and quit all at once and without assistance. Cold turkey is still the most widely applied option, but it is important to keep in mind that this choice is only appropriate for those who are well prepared to quit. For others, research demonstrates that reducing the number of cigarettes you smoke is another excellent way to progress.

We have found that individuals in preparation smoke an average of just four fewer cigarettes each day than those in contemplation. Even reducing your smoking by one cigarette a day can make a significant difference. Such a reduction is a good way to apply the "severity effect," which says that decreasing the severity of your problem increases your chances of success. It has been well known that lighter smokers are more successful at quitting than heavier smokers. Originally, it was thought that this was because heavier smokers have a stronger biological addiction to nicotine than lighter smokers do. But several studies have shown that lighter smokers apply change principles and processes more successfully than heavier smokers do. We interpret this to mean that lighter smokers are already applying the "effort effect" (the amount of energy and work it takes to make a change) more so than heavier smokers even before they actually take action. The point here is that they may already be applying self-controls, or self-change processes, to their smoking to counter the effects of biological controls, such as nicotine blood levels.

Interestingly, we also found that female smokers apply the effort effect more than men do, both before and after taking action. It was once believed that women were less successful than men when it comes to long-term abstinence. This belief was held so strongly that the National Cancer Institute spent millions of dollars on special cessation research for women. However, our own research—six large studies in which we applied the approach you are learning and using in this book—showed that the long-term success rates were essentially identical for men and women. Our studies also revealed that women apply the effort effect more, suggesting that women have to work harder to achieve the same success as their male counterparts. The takeaway here is that to keep from regressing back to smoking, women need to be prepared to work a little harder on changing, especially when coping with stress and distress—since they are more prone to becoming depressed, anxious, or emotionally distraught.

Medical Aids: Adding Biological Controls

Another evidence-based choice to strengthen your commitment or willpower is to add biological controls. The following aids have been found to be successful in some cases.

NICOTINE REPLACEMENT THERAPY (NRT)

NRT has been one of the most widely tested and applied means to help people quit smoking by treating their nicotine addiction. The evidence is clear that relying *only* on NRT does not produce the best outcomes— just as relying on a single principle or process of change doesn't lead to the best results. However, many studies show that including NRT as an *additional* strategy for dealing with your nicotine addiction can increase your odds of quitting.

CHANTIX

Chantix (varenicline) is a prescription medication that has been found to be effective when it is combined with behavior change processes delivered through counseling. The ingredients contained in this drug are believed to block nicotine receptors and both reduce craving and decrease the pleasurable effects of smoking cigarettes. Unfortunately, Chantix sometimes has some significant side effects, such as disturbing dreams, sleep disruptions, and depression, so it is important to take it under the supervision of your health care provider. Chantix is generally limited to individuals who have failed to quit smoking using other methods, such as cold turkey or NRT. In our experience, some smokers have found Chantix to be very helpful in reducing craving and reducing the pleasure they get from smoking and they are well able to tolerate the side effects. However, we have also worked with other smokers who find that the side effects are not tolerable and feel they outweigh whatever benefits they might experience from quitting.

E-CIGARETTES

We also want to mention e-cigarettes, since they have received a great deal of press lately. E-cigarettes are "fake" cigarettes that run on batteries to deliver nicotine, flavor, and other chemicals. They turn chemicals into vapor that is inhaled by the user. *There is no evidence to date that they help people stop smoking.* A real downside to e-cigarettes is that they can continue people's addiction to nicotine and encourage nonsmoking youth to start smoking. We don't recommend this option.

Remember, self-liberation involves commitments that go beyond decisions based on evidence and reason. Your challenge is to make your commitment—whether to go cold turkey, use nicotine replacement, or take medication to block nicotine receptors—be the best choice for you. All of the evidence indicates that no matter which option you choose, it is your *commitment* and the efforts that go with it that will have the greatest impact on increasing your chances of success. Once you make a commitment, then, it is important to create an action plan. Here are the steps for doing that.

How to Create an Action Plan

1. *Set a quit date.*

   Research shows that a plan is best when

   - You pick a date within the next month.
   - You choose a day when you have more flexibility, like a Saturday or Sunday.
   - You choose a day that is likely to have low stress.

2. *Commit to quit.*

   Remember that you strengthen your commitment and willpower by going public. Who are you going to tell? Who else will you tell? Those are key questions when answered honestly. These days, posting your quit date on your social media network can increase your commitment. If you are not on social media, post your quit date on your calendar.

3. *Clear the deck.*

   You don't want the cards to be stacked against you, so

   - Remove all the stimuli that trigger smoking, including all cigarettes, ashtrays, and lighters from your home, car, and workplace.

   - Stack the deck, by loading up on substitutes for smoking, such as sugarless gum, hard candy, healthy drinks, toothpicks to chew on, or a handy rubber ball or worry beads (a string of beads manipulated with one or two hands and used to pass time) to hold.

4. *Go for the quad-fecta of change.*

   "Trifecta" is a horse racing term where you bet that you can pick the top three horses in a race. Here you are betting on four powerful change principles that can make you a winner each day.

   Make a to-do list starting with "Quit to lower my blood pressure" (which begins happening in the first twenty minutes after quitting). Each day, quit for a different benefit, such as, "Quit for my heart" or "Quit for my kids." This single technique above the surface triggers four complex and powerful principles of change, the "quad-fecta":

   1. *It increases the pros,* which increases your motivation over time, especially at times when you question whether your efforts to stay quit are worth it.

   2. *It increases your commitment,* which increases your willpower or self-control to counter the biological or social controls that can tempt you to smoke. This also affirms that quitting smoking is a top priority each day of the week.

   3. *It increases stimulus control* by reminding you to stay quit whenever you look at your list.

   4. *It reinforces your daily successes* when, at the end of the day, you scratch your commitment to quit for that day off your list.

Taking Action: Counter Conditioning—Substituting Healthy Alternatives to Counter Smoking

A common mistake when quitting cold turkey is to rely just on willpower or a commitment to quit. You are supposed to just curl your fists, grit your teeth, and stop smoking. Many of the self-changers we've worked with taught us about the many techniques they used to deal with temptations or cravings to smoke. The following exercise outlines just some of the healthy alternatives they used.

––––––––––––––– EXERCISE –––––––––––––––

Behavior Substitutes for a Day in the Life of a Quitter

Check the behaviors under "New Self" that you may want to use to increase your commitment.

TIME/EVENT	OLD SELF	NEW SELF
Wake up	Light up to relax	☐ Take a warm shower
Wake up	Light up to wake up	☐ Take a cold shower
Breakfast	Finish with a cigarette	☐ Finish with a cup of tea
Driving in the car	Fill up the car with smoke	☐ Fill the car with music
Stuck in traffic	Stuck on smoking	☐ Listen to your favorite sports, talk, or music radio station
Arrive at work or a store	Light up to relax	☐ Park a little farther away so you can walk to relax
First break time	Break to smoke	☐ Break from smoking by talking to a friend indoors
Lunch break	Break to smoke	☐ Break by having a healthy lunch

TIME/EVENT	OLD SELF	NEW SELF
Another break	Break to smoke	☐ Break your habit by eating a carrot or other healthy snack
Driving home	Smoke to celebrate the end of work	☐ Sing to celebrate the end of a deadly habit
Entering your house	Tell yourself: "This is my castle and I can smoke a king-sized cigarette in here"	☐ Tell yourself: "If I am king or queen, I cannot be a slave to smoking"
Having a drink	Triggers a cigarette	☐ Triggers letting go of such temptations
Eating dinner	End with a cigarette	☐ End with a healthy dessert
Watching TV	Watch through smoke	☐ Watch with healthier eyes
Getting ready for bed	Last chance to light up	☐ Last chance to relax without smoking
Waking up craving	Cave to the crave	☐ Counter the craving

Years ago we followed one thousand self-changers who wanted to quit smoking. Back then, those smokers faced more tempting situations since smoking regulations were not yet in place—they could still smoke anywhere at any time. Today there are fewer times and places where you are "free" to smoke. The following chart shows thoughts and temptations that might arise in a typical day in the life of a smoker and the reasoning (cognitive counters) such a person might use to challenge those temptations as he or she quiets the urges to smoke and changes a possible negative into a positive.

EXERCISE

Cognitive Counters for a Day in the Life of a Quitter

Check which cognitive counters you may want to use. Remember, the act of checking these possibilities increases your commitment.

ACTIVITY/EVENT	BELIEF	CONSEQUENCE	COGNITIVE COUNTER
Waking up	That first cigarette I light up is so helpful.	Light up	☐ That first cigarette is the start of a deadly day.
Stuck in traffic	I can't stand commuting.	Smoking another cigarette	☐ The stress of commuting is one of my biggest drags on well-being, but taking a drag on a cigarette is the biggest threat to my health and well-being.
Arrive at work	I need to smoke to be productive.	Smoke	☐ Being a smoker costs my employer $4,000 each year, half of which is lost productivity.
First break time	I am free to smoke.	Smoke	☐ I am free to talk with a friend.
Lunch break	I am free to smoke.	Smoke	☐ I am free to eat healthier.
Driving home	I'll smoke to celebrate the end of a hard day.	Smoke	☐ I'll celebrate the success of another day of beating a hard habit.
Entering my home	This is my refuge from a controlling world.	Smoke	☐ This is my refuge where I can be free from smoke.
Having a drink	Drinking is a cue to smoke.	Smoke	☐ Don't shoot yourself in the foot (or heart)!
Watching TV	It's time to let go of control.	Smoke	☐ It's time to be happy being freer from my biggest threat.

ACTIVITY/EVENT	BELIEF	CONSEQUENCE	COGNITIVE COUNTER
Getting ready for bed	I need to relax.	Smoke	☐ Nicotine disrupts sleep.
Waking up craving a cigarette	What a desirable dream.	Smoke	☐ When I am fully free from smoking, I will be free from what can turn out to be a nightmare.

Reinforcing the Steps to Free Yourself from Smoking

Let's look at how you can work to overcome one of the biggest threats to your health and happiness. For years, you were controlled by the rapid pleasure rush that smoking delivered through the dopamine (a neurotransmitter that helps control the reward and pleasure centers) pathways in your brain. Taking hit after hit on a cigarette, day after day, had you puffing like a steam engine. You now know that your habits are housed in your brain and you are in the process of rewiring your brain. Your increased consciousness has brought more light into your brain, and you can see more clearly now how you can continue to change your brain and your behavior.

As successful self-changers can tell you, it's important to follow each step of change you take during your early days of action with consistent self-reinforcements. Fill each day with "attaboys" or "attagirls." Tell yourself, "You countered that temptation well." Congratulate yourself with thoughts like, "I disputed my emotional belief that I can't stand being stuck in traffic without smoking." Maybe you still think you cannot stand being stuck in traffic, even though you may have to deal with it in your daily commute. But, even though the stress of commuting might be a regular challenge to happiness and well-being, it doesn't have to be made much worse by driving in smoke each day.

The following chart shows some basic healthy reinforcements you can use to help yourself remain free from smoking over time. Reinforcing yourself for each milestone you reach helps you to appreciate what an important accomplishment you are making to enhance your health and well-being.

--- **EXERCISE** ---

Milestones to Becoming Healthier and Happier

Check off each milestone when you reach it.

Twenty Minutes

☐ Blood pressure and pulse drop to normal.

☐ Circulation in your hands and feet improves.

Appreciate your immediate gains.

Eight Hours

☐ Oxygen level in your blood returns to normal.

☐ Carbon monoxide levels drop to normal, reducing the risk of cholesterol in your arteries.

Breathe deep.

Three Days

☐ Breathing is easier because bronchial tubes relax.

☐ Your risk of headaches and migraines has decreased.

☐ Nicotine has left your body.

Breathe deeper.

Three Weeks

☐ Chronic bronchitis disappears.

☐ You have more energy.

☐ Cilia in lungs start to work again to clean the air you breathe and fight infections.

Feel energized.

One Month

☐ You sleep better.

☐ Your vision at night improves.

Sleep well.

Three Months

☐ Your blood is flowing better.

☐ Your lung function has improved as much as 30 percent.

☐ Your risk of flu and pneumonia is reduced.

☐ Your stress levels have decreased.

Keep relaxing.

Nine Months

☐ You have less coughing, shortness of breath, and stuffiness.

☐ You have fewer colds.

☐ Your digestive system is back to normal.

Eat healthy.

One Year

☐ Your risk of heart disease is now cut in half.

☐ Your risk of osteoporosis has been reduced.

☐ Your asthma is likely to have improved.

Celebrate.

Five Years

☐ Your risk of stroke is now the same as a nonsmoker.

☐ Your risk of mouth, throat, and esophageal cancers is cut in half as compared to a smoker.

☐ Your risk of lung cancer is now half that of a smoker.

☐ Your risk of heart disease continues to go down.

☐ You stop dreaming about smoking.

Appreciate what a good healer you are.

Fifteen Years

☐ Your risk of heart disease, stroke, and lung cancer is the same as for someone who never smoked!

Look forward to a fuller life.

Sharing these milestones with your family and friends, who are part of your support team, allows them to add their own rewards and to show how they care about your progress. In this way, no one is taking your successful efforts for granted.

Please note, however, that while it is very helpful to get support from family and friends, it can be at least as helpful that you not get "reactance" from those you care most about. Reactance is when people react negatively to change. If you are a smoker, one or more of your family members or friends probably also smokes. These people can react defensively, angrily, or insensitively to your quitting, because it can be a threat to your relationship or to their smoking.

You may get the best help from them by first helping them learn about the Stages of Change. Let them know you regret where they are at. In fact, you are prepared to share this book whenever they may want to check it out. Communicating this way says that you are committed to quitting, but that you are not going to abandon them. You are prepared to be supportive and you would welcome their support in times when you are feeling most tempted to lapse or relapse.

Preparing for Disasters: Making a Relapse Prevention Plan

In a recent review of one of our grant proposals, experts representing Homeland Security told us that our particular research project had the potential to transform the way individuals and entire populations prepared for disasters such as hurricanes and floods. In this section of this book, we are trying to prepare you for what many smokers experience as psychological disasters when they are flooded with urges to smoke and do not have enough resources to cope without relapsing. While we showed Homeland Security how people can survive on their own for at least five days following a natural disaster, our goal here is to teach you to be a self-sufficient nonsmoker not just for five days, but for *all* of your days.

Chances are that you have tried to quit smoking in the past but failed. Rest assured, you are not alone. The average smoker makes about seven serious attempts to quit over seven to ten years before finally succeeding for a lifetime. We encourage you to reframe "relapse" from failure to a *learning opportunity*. The following exercise provides an assessment of four areas to help you learn from the past in order to prevent relapse in the present. If you are still in the preparation stage and this is the first time you are preparing to quit, you can also learn from assessing what are your highest risks for relapse. Then we will guide you on what relapse prevention strategies to emphasize in your action plan. Finally, you will learn strategies for rapidly recycling to prevent a "lapse" from becoming a relapse.

--- **EXERCISE** ---

Evaluating Your Relapse History and Level of Dependence

A. Reasons for Relapse and Your Plan for Relapse Prevention

Please rate how much of an influence the following factors had in causing a previous relapse to smoking. If this is your first quit attempt, rate how much you expect these factors to increase your risk for relapse.

1. Craving to smoke

NO INFLUENCE			VERY LARGE INFLUENCE	
1	2	3	4	5

2. Withdrawal symptoms

NO INFLUENCE			VERY LARGE INFLUENCE	
1	2	3	4	5

3. Gaining weight

NO INFLUENCE			VERY LARGE INFLUENCE	
1	2	3	4	5

4. Drinking too much alcohol

NO INFLUENCE			VERY LARGE INFLUENCE	
1	2	3	4	5

5. Too much stress

NO INFLUENCE			VERY LARGE INFLUENCE	
1	2	3	4	5

6. Depressed, distressed, or unhappy

NO INFLUENCE				VERY LARGE INFLUENCE
1	2	3	4	5

7. Doubts that the efforts are worth it

NO INFLUENCE				VERY LARGE INFLUENCE
1	2	3	4	5

B. In your former attempts to quit, how long did you typically stay smoke free and what was your longest length of abstinence?

1. Three days or less

    ☐ TYPICAL   ☐ LONGEST

2. One week

    ☐ TYPICAL   ☐ LONGEST

3. One month

    ☐ TYPICAL   ☐ LONGEST

4. Three months

    ☐ TYPICAL   ☐ LONGEST

5. Six months

    ☐ TYPICAL   ☐ LONGEST

6. One year or more

    ☐ TYPICAL   ☐ LONGEST

C. How many times have you tried to quit in the past?

0	1	2–4	5–6	7 or more

D. A Brief Test for Nicotine Dependence	Score
1. How soon after you wake up do you smoke your first cigarette? Within 5 minutes = **3 points**; Within 6-30 minutes = **2 points**	
2. Do you wake up in the middle of the night and smoke a cigarette? Yes = **3 points**; No = **0 points**	
3. Which cigarette would you most hate to give up? First one in the morning = **1 point**; Any other = **0 points**	
4. How many cigarettes do you smoke each day? 31 or more = **3 points** 21-30 = **2 points** 11-20 = **1 point** 10 or less = **0 points**	
Scoring: 0-2 = **Very low dependence** 3-4 = **Low dependence** 5 = **Medium dependence** 6-7 = **High dependence** 8-10 = **Very high dependence**	**TOTAL**

Add your points and check your level of dependence.

---

*Tailoring Your Relapse Prevention Plan to Address
Your Risks for Relapse*

Please review your answers in the four areas, A through D, in the previous exercise and see where you are at for risks for relapse. Compare your answers to the following description.

HIGHEST RISKS FOR RELAPSE

Of the items on the four brief assessments, the following put you at the highest risk for relapse:

A. Cravings or withdrawal are your most important concerns.

B. Your longest period of abstinence from smoking was a month or less.

C. You have tried to quit seven or more times.

D. You have a high or very high dependence score.

If you meet three or more of these criteria, then you should, at a minimum, consider including nicotine replacement therapy (NRT) as part of your relapse prevention plan. You should talk to your health care provider or pharmacist about your plan to use NRT to make sure it is safe with your particular health history. If you have used NRT in past efforts to quit, or if you have a very high dependence score, ask your health care provider about including a prescription medication, such as Chantix, as part of your relapse prevention plan.

The more severe your smoking problem, the more intensive your treatment should be. This would include working with a certified smoking cessation counselor as a key part of your plan. In addition, you could consider using Pro-Change's Smoking Cessation TTM Computerized Tailored Intervention (CTI) by going to www.prochange.com/myhealth. The latest breakthrough with our CTI, plus tailored text messages, has produced dramatically increased impacts when working with smokers who were ready, getting ready, or not ready at the start of the program.

Coping with Cravings

Here are some strategies that self-changers have used to cope with cravings. Check which ones you plan to include in your relapse prevention plan. Remember that most cravings and urges to smoke last for a limited time. The better you cope, the faster and the more effectively you counter such cravings.

Strategies to Cope with Cravings

☐ Walk away from them.

☐ Breathe deeply and exhale slowly.

☐ Distance yourself with a distraction.

☐ Call on a friend.

☐ Sip on some water.

☐ Tell yourself you are going to help beat the tobacco industry.

☐ Relax your muscles and your mind.

☐ Tell yourself that this, too, shall pass.

☐ Tell yourself you can counter such cravings.

☐ Chew away your cravings with a stick of sugarless gum.

☐ Chew away your cravings with a stick of NRT gum.

☐ Use the medication Chantix.

☐ Think of all the benefits you are generating.

☐ Tell yourself that as you win each battle, you are winning the war against smoking.

☐ Think about how good you will feel as you get freer and freer from cravings.

☐ Do something with your hands.

☐ Tell yourself a carrot can keep the craving away.

Solutions for Withdrawal

The following chart provides more solutions for countering withdrawal symptoms. Check which ones you plan to include in your relapse prevention program.

SYMPTOM	SOLUTION
Tired	☐ Take a nap. ☐ Take some extra time to sleep. ☐ Don't push yourself. ☐ Exercise.
Headache	☐ Try lying down. ☐ Do deep breathing. ☐ Take a warm shower or bath. ☐ Take an aspirin or Tylenol.
Nervous	☐ Take a walk. ☐ Soak in a hot bath. ☐ Do something relaxing. ☐ Call a friend.
Irritable	☐ Tell people close to you that you're quitting and ask for their understanding if you are somewhat edgy over the next few days. ☐ Be patient with yourself. ☐ Do some physical activity.

SYMPTOM	SOLUTION
Insomnia	☐ Avoid caffeine after 3 p.m. Some people may need to avoid it even earlier. ☐ Try exercising in the morning or early afternoon. ☐ Do something relaxing before going to bed.
Sore throat, coughing	☐ Drink plenty of fluids (try hot tea). ☐ Try cough drops. ☐ Tell yourself you are coughing more because you are cleaning out your system.
Hungry	☐ Drink water or low-calorie liquids. ☐ Be prepared with healthy snacks.
Dizzy	☐ Take extra caution. ☐ Change positions slowly.
Stomach pain or constipation	☐ Drink plenty of fluids. ☐ Add foods with fiber to your diet (such as fruits, vegetables, and whole grains). ☐ Exercise.
Trouble concentrating	☐ Make lists. ☐ Remove distractions, like turning off the TV. ☐ Ask others not to distract you. ☐ Be patient with yourself.

Successful Weight Management

If the fear of gaining weight is one of your key concerns that could lead to relapse, here are some things that can help you win on weight while preventing relapse.

First, you need to know that after quitting smoking your sense of smell and taste improve, especially for women. With that in mind, a primary prevention measure is to be *mindful of your sugar intake*. So far, whenever we have discussed eating and drinking behaviors as a way to counter cravings, the solution was to rely on sugarless gum or hard candies, carrots, water, or sugar-free beverages. Other healthy options are celery, sunflower seeds, or raw nuts like almonds. If you already have the habit of relying heavily on comfort foods, you are likely to get heavier when you quit smoking, so you need to be prepared to seek comfort that can help you to be healthier or happier. Walk with a friend, talk with a friend, play with a pet, read a fun book, or watch a favorite television show when you're tempted to turn to comfort foods with all their sugar, salt, and fat.

Thus far, we have also included physical activity as a primary way to prevent relapse. Once again, you can walk to help manage your weight when coping with other primary causes of relapse, such as being tired or having sleep problems, irritability, or constipation. Taking nicotine out of your daily diet can affect your metabolism, which affects how quickly you burn off calories, so you may want to walk faster or exercise more vigorously for a while at least.

When faced with the possibility of weight gain, you may need to *reevaluate your self-image* if you add the average of five to ten pounds after quitting. First of all, for most people, this extra weight withers away over time. You can make sure that happens with the help of the chapter on healthy eating. But recognize that there is serious debate over whether trying to quit smoking and losing weight should be done simultaneously. The evidence isn't clear, and we will discuss this issue more in our chapter on changing multiple behaviors. For now, we recommend that you keep smoking cessation as your primary goal. But generally limiting sugar intake, eating a healthy diet, and exercising are great ways to help prevent relapse. After six months of successful abstinence from smoking, you can add "loss of your new pounds" to your behavior change plan. The healthy eating chapter discusses ways that can help you lose your new weight in a month or two, while enhancing your health and happiness for years to come.

Meanwhile, here is a checklist you can use to prevent weight gain while quitting smoking and beyond. Check which ones you plan to apply.

Paths to Prevent Weight Gain

☐ Limit your sugar intake.

☐ Eat healthy snacks, such as carrots, celery, and seeds.

☐ Use smaller plates and bowls for portion control.

☐ Use sugarless gum, hard candy, and cough drops to cope with cravings or coughing.

☐ Drink some water.

☐ Drink coffee or tea without sugar or caffeine.

☐ Go for a walk, swim, or bike ride.

☐ Walk, swim, or bike faster if feasible.

☐ Eat slowly, walk fast.

☐ Make comfort calls to friends instead of eating comfort foods.

Maintenance: Staying Free from Smoking

Staying free from smoking in the maintenance stage requires ongoing application of

- social liberation to take advantage of supports in your environment
- stimulus control to manage your environment by controlling yourself
- managing emotions to deal with the stress and distress in your life

Social Liberation: How Changes in Your Environment Can Help You and Others Stay Quit

In chapter 6, we discussed the transformation that occurred with policy changes to ban smoking in public places—smoking shifted from being more under biological stimulus control (nicotine blood level) to being under social stimulus control (no smoking in public places). The tobacco industry spent fortunes for decades to fight such policies. For instance, tobacco companies argued that smoking was a personal choice that only affected the individual smoker, and they tried to dispute evidence on the damaging and deadly effects of secondhand smoke. The public health policies that finally banned smoking in public settings changed the environment to protect others in the environment from the effects of smoking. But they also changed the environment in ways that could help you to quit.

Today if you go to a smoke-free restaurant or bar, you won't be as tempted to smoke. In other words, this "social liberation" has increased your options when you are working to stay free from smoking and from secondhand smoke. Such changes in society were facilitated and accelerated by advocacy groups who generated support for healthier policies and programs. You, too, could be an advocate for greater social liberation that can help you and many others get free from smoking.

Social networks are a more recent innovation that can help smokers get free and stay free from smoking. Remember our reference to the study about how someone quitting smoking in California can influence someone else to quit in Maine? These connections happened well before online social networks were developed. Now there are social networks, such as QuitNet, just for smokers who are working to get quit and stay quit. QuitNet is especially helpful for those in preparation or action.

Stimulus Control: Controlling Your Environment by Controlling Yourself

One sure way to control your environment is to remove all cigarettes, along with all ashtrays, from your house and car. You may also want to place red dots on stimuli that have been triggers to smoke, such as your smartphone, tablet, or computer, and the refrigerator. Next, you can stock up on carrots, sugarless gum, or hard candy to counter urges to smoke by turning to other oral gratifications. Hanging up no-smoking signs in your home can protect you from being triggered by other people smoking. Early in the action stage, it is wise to use the coping strategy of distancing yourself from stimuli strongly associated not only with smoking but also with loosening of self-controls. Such strong stimuli include taking breaks at work with smokers or going to a favorite bar where too much drinking can trigger smoking.

As you build up your confidence by remaining smoke-free over time, you can gradually start to be around stimuli you used to associate with smoking. But you may choose to avoid returning to clubs or bars that have been triggers to risking your health and happiness.

Here is a more dramatic and creative way that one of our self-changers used stimulus control to quit and stay quit. Diego, a forty-five-year-old construction worker, had tried to quit smoking five times. Each time he relapsed at home, most often because of stress or distress.

Clearing his house of stimuli that had controlled his smoking helped him counter many cravings. But he needed to learn that his home was still where he was most at risk to smoke, because there were so many social controls that extended into his home. So he decided to create his own personal health policy: He would only smoke in his comfortable chair in his basement.

This "rule control" would seriously limit automatic, mindless smoking that could urge him at any time to light up anywhere in his house. Using our terminology, he was making his smoking more mindful. He was also dramatically reducing all the stimuli in his house that were paired with and conditioned to stimulate smoking. Over time, he increased his confidence, or self-efficacy, that he would not light up anywhere but in his basement chair. He had dramatically cut back from eighteen to eight cigarettes a day. This was, in part, because of the extra effort it required to go to the basement. He was also finding smoking to be less pleasurable, because it occurred in the absence of TV, food, family, and the warmer parts of his house.

Finally, he determined that it was time for him to part company with his comfortable chair. He decided to donate it to charity as a symbol of helping others while he helped himself. Diego was surprised to discover that he grieved his favorite chair more than the loss of his cigarettes.

Managing Emotions to Prevent Relapse Due to Stress and Distress

In chapter 4, we hope you made significant progress in preparing yourself for managing stress, distress, and depression. You have learned that those emotional behaviors are major drivers for engaging in the four biggest threats to your health and happiness. Congratulations for being willing to tackle the biggest threat: smoking. You also have learned that stress and distress are major causes for relapsing back to smoking, as well as to the other three major threats. Here are some ways to manage your emotions while maintaining your abstinence from smoking.

1. Breathe deeply and exhale slowly.
2. Drink healthy beverages, such as water or tea.
3. Eat healthy foods, such as carrots, celery, or seeds.
4. Move more; for example, walk; then walk faster.

Look at how each of these four fundamental processes of life can be called on to avoid relapsing back to smoking, the biggest threat to life. But also recognize how toxic forms of these fundamental processes of life can lead to relapsing back to breathing toxic smoke. Drinking too much alcohol, eating too many "comfort foods," and moving too little can contribute to relapsing back to smoking. You are starting to learn how interconnected these behaviors can be. There can be positive connections or networks of behaviors, just as there can be positive neural networks and positive social networks that can enhance health and happiness. Unfortunately, there can also be negative networks of behaviors, just as there can be negative neural networks and negative social networks that can harm health and happiness.

Hopefully you are appreciating that your increasing commitment to a healthier life, a happier life, a longer life, and a fuller life will lead you to change your multiple risky behaviors that threaten your health and happiness. But much more about that later.

Now we need to talk more about the fifth fundamental process of life—emotion. Dealing with feelings appropriately helps prevent relapsing back to smoking. Here are some of the ways you have already learned to deal with feelings:

1. Talk to a friend.
2. Read a book.
3. Be reinforced, or supported, by others.
4. Be reinforced, or supported, by yourself.
5. Think more positive thoughts.

Let's focus more on healthy thinking that can support healthy behaviors. Here we will apply the ABCDs when you face a relapse of smoking. We will apply this process to our friend Don, the extraordinary man we got to know who owns the shoeshine stand at our local airport. Don had read the Pro-Change TTM stage-based smoking cessation manual. He had progressed from contemplation to preparation, as he broke out of his profound ambivalence about quitting smoking. Don had a long-term love-hate relationship with smoking, which he had relied heavily upon to deal with major distress, like the loss of a career.

Don dramatically increased the importance of the pros of quitting smoking, including how much less he would have to pay for health insurance and how much more he could save by not buying cigarettes. He also saw how his progressing toward quitting could help his wife begin to seriously contemplate quitting her own unhealthy habit. In his action plan, Don decided that the severity of his smoking and his past failures to quit called for a more intensive treatment, so he decided to try Chantix, hoping it would add biological controls while he was struggling with his self-controls.

Each time Jan and I saw Don at his shoeshine stand, he would share with well-earned pride how well his action plan was working. He wasn't having near the cravings he had in the past because of the Chantix. But he also had joined a low-cost health club near the airport where he could exercise physically and psychologically to reinforce his commitment to quit smoking. Don knew from the past that too much empty time produced stress, distress, and temptations to smoke. So Don's confidence was increasing, and his craving or temptations were decreasing. That is until Don faced a very real crisis.

His brother who had died had left Don a ring that he cherished. The ring reminded Don of the love and caring and the good times the brothers had shared together. Somehow Don lost the ring, and he felt that meant he also lost his special connection to his brother. He didn't know how he lost it. He didn't know where. When he discovered it missing, he hopped in his car and drove back to work, convinced he must have accidentally thrown it in the trash when he was cleaning his stand.

Don desperately searched through the trash container numerous times, but to no avail. Don believed he faced a personal disaster, probably, in part, because he was reliving the loss of his brother. He was also facing a personal disaster because he was flooded with incredible cravings to smoke. In the past, smoking would have provided him with immediate relief from the flood of emotions he was experiencing— anger at himself for messing up, depression over his losses, distress from feeling helpless, and fear that he would not cope with this disaster without smoking. It is similar to what happens to military personnel who are deployed to combat situations. A 2008 study found that military personnel exposed to combat were more likely to either develop a new smoking habit or return to old smoking behaviors than those who were not deployed, likely due to the extreme stress they experienced.[39]

But Don dug deep. He knew if he survived this disaster without smoking, he would deserve some type of medal. That day he saved himself, perhaps, in part, because he thought about what his brother would want him to do. Somehow Don was able to counter his profoundly emotional thinking with reasons that made deep sense to him: To self-destruct at this time would not return his precious ring; it would not return his precious brother; and it would not help his precious wife. These are personally significant reasons to make a deeper commitment to living a longer, healthier, wealthier, and happier life. After he grieved the loss of his ring, we celebrated together how he had won this battle by holding on to his pledge to rid his life of the biggest threat to his health. We are grateful to Don for sharing his story and so glad for him that he was able to honor his commitment to change.

Toward Termination: Being Free from Smoking

With every major temptation Don faces, he builds his confidence that even such distressing situations cannot cause him to start smoking again. He is holding on to all of the Principles of Progress that he applied in those bad days of grief, distress, and temptation. And he knows there will be more bad days. But there are so many good days in between when he is fulfilling his commitment to quit for good—for the good of his health and happiness, his wife, and his family.

Like Don, you have completed a guide for progressing through each Stage of Change. Hopefully you have dramatically increased your appreciation of the multiple benefits of quitting smoking. Later, you will see how building your benefits will not only dramatically increase your physical health, but can also enhance all of the elements of well-being that make up happiness. Now you are going to shift from breathing healthy and happy to being happy by making healthy decisions about your alcohol use.

8

Well-Being and Alcohol Problems
A HOLISTIC APPROACH FOR EVERYONE

Although this chapter deals with alcohol and problem drinking, it isn't just for alcoholics; it's about using the Stages of Change to improve all aspects of a self-changer's life, including alcohol misuse and other high-risk behaviors that often accompany it. The Substance Abuse and Mental Health Services Administration (SAMHSA) has taken a strong stance that people with alcohol problems need holistic health care. In other words, rather than just dealing with alcohol misuse, SAMHSA (and a growing number of others in the field) calls for a treatment approach that deals with the person's overall mental, social, occupational, and financial well-being. Jan and I are excited by how rapidly the concept of holistic health approaches for people with an alcohol use disorder (AUD)—whether mild, moderate, or severe—is spreading across this country and the globe. In a matter of months, we were asked to do workshops and presentations with substance abuse and mental health counselors from Rhode Island, Massachusetts, Illinois, South Dakota, Texas, and Alaska, as well as Portugal and Russia.

It was long assumed that if individuals stopped drinking or abusing another drug of choice, the rest of their health risks could be easily handled. But Tom McLellan, a researcher at the University of Pennsylvania and a former adviser to the president on national drug control policy, was one of the first to demonstrate that treatment agencies improve only what they treat. He concluded that just treating the drug of choice is not a miracle that pulls one's whole lifestyle into a healthy and happy place. For example, most substance abusers smoke, but they are not likely to quit smoking if they stop drinking unless they receive high-impact help for that risky behavior as well. With the Transtheoretical Model

(TTM), this means being matched to the appropriate Stage of Change.

It is not by chance that for decades, alcoholism, like other substance use disorders, has been called a disease of denial. People with drinking problems (especially if they fall within the moderate to severe range) are naturally defensive, which is why it is common for them to be stuck in the precontemplation Stage of Change.

David's Story

When David came to me for help, he was in the precontemplation stage for his alcohol problems, partly out of defensiveness but more out of demoralization. But, besides being a heavy drinker, he was also a heavy smoker, heavy eater, and heavy couch potato who was plagued with anxiety, anger, and stress and distress.

He told me he had read the book *Changing for Good,* and so he was very familiar with the Stages of Change. He seemed down but hopeful. "Until I read your book, I felt like I was destined to die at a young age," he said.

He had told me he inherited the five biggest threats to a person's health and happiness from his parents. I told him how rare he was, since less than 5 percent of adults in the United States have all five threats.[40] "At least I'm distinguished by something," David joked darkly.

"Which of your five big risky behaviors threatens you the most?" I asked David, prepared to address his drinking first. Seeming to read my mind, he said, "You might think I would say my drinking, but it's really my smoking. My dad died of lung cancer. What a terrible way to die."

I told him he was right, that smoking was like a time bomb, but that he still had time to greatly reduce his chance of being plagued by lung cancer. "If you quit before you are fifty, research shows that the odds are in your favor that you won't get cancer from smoking." I was trying to increase his pros, raise his consciousness, and generate dramatic relief by first addressing his biggest fear and then reducing it with some science.

"So, David, would you say smoking is your top priority for change?"

He agreed that it was. He told me how his mom had taken him to see a drug counselor when he was a teenager. "I guess she was in the action stage, and I was in precontemplation," he said.

"What stage was your counselor?" I asked.

"Action, and he and my mother ganged up on me to take immediate action. He wasn't my counselor for long. And that turned me off to counselors. Of course, my mom blamed me."

I told David that he seemed to be going in a good direction already, but I wanted to be clear that we both needed to acknowledge where he was in terms of his drinking. I told him that our recent discoveries have shown that he could be progressing toward action on smoking while still starting to move in the Stages of Change on other threats like drinking and depression. In a review of the research, we have found that people with substance use problems like alcohol abuse who also received help with smoking did better dealing with both issues.[41] Similarly, colleagues in San Francisco found that people with depression who also received stage-based help with smoking did better dealing with both behaviors.[42] I told David that while we would spend our time focused on smoking, we would also spend some time on his drinking and depression, since making progress on them could also help him with smoking. I added that we would hold off working on his diet for good reasons that I would explain later, which he agreed sounded like a reasonable way to proceed.

Since David was in the preparation stage for smoking, we started with the change processes of making a commitment and taking more small steps. And because he was in precontemplation for his drinking, I gave him the following homework—strategies you can use to progress in your own journey of change.

Assess Your Alcohol Use to Determine Your Current Stage of Change

Programs like TTM use public health criteria to assess who is at significant risk with their drinking. Jan and I currently rely on those recommended by the U.S. Substance Abuse and Mental Health Services Administration. To be considered at low risk for alcohol abuse, SAMHSA suggests these limits on alcohol use:

1. No more than fourteen drinks per week *and* no more than four drinks in one day for men under age sixty

2. No more than seven drinks per week *and* no more than three drinks in one day for women and for men over sixty

A standard drink equals approximately 12 ounces of beer or wine cooler, 5 ounces of wine, and 1.5 ounces of 80-proof alcohol in a mixed drink. The experts at SAMHSA add this caveat: "Some people should not drink at all, like individuals in the past who have not been able to keep their drinking to low-risk levels."

Look carefully at the limits listed. Do you limit your drinking to fall within SAMHSA's low-risk criteria?

Check which of the following statements best applies to you:

☐ No, and I do not intend to in the next six months (precontemplation).

☐ No, but I intend to in the next six months (contemplation).

☐ No, but I intend to in the next month (preparation).

☐ Yes, but I have been for less than six months (action).

☐ Yes, and I have been for more than six months (maintenance).

Just taking this assessment can produce a defensive reaction or resistance in self-changers. Why should all women and men over sixty be limited to just seven drinks a week or an average of one per day? You might think that such limits don't seem fair. Pause to think about how you reacted to SAMHSA's guidelines. Did you want to dispute these recommendations? How might you look at them?

First, you might say that no one is limiting you—these guidelines are recommendations that can help you to limit your drinking habits in order to reduce your risk of experiencing the harmful consequences of alcohol abuse and enhance your health and well-being. Next, examine the truly small differences between each of these criteria: For men under sixty, the average number of drinks per day should be limited to two. For all women and for men over sixty, the average should be limited to one. For those who have been unable to keep their drinking at such low-risk levels, the average should be zero. The differences are just zero, one, or two drinks.

These differences seem pretty small, but they can have such big consequences. According to SAMHSA, individuals who are able to live within these recommended limits have only about a 2 percent chance of developing an alcohol use disorder. (An AUD includes both what recently was commonly called "alcohol abuse" *and* "alcohol dependence"—problems that were, and still are, commonly called "alcoholism.")

Compare the 2 percent risk to the fact that about 25 percent of people who drink at high-risk levels have an alcohol use disorder. These statistics show that a small difference in drinking can predict a big difference in developing a life-threatening AUD.

Our intention here is not to scare self-changers. Rather, we want to increase your consciousness to help you decrease your defensiveness so you can be more open to progressing through the Stages of Change. Here is a quiz that can help you become more aware of the arguments people often use to defend their risky drinking—defenses that increase their risk of developing even more serious drinking problems.

──────── **EXERCISE** ────────

Signs of Alcohol Problems

Circle whether you believe each statement is true (T) or false (F).

Your drinking is not a significant problem if

1. You only drink after 5 p.m.	T	F
2. You only drink beer.	T	F
3. You only drink with others.	T	F
4. You only have three or four drinks a day.	T	F
5. You only drink fine red wine.	T	F
6. You only drink with food.	T	F

7. You only drink with someone.	T	F
8. You don't have a hangover in the morning.	T	F
9. You can control how much you drink.	T	F
10. You only drink at home to prevent problems.	T	F

Now look at what you've circled. Any of the statements you marked as true are defenses for your drinking. So, we urge you to stay open to facts and feedback. Now let's progress from decreasing defenses to increasing the pros of changing to a healthier lifestyle that includes low- or no-risk drinking.

To help David prioritize the pros for progressing on his problem drinking, I asked him to rate how concerned he was about each of the following parts of his body. I also encourage you to do your own ratings. Soon we will see how concerns about many parts of your body can be addressed by the pros of changing your drinking. You may be surprised by much of what David shared next and how his ratings compare to yours.

———— EXERCISE ————

Concerns about Your Body

Please circle the number for each body part that best reflects your overall concerns:

BODY PART	NOT AT ALL CONCERNED	A LITTLE CONCERNED	MODERATELY CONCERNED	VERY CONCERNED	EXTREMELY CONCERNED
Your brain	1	2	3	4	5
Your eyes	1	2	3	4	5

BODY PART	NOT AT ALL CONCERNED	A LITTLE CONCERNED	MODERATELY CONCERNED	VERY CONCERNED	EXTREMELY CONCERNED
Your mouth	1	2	3	4	5
Your throat	1	2	3	4	5
Your lungs	1	2	3	4	5
Your heart	1	2	3	4	5
Your stomach	1	2	3	4	5
Your liver	1	2	3	4	5
Your kidneys	1	2	3	4	5
Your pancreas	1	2	3	4	5
Your colon	1	2	3	4	5
Your genitals	1	2	3	4	5
Your bladder	1	2	3	4	5
Your hands	1	2	3	4	5
Your feet	1	2	3	4	5

After doing this exercise, David told me, "You may be surprised that I am as concerned about my brain as my lungs. I see myself as a bright guy. I went to college, but I was suspended my second semester because I partied too much. There was tons of drinking there, and I sure felt at home. I wanted to become a psychologist, maybe to understand my family and myself. But my parents wouldn't let me. I had to go into the family business, which was banking. I discovered there's a lot of drinking at business events too."

I asked David if part of his ambivalence about giving up drinking might be because he thought it could negatively affect his business and social life. He said I was probably right. I knew that for David to make progress in the Stages of Change, we would have to increase his positives and decrease the negatives for changing his high-risk drinking habits.

Increasing Your Pros to Change Your Drinking Habits and Move from Precontemplation to Contemplation

So now let's look at your own pros for changing from high-risk to low- or no-risk drinking. To repeat what we stressed in the last chapter, the bigger goal in making significant lifestyle changes is *well-being*. As your body, your mind (self), your spirit, and your relationships improve, your happiness grows. When you use TTM to lower (or eliminate) high-risk alcohol use and learn to change multiple behaviors, you will benefit in many ways. The following lists identify some of those benefits. As was the case in previous chapters, the pros are organized into areas of well-being because these are among the best predictors of success.

--------------------------------- EXERCISE ---------------------------------

Pros of Changing to Low- or No-Risk Drinking

Look over these lists and check the pros that are important to you when it comes to drinking. Remember, the more pros you have to gain, the more likely you will keep progressing. Focusing on the pros you choose will help you move from precontemplation to contemplation.

Physical Well-Being

☐ Reduce your risk of cancer of the digestive systems

☐ Reduce your risk of cancer of the ovaries

☐ Reduce your risk of cancer of the mouth

☐ Reduce your risk of Alzheimer's disease

☐ Reduce your risk of gallstones

☐ Reduce your risk of heart disease

☐ Reduce your risk of stroke

☐ Reduce your risk of colon cancer

☐ Reduce your risk of breast cancer

☐ Reduce your risk of esophageal cancer

☐ Reduce your risk of liver disease

☐ Reduce your risk of bladder problems

☐ Reduce your risk of prostate cancer

☐ Reduce your risk of pancreatic cancer

☐ Reduce your risk of obesity

☐ Reduce your risk of arteriosclerosis

☐ Reduce your risk of kidney cancer

☐ Reduce your risk of diabetes

☐ Better manage any health conditions

☐ Reduce your body fat

☐ Reduce triglycerides

☐ May lower your blood pressure

☐ Reduce risk of high blood sugar

☐ Improve your sleep

☐ Improve immune system function

☐ Help your body use insulin

☐ Lower the risk of erectile dysfunction

☐ Prevent weight gain

☐ Improve health of teeth and gums

☐ Decrease your risk of heart attack

☐ Reduce malnutrition

Note: Long-term use of alcohol is capable of damaging nearly every organ and system in the body.

Functional Well-Being

- ☐ Have more energy
- ☐ Promote effective problem solving
- ☐ Promote feelings of control
- ☐ Increase confidence
- ☐ Be more productive
- ☐ Increase stamina
- ☐ Be more alert
- ☐ Be better coordinated
- ☐ Reduce your risk of falling
- ☐ Have fewer illnesses and absences from work
- ☐ Improve your balance
- ☐ Improve your brain power

Financial Well-Being

- ☐ Manage your money better
- ☐ May save money
- ☐ Lower health care costs
- ☐ Get a promotion or better paying job

Social Well-Being

- ☐ Reduce blowups with others
- ☐ Improve your relationship with others
- ☐ Set an example about making healthy choices
- ☐ Gain pride from your friends
- ☐ Improve your sex life
- ☐ Cause your loved ones to worry less about you
- ☐ Make it easier for people in your home to change their drinking
- ☐ Feel happier around other people
- ☐ Prevent alcohol-related accidents and DUIs

Appealing Well-Being

- ☐ Be more appealing to other people
- ☐ Improve your appearance
- ☐ Have a healthier image
- ☐ Look better
- ☐ Make your skin look better
- ☐ Age slower

Emotional Well-Being

- ☐ Mange your anger better
- ☐ Avoid embarrassing yourself
- ☐ Feel better about yourself
- ☐ Make your emotional life healthier
- ☐ Learn new ways to cope with distress
- ☐ Manage your stress better
- ☐ Spend less time worrying about your drinking
- ☐ Feel more relaxed and at ease
- ☐ Feel like you're taking better care of yourself
- ☐ Show you care about yourself
- ☐ Reduce depression

Purposeful Well-Being

- ☐ Live longer
- ☐ Live better
- ☐ Affirm life has not passed you by
- ☐ Use your talents more effectively
- ☐ Improve your quality of life
- ☐ Improve your self-worth
- ☐ Reduce health care costs for you and society

Keep the list of the pros you have checked in mind as you move forward in the Stages of Change.

Raise Your Consciousness by Assessing Your Risk for Alcohol Use Disorder (AUD)

The following assessment questions for AUD are adapted from the National Institute on Alcohol Abuse and Alcoholism (NIAAA).[43] The more honest you can be when answering the questions, the more accurate your assessment will be.

--------------------------------- EXERCISE ---------------------------------

Alcohol Use Disorder Questions

Circle whether or not you have done each behavior in the past year.

In the past year, have you

1. Had times when you ended up drinking more or longer than you intended?	Yes	No
2. More than once wanted to cut down or stop drinking, or tried to, but couldn't?	Yes	No
3. Spent a lot of time drinking, being sick, or getting over other aftereffects of drinking?	Yes	No
4. Wanted a drink so badly you couldn't think of anything else?	Yes	No
5. Found that drinking—or being sick from drinking— often interfered with taking care of your home or family?	Yes	No
6. Continued to drink even though it was causing trouble with your family or friends?	Yes	No
7. Given up or cut back on activities that were important or interesting to you, or gave you pleasure in order to drink?	Yes	No

In the past year, have you

8. More than once gotten into a situation while or after drinking that increased your chances of getting hurt (e.g., driving, swimming, using machinery, walking in a dangerous area, or having unsafe sex)?	Yes	No
9. Continued to drink even though it was making you feel depressed or anxious or adding to another health problem—or after having had a memory blackout?	Yes	No
10. Had to drink much more than you once did to get the effect you want? Or found that your usual number of drinks had much less effect than before?	Yes	No
11. Found that when the effects of alcohol were wearing off, you had withdrawal symptoms, such as trouble sleeping, shakiness, restlessness, nausea, sweating, a racing heartbeat, or a seizure—or sensed things that were not there?	Yes	No

According to the NIAAA, having at least two of these symptoms may indicate an alcohol use disorder. The severity of the AUD is defined as either mild (two to three symptoms), moderate (four to five symptoms), or severe (six or more symptoms). It is important to raise your consciousness of the serious consequences of your drinking. This will help guide the best strategies for you.

Use Dramatic Relief to Pay Attention to Your Feelings

Reading and answering the previous questions can be emotionally upsetting, because the exercise can dramatically reflect the multiple ways that risky drinking can get out of control and deteriorate your health and happiness. If you think you have an alcohol use disorder or are moving in that direction, the best way to reduce some of your upset is to add professional counseling to your change plan. David did this when he made an appointment with me—even though he was still in precontemplation about his alcohol use.

What David demonstrated is that self-changers don't have to be prepared to take action to benefit from professional help. Most licensed or certified alcohol or substance abuse professionals have been trained in TTM using the Stages of Change and/or motivational interviewing (discussed in chapter 5). Each of these approaches is designed to start where you are in your change process and help you to progress from there. If you are working with a substance abuse professional, this book can be a friendly companion that can help you to progress before, during, and between counseling sessions. So, take the next best step toward progressing to low-risk drinking or stopping drinking. You can find such help by calling professional organizations like your state's psychological or psychiatric, counseling, or substance abuse association. Tell them the type of expert guidance you are seeking so you can find therapy to meet your needs. SAMHSA's national locator can help you find the drug and alcohol treatment program nearest you. Just go to https://findtreatment.samhsa.gov/TreatmentLocator/faces/quickSearch.jspx and click on your state, or call SAMHSA's free treatment and referral helpline at 1-800-662-HELP (4357).

In Contemplation, Lower the Cons for Changing Your Drinking Habits

We've mentioned some of the reasons David had for not wanting to give up his risky drinking habits (negative effects on his social and business life). No doubt, you—like other self-changers—have your own list. Here are some of the most commonly claimed cons that we've come across in our many years of working with the Stages of Change. Ways to counter each con are also included. Study this chart to see how you might deal with your own risky drinking by overcoming the negatives and increasing the positives for cutting back on or eliminating alcohol from your life.

COMMONLY CLAIMED CONS	COUNTERING THE CONS
Drinking can be healthy.	Drinking a little or none can be, but not a little more.
Dramatically reducing or stopping drinking is much too hard.	It is much too hard when you're not prepared, but getting prepared isn't too hard.

COMMONLY CLAIMED CONS	COUNTERING THE CONS
I might lose all my friends who drink.	Like David, you can find your friends who also want to change.
The best parties are drinking parties.	Who says you have to drink to party? And you don't have to pay the price of drinking to party.
I feel most free when I am drinking.	Read again the eleven consequences in the previous exercise that can come with risky drinking. How free is that?

Environmental Reevaluation: Notice Your Effects on Others

It's important to reevaluate how your changing affects others in your social environment. When we change our drinking habits, we learn a key lesson: *The change processes can have negative effects and end up stopping or reversing our progress.* Look at David who was so deeply embedded in a drinking culture. He was rightfully worried that his changing would threaten family, friends, and business contacts where social and emotional lives revolved around alcohol. He was demoralized by what he perceived as his biological and social destiny. The homework I assigned David was to try to identify who in his social network might be most open to pull together with him toward progress rather than pushing him to regress.

Being the bright guy he was, David risked sharing the following message on his social network sites: "I'm tired of wasting too much time and resources on drinking. Open to joining me in a journey toward a better life?" He was surprised by the number of rapid responses he received, like "Me too, David. Count me in." "Thanks for taking the lead. I'm sure there is a better life down a new path together." "David, you've been my role model for drinking. Tell me you're ready to model a way to be freer from drinking."

The lesson here is don't assume everyone in your drinking environment has no interest in changing. Remember that even in precontemplation, most people want to change their threatening behaviors. They just aren't currently intending to take immediate action. Being proactive and reaching out to them can help them move into contemplation and eventually to preparation and action. Who in your social network might be willing to support you in such movement? How can you reach out for such support?

Progressing to Preparation

How do you think you would feel about yourself if you changed to low-risk or no-risk drinking? Self-reevaluation is a key process to determine the answer to this question—a process that prepares us for taking action. It is much easier to answer these key questions when it comes to smoking. Remember in chapter 7 when self-changers were asked how they think and feel about themselves as a smoker versus how they imagine they would think and feel about themselves as a nonsmoker? Being a smoker is part of the identity of most people who smoke. But many people who drink would not call themselves drinkers, in part because it is not an important part of their identity. Also, calling oneself a drinker seems associated with being a heavy drinker—as in, "Oh you know Chris—she's quite the drinker."

Using Self-Reevaluation to Create a New Self-Image

Here is an exercise for evaluating your self-image as a drinker.

———————————————— EXERCISE ————————————————

Self-Reevaluation

If the earlier self-assessment about your drinking habits indicated that you drink too much (more than seven to fourteen drinks per week and more than three to four drinks on any occasion), check how you think and feel about yourself now and how you imagine you'd feel if you changed to be within the low- or no-risk limits.

SELF-IMAGE NOW—I SEE MYSELF AS	SELF-IMAGE IF I CHANGE—I THINK I WOULD BE
☐ a heavy drinker	☐ a light or moderate drinker
☐ a risky drinker	☐ a nondrinker
☐ a problem drinker	☐ a low-risk drinker

SELF-IMAGE NOW—I SEE MYSELF AS	SELF-IMAGE IF I CHANGE—I THINK I WOULD BE
☐ having the potential to become a problem drinker	☐ a healthy drinker or nondrinker
☐ having the potential to be an alcoholic	☐ at little risk of becoming dependent
☐ a defensive drinker	☐ at little risk of becoming an alcoholic
☐ not too smart of a drinker	☐ a smarter drinker or nondrinker
☐ not controlling my drinking enough	☐ a more controlled drinker

Now consider how you would see yourself as a drinker if you had two or more of the consequences discussed in the alcohol use disorder self-assessment you completed earlier. First, think about how you see yourself as a drinker, then how you think you would see yourself if you limited your drinking.

DRINKER	LIMITED DRINKER
☐ Irresponsible	☐ Responsible
☐ Disappointed	☐ Proud
☐ Sluggish	☐ Productive
☐ Unhealthy	☐ Healthy
☐ Unsure	☐ Confident
☐ Weak	☐ Strong
☐ Hooked	☐ Free
☐ Depressed	☐ Centered
☐ Deteriorating	☐ Growing
☐ Embarrassed	☐ Pleased
☐ Uncontrolled	☐ Controlled

Now, look at this list from the perspective of your family and good friends. How do you think they see you now? How do you think they would see you if you changed?

HOW YOU ARE SEEN NOW	HOW YOU WOULD BE SEEN IF YOU CHANGED
☐ Irresponsible	☐ Responsible
☐ Disappointing	☐ Proud
☐ Sluggish	☐ Productive
☐ Unhealthy	☐ Healthy
☐ Unsure	☐ Confident
☐ Weak	☐ Strong
☐ Hooked	☐ Free
☐ Depressed	☐ Centered
☐ Deteriorating	☐ Growing
☐ Embarrassing	☐ Pleasant
☐ Uncontrolled	☐ Controlled

Reflect on the differences in your present self-image and how your self-image could be if you made the change to responsible drinking.

Make a Commitment to Move from Preparation to Action

You are on your way to action when you make commitments to change. As you learned previously, having two choices strengthens your commitment more than if you have only one choice. And having three choices is even better when it comes to making a commitment.

Check which alternative to drinking you are ready to commit to.

I am ready to

☐ gradually reduce how much and how often I drink

☐ immediately reduce to recommended limits

☐ stop drinking entirely

Based on the self-assessments about the consequences of your drinking, which of these three alternatives would you commit to?

I will

☐ apply the recommendations in this book as long as I am progressing

☐ add a professional counselor to my plan

☐ add a recovery group to my plan

If your self-assessment indicated that you may have an alcohol use disorder, you should commit to the second alternative (adding a professional counselor to your plan). If you are not ready to do that, you should at least talk to your health care provider. The more severe your AUD, the greater the risk if you take action without medically supervised alcohol detoxification.

Another effective way to increase your commitment is to go public. But a lot of people try to keep their drinking private, especially from their families. Often they are only fooling themselves. Ask yourself, "Who knows about how much and how often I drink?" and, "Who knows some of the serious consequences of my drinking?" If no one knows, you should seriously consider adding a counselor or self-help group to your plan. This step alone can increase your commitment by telling at least one or more people about your drinking. Of those who know your drinking habits and consequences, who could you tell about your plans to change your drinking patterns? Who else can you tell?

Go to Action by Using Counter Conditioning to Substitute Your Drinking Habits with Healthy Habits

As we've talked about, stress and distress are top reasons that people relapse to drinking. So if you progressed in chapter 4 where we discussed managing stress and distress effectively and healthfully (you might go back and reread that chapter to see where you stand now), you will be well prepared to apply these strategies to alcohol and keep progressing in the Stages of Change.

This applies to the other risky behaviors as well. If you have already quit smoking, you won't turn to cigarettes when craving a drink. In the next chapter, you will learn more about healthy foods. When you are feeling in poor physical shape from too much drinking, you can add regular exercise to your healthy habits. When you progress to low- or no-risk drinking, you will be even better prepared to change your diet and enhance your exercise, because too much alcohol reduces too many controls related to eating and moving, not just to drinking. As you make increasing commitments to your *whole* health, you are participating in a new kind of recovery that is driven by increasing commitments to life— a longer life, a healthier life, and a better life.

Now let's look at some of the ways you can counter your risky drinking habits with healthy habits. Then you will see later how these new habits can enhance your whole health—not just your "alcohol health."

Developing New Habits to Move toward Maintenance

Want a simple but powerful strategy to help you drink within your limit? Just replace old habits with new ones. Rather than doing something that might trigger your desire to drink, you do something else instead.

Which situations listed next might tempt you to drink more than you want? Read the lists under each situation to discover some healthy substitutes that you can do instead of drinking too much. Select the substitutes that you would do.

When I'm planning something with friends or family, instead of doing something that involves alcohol, I will

☐ Go to a movie

☐ Go to a coffee shop

☐ Go shopping

☐ Go to a restaurant that doesn't serve alcohol

☐ Invite them over for a healthy meal

☐ Plan an outdoor activity

☐ Play a sport

☐ Explore a new place or city

☐ Go to a museum, aquarium, or play

☐ Work on a project together

When I'm stressed or distressed and feel like I need a drink to relax, instead I will

☐ Do deep breathing

☐ Talk with others

☐ Walk

☐ Do a hobby

☐ Take a shower or bath

☐ Play a sport

☐ Garden

☐ Listen to music

☐ Meditate

☐ Start a project

☐ Read for pleasure

When I'm in a social setting where there is alcohol, instead of drinking more than my limit, I will

☐ Be a designated driver

☐ Drink water

☐ Drink some nonalcoholic beverages

☐ Talk, engage with others

☐ Hold something in my hand

☐ Chew gum or suck on candy

☐ Leave early

☐ Have a reason to explain why I am not drinking much

☐ Ask a friend to cut back on drinking too

☐ Ask someone to "cut me off" after a certain number of drinks

☐ Set a reminder on my phone to stop drinking or to leave

☐ Ask a partner or friend to call me to remind me to stop or to leave

Get Support through Helping Relationships

Hopefully, you have at least one person with whom you can share your commitment to quit or reduce drinking. Such a friend or family member can not only strengthen your commitment but can provide the emotional and social support you need to get through distressing times that tempt you the most to relapse.

Ask yourself if someone in your life who cares about you might be able to offer you this kind of support. Could they be threatened by your commitment because of their own drinking patterns? Could they listen and be empathetic? Could they respect the progress you are making without pressuring you to take immediate action? If you don't have supportive help available, consider adding a counselor to your plan if you haven't already. This could be a clergyperson, a doctor or nurse, a qualified substance abuse counselor, or a phone counselor available from your work or health plan. There are also online support groups where you can go public and receive support when you need it. In that kind of support community, you can stay anonymous if you prefer. Over time you may feel free to be more open, not only with folks you didn't know before but also with family and friends. Remember, the more open you become, the less defensive you will feel, the more support you will receive, and the more likely you will be to succeed over the long term.

Maintaining Self-Liberation through Social Liberation

When it comes to applying the principle of social liberation, many societies, including ours, have profound ambivalence at best. On the positive side is what we described in chapter 5 as one of the public health wonders of the world. This is the free positive social network founded decades ago by Bill W. to help people find recovery from alcoholism. Alcoholics Anonymous is by far the best known and largest social network that makes the Twelve Step approach available to unlimited numbers of people worldwide, creating positive connections between new and old members.

The Twelve Step approach was compared to the leading evidence-based treatments of motivational interviewing—which was designed to enhance motivation to quit and stay quit—and cognitive behavioral therapy—which emphasizes skills to take action and sustain action. Project Match, the largest comparative study of treatment methods ever funded by the National Institutes of Health (NIH), made a striking discovery: The three treatment approaches they reviewed had similar long-term results. But the Twelve Step program offered some advantages for people with more severe alcohol use disorders. Further, for all of the different methods, individuals who also attended a recovery group as part of their maintenance plan were more successful.

That is the good news. The bad news includes the fact that evidence-based treatments have been seriously underfunded by health care systems and federal, state, and local governments. Not only are the amount of services inadequate, but the compensation, continuing education, and effective tools like computer-tailored interventions are inadequate.

The "free" choices available for social liberation for long-term maintenance include AA; other Twelve Step groups, such as Narcotics Anonymous (NA), Marijuana Anonymous (MA), and Cocaine Anonymous (CA); and non–Twelve Step organizations, such as SMART Recovery and Women for Sobriety. One of the drawbacks of AA and related recovery groups is that they are designed more for people who are prepared to take action, or are in the action stage because of a crisis or feeling they have "hit bottom," than for people in the earlier Stages of Change.

However, if you have a moderate to severe alcohol use disorder and have progressed through the early Stages of Change using the information in this book to prepare for action and maintenance, then you are more likely to be ready for recovery and will have an excellent chance for success if you join a recovery community like AA.

On the next page is a self-assessment to help you decide whether to include a recovery group as part of your maintenance plan.

EXERCISE

Pros and Cons of Recovery Groups

Circle how important each pro or con is to you.

PROS	NOT AT ALL IMPORTANT				VERY IMPORTANT
1. Free	1	2	3	4	5
2. Help available most any place	1	2	3	4	5
3. Help available most any time	1	2	3	4	5
4. Can provide a positive social network	1	2	3	4	5
5. Can complement professional help	1	2	3	4	5
6. Help available for family and friends to help me	1	2	3	4	5
7. Real people who face the serious challenges of staying sober	1	2	3	4	5
8. Positive outcomes comparable to professional treatments	1	2	3	4	5
				TOTAL	

CONS	NOT AT ALL IMPORTANT				VERY IMPORTANT
1. Takes lots of time	1	2	3	4	5
2. Takes lots of effort	1	2	3	4	5
3. Have to be prepared to quit	1	2	3	4	5
4. Lacks experts in behavior	1	2	3	4	5
5. Have to believe you are an alcoholic	1	2	3	4	5
6. Only for people with moderate to severe alcohol use disorder	1	2	3	4	5
7. Some groups aren't so positive	1	2	3	4	5
8. Stigma of going to a group	1	2	3	4	5
				TOTAL	

Total your scores for the pros and the cons. If your pros are five points higher than your cons, you would likely benefit from a recovery program like AA. If your pros and cons are about tied, we urge you to still give a recovery program a try. You may want to share your concerns with a trusted member of a recovery group who has long-term sobriety and ask for some feedback in your decision-making process. If your cons are clearly higher than your pros, you are at risk of dropping out quickly, because you are probably not ready for such a group. You should then ask yourself, "Do I have a positive social network that can support me while I am staying free from risky or all drinking?"

The Public Health Policy for Social Support
It's interesting to compare the public health policies for smoking versus drinking alcohol. For decades, tobacco ads have been banned from TV and other media. Yet today we are bombarded by ads for booze. Who do you think the ads target? Young people who are known to be most influenced by mass media. How is drinking portrayed? As fun and free, social, sexy, glamorous, and harmless: happiness in a bottle. The ads are similar to old tobacco ads that were banned because they were known to be influential—even though they were misleading.

Look at how many public places prohibit smoking. Almost all of them now, including places where drinking is promoted, like bars, restaurants, sporting events, weddings, and most social gatherings.

Here are some reasons why alcohol calls for higher impact policies. As of this writing

- About 90,000 deaths in the United States each year are alcohol related.[44]
- Every day in the United States, twenty-eight people die as a result of alcohol-related car crashes.
- Alcohol is involved in more homicides than any other substances combined.
- One-fourth of suicides involve drinking.
- Alcohol is involved in a high number of emergency room visits.
- Alcohol-related auto accidents are the number one cause of teenage death in the country.[45]
- The majority of domestic violence is related to drinking.

And yet, when asked what are the most dangerous and abused drugs, many people would probably pick heroin, cocaine, and tobacco over alcohol.

So what is a person to do now that drinking is the social norm? First, it should be recognized that about 25 percent of adults in the United States never drink. The vast majority of those folks were born into religious groups, like Mormons, Seventh-day Adventists, and most Southern Baptists. Some people seek out such religious communities to support their sobriety. And the largest secular (nonreligious) subculture that is alcohol-free—the network of Twelve Step recovery programs like Alcoholics Anonymous—include spiritual as well as emotional and physical well-being as an important part of maintaining sobriety.

Because people who are active in a religious organization are less likely to abuse alcohol, consider checking out churches that might match your values and your lifestyle to support you in cutting back or eliminating alcohol from your life. A major benefit of being part of a religious community is that such members have been shown to have higher levels of happiness and well-being. But there are also other non-religious organizations that are devoted to enhancing social well-being, such as local YMCAs, community clubs, or other places dedicated to cultural needs—like live theaters, libraries, book clubs, film clubs, or community education classes. Or you could do your own creative searches in your community and online to find like-minded people who gather in an alcohol-free environment for mutual support.

While alcohol-free subcultures do exist, the majority of the people who drink are moderate drinkers who are able to live within the limits of low-risk drinking. In most of this country, heavy and risky drinking is not the social norm, and most adults can enjoy a cocktail, a glass of wine, or a beer with friends without worry. Your challenge is to identify where and with whom you can make progress toward low-or no-risk drinking in a safe environment. Finding refuge from unsafe drinking is an example of social liberation.

Use Stimulus Control to Control Your Environment Rather Than Having Your Environment Control You

We just discussed how difficult it can be to find alcohol-free environments. Yet, it is relatively easy to remove all alcohol from your home and to go to alcohol-free activities, such as movies, museums, and plays. You might also want to think about removing all cocktail, wine, and beer glasses from your house, just as you would remove all cigarettes and ashtrays from your home and car if you were quitting smoking.

But living in an alcohol-free family or network of friends is a much greater challenge, given how many people still rely on alcohol for their social, financial, sexual, and emotional needs. At times, it can seem like an insurmountable challenge for those who have been embedded in families, friendships, and social clubs where heavy and risky drinking is the norm. For most of us, it would be much too costly to totally give up such social networks, which is why it's so important to find a safe haven for recovery. The more severe the alcohol problem, the more likely the person has been embedded in a culture of alcohol. Those folks so often need to change not only their drinking habits; they also need to change their social environments—yet rarely can they change such hard-wired habits alone. So, the more severe your alcohol problem, the more your maintenance of an alcohol-free life will need the support of a surrogate family or community like AA or another peer support group that is dedicated to your recovery.

For those who have not yet developed such severe alcohol problems, your challenge is to reduce your risk significantly to avoid more severe consequences from your alcohol misuse. You have begun to do that by following the protocols presented in this chapter to progress through the Stages of Change toward a life not threatened by your drinking. Part of your plan also needs to include thriving. So, keep progressing through this book and you will raise the bar to increase your health, happiness, and overall well-being. Those who have problems with alcohol frequently have problems with not only smoking, but healthy eating and exercise as well—the focus of the next two chapters.

9

Healthy Eating for Well-Being and Weight

Eating healthy isn't always easy. In fact, changing our bad eating habits can be more complex than quitting smoking or reducing alcohol consumption. To begin with, unlike tobacco and alcohol, we need food to survive and can't just give it up entirely because our dietary habits are threatening our health. But even for a non-necessary food like sugar, there are different opinions and approaches about the amount of intake that's considered healthy—is it none, like tobacco, or is it the same as alcohol for non-addicts: A little is okay; a lot is not?

You'd think that when experts can agree on what makes a healthy diet, our decisions would be simple, but that's not always the case. For example, health professionals strongly agree that we should eat a lot of fruits and vegetables—about five cups a day. And many experts can make a compelling case for an all-plant diet. But in Western cultures, not many of us are willing or ready to eat that much fruit and vegetables and probably even fewer can make the leap to become strict vegetarians.

Diets are further complicated by the fact that different diets are appropriate for different people and for some, such as people with diabetes or food allergies, the best advice will come from their health care provider or, ideally, a dietitian who can design a diet for their unique dietary needs.

When it comes to weight loss, there have been too many fads and fashions and too few facts to create a strong agreement about the sanest and safest way to achieve and maintain a healthy weight. Perhaps the most common recommendation given to people who need to lose weight is to cut about 500 calories per day from their diet until they reach their weight goal. But if people have an unhealthy diet that includes a lot of sugar and few fruits and vegetables, they are still at risk for losing their health (and even their lives) too early regardless of how many calories they cut each day. Contrary to what many ads and weight-loss programs would have us believe, there is no "one diet fits all" or no magic bullet for self-changers who want or need to lose weight and eat healthy.

We encourage you not to sacrifice truth for certainty. Stay open to the complexities of diet as we introduce you to alternatives that we know to be safe and healthy, and to work well with other self-changers. Remember that when people face only one choice, their willpower will not be as strong as when they are given two choices. Three choices are even better. The good news is that the Transtheoretical Model (TTM) approach you are learning about for other risk behaviors has also been proven to be effective in helping self-changers manage their weight and improve their eating habits.

Years ago, the growing epidemic in obesity and overweight individuals became obvious—not just in the United States but throughout the world. Some of the statistics were startling. For instance, in 1977, only 2.7 percent of the men and women in the United Kingdom were obese. By 2014 the situation had changed dramatically, and 25.6 percent of adults were obese in the United Kingdom.[46] The pounds continued to pile on with the years, but as leading behavior change scientists, we were stuck in chronic contemplation: Should we commit ourselves to tackling this big problem?

We knew that healthy weight management was a multiple behavior problem and so the solution would call for multiple behavior changes. We also realized that the solution would need to include healthy eating, adequate exercise, and managing emotional eating. But we had not yet proven to ourselves and to others that our TTM approach, which had already produced significant results with single major threats like smoking and stress, could be as effective when trying to change multiple risk behaviors simultaneously.

Prior to our efforts, our field had failed dramatically when it came to creating programs that dealt with the multiple behavior risks for heart disease—smoking, unhealthy eating, inadequate exercise, and stress. For example, decades ago Stanford University, the University of Minnesota, and Brown University were given large grants and five years to develop "Healthy Heart Projects" to reduce the identified threats for heart disease in specific treatment communities. Unfortunately, they failed in their efforts.[47]

Our analysis of the Healthy Heart Projects results suggested that their biggest failure was the inability to engage a high percentage of at-risk populations into their best treatments. With smoking, for example, in one year, they engaged only 4 percent of smokers in the smoking cessation clinics in their Minnesota target communities compared to 3 percent in "no treatment" communities. With such low participation, their success rates were destined to be very small. From our perspective, they were trying to treat populations of smokers with *action-oriented* cessation clinics even though more than 80 percent of their smokers were not ready to take action. The same problem existed for diet and exercise.

One of the major fallouts of these failed programs was that leaders at the National Institutes of Health (NIH) became demoralized about population-based treatments for multiple risk behaviors. There was no consensus on how multiple behaviors might be changed or even if they could be changed. So when we applied for a large grant for a cancer prevention program that also reduced multiple risks, our expert grant reviewers thought we were also likely to fail. However, after reviewing our innovative TTM change model and our intervention methods, they eventually concluded that it was worth taking a big risk on our ambitious project. At minimum, the funders decided that—no matter the outcome—at least we (and they) would learn a great deal about what worked and what didn't when using TTM to simultaneously treat three or four risky behaviors.

In the end, the lessons we learned from using TTM to effectively change multiple behaviors in cancer prevention broke us out of our state of chronic contemplation and we decided to tackle weight management problems. In this chapter we'll share what we discovered. We'll help self-changers reduce and change a number of risky behaviors that have prevented them from managing their weight in a healthy and long-lasting manner. When readers discover how easy it is to change multiple behaviors using the Stages of Change, they will realize the lessons they've learned here can extend far beyond weight management issues. You might say TTM is the gift that keeps on giving!

Predicting Success

Recently a student and I made a discovery that has to do with what predicts long-term success with weight loss. When we completed a comprehensive review of weight-loss research from the past twenty years, we were distressed to see that there were very few baseline predictors of success. The good news is that we've learned what works with TTM— the "dynamic variables" you can control and change that help you move toward and eventually succeed in achieving your desired behavior change. You have already been increasing your behavior change IQ by using things like the Stages of Change and examining the pros of changing. Now you are ready to apply your increasing knowledge and new skills to healthy eating, exercise, and emotional eating.

When we studied TTM predictors of success like the pros of changing, we found they had more to do with an individual's well-being (increasing happiness, self and social respect, and so on) than preventing or treating diseases like diabetes. That is why this chapter will focus on ways to enhance your well-being and happiness as you take steps to decrease your risky behaviors and your weight. As the title of this book suggests, you are changing to grow healthier indeed—but you are also changing to *thrive*.

Harry's Story

Harry, a carpenter in his mid-thirties, was 350 pounds and developing diabetes and hypertension. His weight was also affecting his ability to do his job, as well as his marriage. Harry decided he was prepared to take dramatic action and commit to what he called a "starvation diet." He joined a program at an outstanding hospital where I consulted. This multidisciplinary program included psychologists specializing in behavior change, especially for emotional eating. The physician who headed the program was internationally known and supervised the medical monitoring needed for a program that involved six months of abstinence from "real" food. Patients consumed only special nutrition packets and followed a daily exercise program that emphasized walking for weight loss and for managing stress and distress.

Harry added his own innovation: He removed all food from his home. His wife, Hilary, was supportive, since she viewed her husband as a food addict. Part of the way Hilary would support Harry was to eat away from home. She would have breakfast on the way to work, lunch at work, and dinner after work, usually with colleagues, friends, or family, before arriving home. She joked that she paid a price but she benefited by not having to prepare meals or shop for food.

Harry's dramatic action plan seemed brilliant, because as we shall see, so much of eating habits are under stimulus control—that is, a behavior is triggered by the presence or absence of some stimulus. For example, most of us were conditioned by our parents to eat everything on our plates, after which we were reinforced and rewarded with more food, namely dessert. Harry learned early on to stuff down the huge amount on his plate even after he was full.

With no food in the house, Harry was "free from food," as he called it. But he wasn't free from all of his old habits. When he got bored, he would open his refrigerator and cupboards and sigh when he found them bare. Time after time, he repeated this pattern, just like the famous psychologist and behaviorist B. F. Skinner's pigeons that rushed to peck for food when a stimulus like a light or sound came on. Over time, Harry became "habituated" and no longer looked for food in his house.

Harry lost what he called "a ton of weight." In less than six months, he lost 150 pounds and reached his goal of 200 pounds. He also lost the symptoms of diabetes and high blood pressure. He gained the healthy habit of walking for at least sixty minutes a day and enjoyed taking his companion dog with him.

Harry had no desire to return to "real" food. He was confident he could control his weight *if* he didn't have to eat and could remain on the nutrition packets. But he had no choice—he got an unusual doctor's order: He had to eat to stay healthy. Harry joked, "First they tell me I can't eat; then they tell me I have to eat. The only way I can be free from fat is to be free from food!"

Harry had reason to fear his return to eating. His new habits had been under the most powerful approach to controlling behavior, stimulus control: He lost weight when he removed the stimuli that controlled his eating. Harry now had to rely heavily on a much less powerful approach, *decision control*. When people who are losing weight go out to eat, they are much more likely to lapse in their weight management behavior. In restaurants, they have to *decide* what they are going to eat based on all the tempting options on the menu. They have to decide if they will have to eat all of the super-sized servings provided in most restaurants. Good luck with that! Here is where the ingrained habit of eating everything on your plate comes into play.

Harry now had to make many daily decisions. What was he going to eat that day? How much was he going to eat? When? Where? With whom? How fast would he eat? How long? How much would he have to struggle? How long would he have to struggle? Why not eat more when his huge hunger was returning? Why deprive himself of his favorite foods? Harry was discovering that falling back into old habits that were still hardwired in his brain was much, much easier and faster than developing new healthier habits. Plus, his new routine of not eating regular food was no longer a choice: Eating real food was doctor's orders.

Although we are wired to make demanding decisions, it is a skill that is supposed to be reserved for special occasions, like managing a crisis or embarking on a major change in our lives. When we are required to make too many decisions, we can feel overwhelmed and overly stressed and distressed. And we know what can happen when stress takes over. Harry knew he was on the road to relapse. Although his dramatic diet innovation of a house free of food had a dramatic effect on his weight, it was not sustainable.

We will return to Harry later, but now we need to help you prepare for one of the toughest challenges of our time—the challenge of losing weight or not gaining weight in an era and a culture that still produces too many overweight and obese children and adults. The good news is that there are innovative approaches to losing weight and preventing weight gain. These innovations are not as dramatic as Harry's solution, but they are sustainable. And they are much more joyful than a home without food.

First we will share how we've integrated some of these innovations into TTM. Then we will immediately get you started on your personal journey to "well-being weight management" that includes becoming healthier and happier.

Increasing Consciousness: What Is New That Can Help You Win with Weight?

In 2013, a very exciting discovery was published confirming that the multiple behaviors that produce long-term weight loss are positively linked.[48] This means that if you change one behavior, such as exercise, you are two and a half times more likely to change a second key behavior, like healthy eating. This phenomenon is called "coaction." Coaction occurs mainly with individuals who participate in a TTM program, like the one described in this book. Coaction produces "synergy," in which the whole is greater than the sum of the parts. This means that the total amount of behavior change you produce is considerably greater than if you worked on each behavior separately. What synergy does is create more success with no greater effort. It is as if these linked behaviors pull each other in a positive direction.

This book is the first one to apply the coaction phenomena to improve your chances of success without increasing your effort. You will be working *smarter* rather than harder, guided by the latest science of behavior change. Coaction is also critical to greater success with weight loss because the best predictors of long-term success include moving through the Stages of Change for both healthy eating and exercise. The message here is that the more we can help you start progressing from one stage to the next, the greater success you will enjoy. For example, if you progress from precontemplation to contemplation early in this program, you will be about two and a half times more likely to achieve long-term weight loss. If you then move on to the preparation stage, you will be about four and a half times more likely to win with weight. If this challenge was like a horse race, those would be excellent odds to bet your time and efforts on! So, let's start the race and get you on your way to becoming a big winner.

Assess Your Eating Habits to Determine Your
Current Stage of Change

Our program relies on the best advice that experts agree leads to healthy eating for healthy weight management. Because people in this country eat so many types of different foods, coming to an agreement on all types of foods is tricky at best. With TTM, we have identified a few behavior changes that represent overall best practices for healthy eating and healthy weight management.

Here are four questions to help you assess which stage you are in for eating a healthy diet. Later we will add more components of a healthy diet.

———————————————— EXERCISE ————————————————

Assessing Your Stage of Change

Circle the answers that best describe your current eating habits.

1. Do you eat 2-1/2 cups of vegetables a day?	Yes	No
2. Do you substitute low-fat dairy products and dressings for regular products?	Yes	No
3. Do you minimize fast foods (such as cheeseburgers and french fries) and comfort foods (such as cookies, chips, and ice cream)?	Yes	No
4. Have you reduced the number of daily calories you eat by 500 calories to lose weight or 200 to prevent weight gain?	Yes	No

Now, please answer the following:

A. If you answered no to any of the four questions, do you   Yes   No
intend to make changes in the next six months, so you
can answer yes to all four questions?

B. If you answered no to any of the four questions, do you   Yes   No
intend to make changes in the next month, so you can
answer yes to all four questions?

C. If you answered yes to all four questions, have you been   Yes   No
practicing all four behaviors for more than six months?

→ You are in precontemplation if you answered no to question A.

→ You are in contemplation if you answered yes to A and no to B.

→ You are in the action stage if you answered no to C.

→ You are in the maintenance stage if you answered yes to C.

How to Progress from Precontemplation to Contemplation: The Pros of Healthy Eating

To move from precontemplation to contemplation, you have to increase the pros that represent many of the reasons *why* you should contemplate changing. What are the most common pros that attract people to weight-loss programs? When I worked with one of the leading weight-loss programs to help them with people in precontemplation, I learned that—contrary to what I thought—improved health was not their clients' number one concern. It was appearance.

Appearance is important, no question about it. But does appearance become less important when you are surrounded by people who are overweight or obese? And is appearance a strong enough reason to lose weight when you are craving chocolate or more of your favorite comfort foods?

Jan and I witnessed the power of craving when we were treated to a stay at a famous health ranch to help their wealthy clients progress from action to maintenance after spending a month or two at the ranch. The number one problem their clients used to have was alcohol abuse. When we were there, it was weight. The ranch had three rules: You could not bring cigarettes, alcohol, or chocolate with you. We learned about serious incidents where a distressed overweight client would walk "over the hill" to town on a sunny 115 degree day, desperate to buy some chocolate and satisfy a craving. The ranch had to send one of its rescue wagons to avoid losing a client to craving.

Besides appearance, the other most common pro to losing weight is health, especially in clinic- and hospital-based programs. This was clearly the case in a prominent hospital-based program with some of the best outcomes—that is, the best outcomes for those who completed the action-oriented program. However, 80 percent of the participants did not complete the twelve-session program. So I was invited to collaborate on a study designed to identify the best predictors of program participation and program success. Not surprisingly, the best predictors of participation and success for this action-oriented program was being in the action stage at the start and applying the change principles and processes emphasized in the action and maintenance stages.[49]

The lesson here is that programs designed to take immediate action are most likely to succeed with self-changers who are already taking action, and they are most likely to fail with participants in earlier Stages of Change. Health is a very important pro, as is appearance. But neither alone will prompt people in the early Stages of Change to adopt one or more of the multiple behaviors needed for long-term success.

Assessing Your Pros

We have just discovered a broad set of pros that predict progress and success. The following assessment can help you determine whether your current pros are sufficient to help you maintain your weight. This assessment can also help you see how changing multiple key behaviors may benefit you in unexpected ways or ways that lead you to win with weight.

---- **EXERCISE** ----

Assess Your Pros

Please circle the number that indicates how important each of these "pros" is to you.

---

1. Being happier by exercising regularly.

NOT IMPORTANT			EXTREMELY IMPORTANT	
1	**2**	**3**	**4**	**5**

---

2. Increasing self-control by losing weight.

NOT IMPORTANT			EXTREMELY IMPORTANT	
1	**2**	**3**	**4**	**5**

---

3. Gaining more self-respect by eating healthier.

NOT IMPORTANT			EXTREMELY IMPORTANT	
1	**2**	**3**	**4**	**5**

---

4. Looking better by losing weight.

NOT IMPORTANT			EXTREMELY IMPORTANT	
1	**2**	**3**	**4**	**5**

---

5. Approval of friends and family for not relying on eating to manage distress.

NOT IMPORTANT			EXTREMELY IMPORTANT	
1	**2**	**3**	**4**	**5**

---

6. Having more energy for family and friends by exercising regularly.

NOT IMPORTANT			EXTREMELY IMPORTANT	
1	**2**	**3**	**4**	**5**

---

7. Becoming more productive by losing weight.

NOT IMPORTANT			EXTREMELY IMPORTANT	
1	**2**	**3**	**4**	**5**

---

8. Becoming more positive about life by exercising regularly.

NOT IMPORTANT   EXTREMELY IMPORTANT

1   2   3   4   5

9. Improving quality of life by managing emotions without relying on eating.

NOT IMPORTANT   EXTREMELY IMPORTANT

1   2   3   4   5

10. Feeling healthier by eating more fruits and vegetables.

NOT IMPORTANT   EXTREMELY IMPORTANT

1   2   3   4   5

Total up the numbers you circled: _____

If you scored 40 or above, your pros are in good shape. If your total is under 40, it would be helpful to learn more about the benefits of weight management.

Seventy Pros of Healthier Eating for Weight and Well-Being

The following lists identify the many potential benefits of healthy eating to manage your weight and your well-being. The pros are organized into areas of well-being because these are among the best predictors of success for clinically significant weight loss. Remember, your goal is not to just lose weight or prevent weight gain. The bigger goal that will help you maintain a healthy weight long term is to enhance your *overall* well-being—the well-being of your body, your self, your spirit, your social relationships, and your society.

───────────────── **EXERCISE** ─────────────────

Pros of Healthy Eating for Weight and Well-Being

Look over these lists and check which goals you would like to achieve—remembering that when it comes to well-being and weight, the more you have to gain, the more you are likely to lose.

Physical Well-Being

- ☐ Reduce your risk of heart disease
- ☐ Reduce your risk of stroke
- ☐ Reduce your risk of colon cancer
- ☐ Reduce your risk of breast cancer
- ☐ Reduce your risk of esophageal cancer
- ☐ Reduce your risk of prostate cancer
- ☐ Reduce your risk of pancreatic cancer
- ☐ Reduce your risk of obesity
- ☐ Reduce your risk of arteriosclerosis
- ☐ Reduce your risk of kidney cancer
- ☐ Reduce your risk of diabetes
- ☐ Reduce your risk of endometrial cancer
- ☐ Reduce your risk of sleep apnea
- ☐ Reduce your body fat
- ☐ Reduce triglycerides
- ☐ May lower your blood pressure
- ☐ Reduce your risk of gaining weight
- ☐ Improve your blood flow
- ☐ Decrease your risk of clogged blood vessels
- ☐ Decrease pressure in your joints
- ☐ Reduce risk of high blood sugar
- ☐ May improve your breathing
- ☐ Improve your sleep
- ☐ Reduce pain

- ☐ Improve immune system function
- ☐ Help your body use insulin
- ☐ Improve bowel regularity
- ☐ Lower the risk of erectile dysfunction

Functional Well-Being

- ☐ Have more energy
- ☐ Promote effective problem solving
- ☐ Promote feelings of control
- ☐ Feel better about yourself
- ☐ Increase confidence
- ☐ Be more productive
- ☐ Increase stamina
- ☐ Be more alert
- ☐ Have fewer illnesses and absences from work

Financial Well-Being

- ☐ May save money
- ☐ Lower health care costs

Social Well-Being

- ☐ Improve your relationship with others
- ☐ Set an example about making healthy choices
- ☐ Be around longer for your family
- ☐ Gain pride from your friends
- ☐ Improve your sex life
- ☐ Cause your loved ones to worry less about your health
- ☐ Make it easier for the people in your home to eat healthier
- ☐ Feel happier around other people

Appealing Well-Being

- ☐ Have better fitting clothes
- ☐ Improve your appearance

☐ Have a healthy image

☐ Look better

☐ Make your skin look better

Emotional Well-Being

☐ Feel better about yourself

☐ Make your emotional life healthier

☐ Learn new ways to cope with distress

☐ Manage your stress better

☐ Spend less time worrying about the food you eat

☐ Feel more relaxed and at ease

☐ Feel like you're taking the best possible care of yourself

☐ Enjoy life more

☐ Be happier

☐ Improve your mood

☐ Feel less nervous or anxious

☐ Keep you more in tune with feelings of fullness

☐ Show you care about yourself

Purposeful Well-Being

☐ Live longer

☐ Improve your quality of life

☐ Improve your self-worth

☐ Healthier for the environment (shifting away from animal products and highly processed food)

☐ Is natural (avoiding chemical additives and food-like substances)

☐ Reduce health care costs for you and society

Use Dramatic Relief to Pay Attention to Your Feelings

When people are stressed or distressed, they often seek relief by eating junk food. We call that "emotional eating." Sweets, like doughnuts, cookies, and candy, are among the most common comfort foods. We should relabel these foods as risky foods, since over time these sweets can turn sour. Here is what has been reported recently. People who add 150 calories to their daily diet increase their risks of diabetes by only a small amount. But people who add those 150 calories *via sugar,* like drinking a 12-ounce can of Coke or eating an ounce of M&Ms, have ten times greater risk of developing diabetes. To make matters worse, about 80 percent of all sugar found in food in the United States has been added by the food industry. The food industry has added the equivalent sugar of two and a half cans of soda or two and a half ounces of M&Ms to the food most people eat each day. With this increased amount of sugar in the average person's diet, the risk of diabetes has multiplied about twenty-seven times.[50] The problem for most people is they have no idea how much sugar they eat on an average day.

How do these facts make you feel? Anxious? That's understandable. Angry? That can be helpful. Smokers who got angry when they learned that the tobacco industry had increased nicotine in cigarettes in order to increase addiction were more likely to contemplate quitting. Just as we can help smokers decrease stress and distress without smoking, so too can we help emotional eaters to decrease stress and distress without relying on sweets and other risky comfort foods.

Reduce the Cons to Reduce Weight

The following is a list of cons that you may have found or expect to be important barriers to losing weight or preventing weight gain. Select the cons that concern you, write them down on a separate digital or paper sheet, and then add your own. We will then discuss how you can counter your cons.

☐ I would experience craving when I feel hungry.

☐ I would have to give up some of my favorite foods.

☐ Comfort foods are such a pleasurable way to reduce stress.

☐ There is such history and tradition to the foods I eat.

☐ I feel vain when I am trying to improve my appearance.

☐ I would feel deprived.

☐ Changing habits is such a hassle.

☐ There are so many decisions I would have to make.

☐ I would risk failing at losing weight.

☐ I can get really irritable or tense when feeling hungry.

☐ Changing takes a lot of time.

☐ I feel demoralized about my ability to lose weight and maintain it over the long term.

☐ Family or friends don't want me to change.

☐ I might feel left out at parties or restaurants.

☐ I may have trouble sleeping.

Add your own barriers on a separate sheet of paper.

Think about countering your cons with statements such as these:

CON	COUNTER
I will miss some of my favorite foods.	Yes, and I will grieve but will I miss my worries over my weight or the way I eat?
But comfort foods are so comforting.	They can also be killers and I am already working on healthier ways to deal with distress.
Changing takes a lot of time.	I am going to learn how to change multiple behaviors with less time and effort.
I would risk failing at losing weight.	I am working to increase my chances of success.
The craving can drive me crazy.	Read on to learn ways to silence the sounds of starving.

Use Environmental Reevaluation to Notice
Your Effects on Others

When I tell audiences of health professionals about a survey of 400 women we conducted to determine who is eating healthy and who is not, I ask them to guess who has the healthier diet—women with children or women without children. Their responses are quick and varied. "With children!" "Without children!" "With children!" "Without children!" The differing voices go on until I reveal that the biggest predictor of an unhealthy diet in women has nothing to do with education, income, age, race, or ethnicity. Rather, we found the biggest predictor is having children, and thus concluded that children are a major risk factor for the family's health.

In psychology we talk a lot about social learning, such as when children learn unhealthy eating habits from their parents. Yet psychologists rarely study how children change their parents' behaviors, like their own eating habits. But marketers for the food industry know that the younger the person, the more marketing is likely to affect an individual's behavior. So marketers spent millions promoting unhealthy foods on television during Saturday morning cartoons. Were the parents watching? Usually not. Young children were the targets.

When I ask professionals when they think women make the biggest changes in their diets, they often answer with confidence, "When they are pregnant." But changes during pregnancy are temporary. A study at Penn State found that women make the biggest positive changes in their diets when the last child leaves home![51]

We've also now learned that even pets like cats and dogs are negatively affected in "overweight" households. I had the opportunity to consult with one of the world's largest makers and marketers of cat and dog food. They took pride in producing quality pet food that could help with the number one health concern of veterinarians and owners—overweight pets. Our multidisciplinary team asked the company to study the prevalence of overweight and obese pets. We were stunned to learn that their findings with pets paralleled what was happening with children. About 40 percent of pets and children in the United States are overweight or obese.[52] We concluded that the biggest problem is not overweight and obese individuals; it is overweight and obese households!

What is the number one problem parents have when trying to help their children change their eating habits in order to lose weight? Setting limits on how much and what their children eat. What is the number one problem that owners have when trying to change how much and what their pets eat to help them lose weight? Setting limits. What is the number one problem people have when trying to change how much and what they eat? Setting limits.

Appreciate that as you learn strategies for limiting what and how much you eat, you will be better prepared to improve the overall health of an overweight household. If you are overweight, chances are that your spouse or partner is too. How hard it must be for parents and partners who are both overweight to help each other set limits on their eating. Together, we can help change history—and self-changers can help change their families (and their pets)—by applying the best that behavior change science has to offer.

Use Self-Reevaluation to Create a New Self and Body Image and Move to Preparation

As self-changers progress, they first examine how they think and feel about themselves, their unhealthy eating habits, and their weight concerns. Then they start to look to the future and reevaluate how they think they will feel about themselves after they adopt healthier eating and healthier weight management.

Here is an easy self-evaluation exercise. First look at yourself as you have been with unhealthy eating and weight management habits, and then look ahead to how you think you will be if you change those habits. Remember our discovery that long-term weight loss was driven in part by the pros of pride that family, friends, and self can have when someone gets leaner, achieves healthy weight loss, and adopts healthy eating habits. So, "lean" on your self-image to be sure you are prepared for a new way of being.

—————— **EXERCISE** ——————

Creating a New Self-Image

As someone who doesn't eat healthy, how do you view yourself? Use this opportunity to take a hard look at yourself. Feel free to add your own ideas to these lists.

HOW DO YOU VIEW YOURSELF AS A PERSON WHO DOES NOT EAT HEALTHY ENOUGH?	
☐ overweight	☐ a healthy weight
☐ active	☐ passive
☐ irresponsible	☐ proud
☐ responsible	☐ dissatisfied
☐ mindful eater	☐ healthy
☐ emotional eater	☐ unhealthy
☐ confident	☐ successful
☐ not confident	☐ regretful
☐ energetic	☐ determined
☐ sluggish	☐ ambivalent
☐ in shape	☐ lazy
☐ out of shape	☐ _____

HOW WOULD YOU VIEW YOURSELF AS A HEALTHY EATER MANAGING YOUR WEIGHT WELL?	
☐ overweight	☐ a healthy weight
☐ active	☐ passive
☐ irresponsible	☐ proud
☐ responsible	☐ dissatisfied
☐ strong	☐ healthy
☐ weak	☐ unhealthy
☐ confident	☐ successful
☐ not confident	☐ regretful
☐ energetic	☐ determined
☐ sluggish	☐ ambivalent
☐ in shape	☐ lazy
☐ out of shape	☐ _____

Use Self-Liberation to Make a Commitment to Increase Your Willpower

Self-liberation is the belief in your ability to change and your commitment and recommitments to act on that belief. Most people call this process willpower, and when they fail to meet their goals with weight, they often blame it on not having enough willpower. They weaken their willpower by weakening their belief in their ability to change. They have learned to view willpower as a stable trait that is strong if you are fortunate and weak if you are unfortunate. They have yet to learn that willpower is a dynamic process that can be strengthened. Here are two ways to strengthen your commitments.

1. *Set Smarter Goals.* You may be familiar with the idea of SMART goals: Specific, Measurable, Achievable, Results-focused, and Time-based goals. While this idea of smart goals can help you achieve a lot of tasks at work or home, they are not "smart" enough to transform your health and happiness for a lifetime. For us, SMART*ER* goals are **Sustainable**—they last for a lifetime, not just a short time (like losing weight for a reunion or wedding). The goals are **Meaningful**—the more the changes mean to you (the more they enhance multiple areas of well-being), the more sustainable and **Achievable** they will be. The more **Realistic** the goals are (like losing one to two pounds per week), the more achievable they will be. The more **Transformative** your goals are, the more they will change your body, your self, your social relationships, your happiness, and your purpose. The more **Effort**-focused you are, the more progress you can make since the change processes are more under your control. And finally, the more **Results** are focused on the long term, the more you can transform your weight and your well-being.

2. *Prepare a Plan for Action.* No single approach for healthy weight management is right for everyone. You may want to consult with a dietitian at your primary care or community health center before you start a weight-loss and management program. They could tailor your diet to your personal health needs. We have worked to identify the best practices from a broad spectrum of approaches. If you are convinced there is a better approach for

you, commit to it as long as it is good for your health and well-being and not just your weight.

Choosing Your Best Weight-Loss and Healthy Eating Option(s)

As we said earlier in this book, research shows that three choices are better than one, and people who have three alternatives have a stronger commitment than people who were given only one or two options. If someone is insisting there is only one correct choice for you, ask them about the two next best choices. Then commit to making the correct choice for you.

For each category that follows, you'll find three good choices you can make to change each behavior for healthy eating. Check the option you would like to try. (Sometimes you may want to choose more than one.)

Eating the Best Number of the Best Calories

☐ Eat 500 fewer calories per day as soon as you take action.

☐ Eat only until you are no longer hungry rather than until you feel full. This should equal about 20 percent less than you currently eat, which will be about 500 calories for many people.

☐ Gradually reduce your calorie intake by about 100 per day for the first week, 200 the next week, 300 the third week, until you reach 500 calories a day or your craving becomes too big of a con. Then you can decide to either exercise more or can take longer to reach your goal.

Increasing Healthy Foods and Decreasing Unhealthy Foods

☐ Start by increasing the most appealing healthy foods (such as berries, nuts, whole grain cereals, or fish). Then increase other healthy choices (such as vegetables, other fruits, and low-fat dairy products).

☐ Start by minimizing fast foods (like cheeseburger and fries) and risky comfort foods (like cookies, candy, and ice cream). This may reduce your diet by more than 500 calories/day.

☐ Limit the foods most connected to weight gain (for example, french fries, potato chips, sugar-sweetened drinks, red meat, and processed meat like lunch meat).

Managing Emotional and Mindless Eating

- ☐ Relax, walk, or talk instead of eating when stressed or distressed.

- ☐ Use mindful eating (for example, eating slower and savoring your food) of 200 fewer calories to prevent craving.

- ☐ Feed your emotions (like boredom and anxiety) with positivity (such as joy and gratitude).

In Preparation, Share Your Commitments with Others

People are particularly prone to keeping quiet about their commitment to alter their diets and lose weight because they have tried and failed so many times in the past. However, such silence only weakens their willpower. If you haven't already, share your Stages of Change journey with others. You are planning to take action and you may want to call on others for some support to keep moving ahead.

Check who you will tell about your commitment to change:

- ☐ friend
- ☐ spouse or partner
- ☐ neighbor
- ☐ physician
- ☐ health care provider
- ☐ coach
- ☐ co-worker
- ☐ friends on Facebook
- ☐ kids or siblings

Use Counter Conditioning to Change Your Unhealthy Eating Habits in Action

Millions of people have been successful in limiting the amount of fat in the milk they drink. Jan and I are among them. We grew up drinking what is called whole milk, but what should be called high-fat milk. When we first tried skim milk after many years of drinking whole, our brains said, "Ugh! This tastes like water!" Fortunately for us, and for millions of others, the food industry provided products that allowed us to apply a fundamental strategy for changing habits. The technical term is called "successive approximation," where you progress in sequence from one small change to the next until you finally achieve or nearly reach your goal.

Here is a simple technique that many people use when changing from whole milk to skim that further describes what we mean by successive approximation. Rather than leap from high- to no-fat milk, their first step was to switch to 2% milk. Their brain and belly did not rebel because they couldn't detect a big difference. Once they had adapted to 2% milk, they then replaced that with 1% to get closer to their ultimate goal of drinking non-fat milk.[†]

Over time, they had conditioned themselves to strongly prefer the taste of non-fat milk, which they found to be much more refreshing. When they find only higher fat milk available, like at many airports, their message from their brain is, "Ugh! This tastes like cream." When I ask both professional and public audiences to raise their hands if they are totally confident they are never going back to whole milk again, the vast majority of them raise their hands. They had reached successfully the termination stage where there is no risk of relapsing back to their previous life-long habit. (Note: Such a goal of non-fat milk is not presently recommended for preschoolers who have been found to gain weight from drinking non-fat milk.)

You can apply this same approach when shifting from the large size soda, buttered popcorn, cheeseburger, fries, etc. to the medium size, small size, and kids' size. Then you may be ready to shift entirely to a much better alternative (e.g., unsweetened beverage, a tuna sandwich with tomato and lettuce but no mayo, a side of fruit instead of fries, and black coffee instead of a flavored latte). The following table shows how many calories you could save by adopting these changes:

---

† With the complexities of diet, recent research has found that low-fat dairy is better than no-fat for vitamin D and calcium absorption and may not contribute to cholesterol increases that other saturated fats do.

OLD	CALORIES	VS.	NEW	CALORIES
20-oz. soda	250		sparkling water	0
16-oz. flavored latte	200		black coffee	0
3-oz. bag of ranch-flavored tortilla chips	424		3.5 cups of air-popped popcorn	110
1 scoop ice-cream waffle cone w/ 1-oz. chocolate pieces topping	660		1 kid-size scoop cup w/o topping	150

Countering the Con of Craving

If you choose the alternative of gradually and successively reducing your calories by 100 for a week to reducing them by 200, 300, 400, and ultimately 500 per week, you would be applying the principle of successive approximation we discussed earlier. The biggest challenge many people face when reducing calories is craving. Here are some techniques that can help counter the con of craving.

Differentiate Cravings Due to Stress and Distress versus Hunger

It can be very difficult to tell the difference between desires to eat because of stress and distress and desires due to hunger. To help you, let's first assess how often you engage in emotional eating. Check the times you are likely to eat more.

☐ when you are worried about something

☐ when you are feeling down or in a bad mood

☐ when you are alone or feeling lonely

☐ when you are bored

☐ when you turn to food for comfort

☐ when you "treat" yourself with food

☐ when you eat even though you are not hungry

☐ when you eat when frustrated or angry

☐ when you are looking for an escape

□ when you eat within a few hours after a meal

□ when you eat to help you sleep

□ when you eat particular foods, such as sweets, when distressed

Now consider times when you eat between mealtimes and how you would answer the following question: "Why do I want to eat this?" If you regularly answer using two or more of the responses that follow, you may be at risk for emotional eating. If so, try applying one of the healthy strategies for managing emotions that you worked on in chapter 4. A good first step is to turn a mindless habit of automatically eating in response to distress into a more mindful approach to eating. The second column in this chart offers some ways to counter automatic eating.

IF THE ANSWER IS	THE COUNTER IS
I am feeling stressed.	Walk away—literally: go for a walk.
I am worried about something.	Talk away your worries with family or friends.
I am feeling really tense.	Let your muscles go in the direction of feeling more and more relaxed.
I don't know why.	Think of some of the many benefits that can come from not eating more.
I am angry.	Don't take it out on yourself. Think about how you might express your anger in a helpful or healthy way.
I am afraid my craving will keep increasing and get out of control.	Imagine your urge to eat as being like a wave that will rise, then crest and flow down. Dive through that wave of an urge as it passes by.
Eating can help me sleep.	Help yourself to sleep better naturally so you can eat better and vice versa. We will help you in chapter 12.
I am really hungry.	Ideally, eat something healthy, such as a piece of fruit rather than a doughnut.

Substitute Healthy Foods for Unhealthy Foods

In previous chapters, we talked about how substituting healthy alternatives for unhealthy or less healthy ones is a key strategy to counter ingrained habits. Fortunately, many foods are healthy in their own right while also being helpful in losing weight. In reviewing research on a broad range of foods, we found it striking that about 75 percent of the most healthy and helpful foods were plant-based. Olive oil, for example, is considered the healthiest oil in the world and can be a very tasty substitute for butter. Avocados are fruits that have low carbs and healthy fats just like olive oil, and they can add excellent taste to salads. Further, eating fats alongside vegetables can help your body better absorb the nutrients from the vegetables—anywhere from two and a half to fifteen times more.

Most berries are very healthy and tasty; they make a good substitute for sugar-sweetened desserts like candies, cookies, cakes, and ice cream. Broth-based soups have lots of water like fruits and vegetables, and they are a filling and tasty alternative for creamy soups. Some whole grains like oats and brown rice can be tasty and healthy substitutes for the refined grains found in many cereals and breads, which can be a disaster to health and weight. Black beans and lentils can be prepared in tasty ways and provide high protein and fiber that are filling; use them as substitutes in meals that have too much unhealthy fat and predict weight gain. Root vegetables like sweet potatoes, turnips, and carrots have high fiber, are filling, and can be flavorful; use them instead of white potatoes, which are often associated with weight gain.

Nuts can be delicious—filled with proteins, fiber, and healthy fats. Though relatively high in calories, they are filling even in small amounts. Eating them is a healthy alternative to snacks like potato chips, and unlike those unhealthy snacks, they do not predict weight gain.

Non-plant foods that are both healthy and helpful with weight management include fish, like tuna, sardines, and salmon. High in protein and healthy fats, they can be prepared in tasty and healthy ways and substituted for meals of fish sticks and french fries. For example, canned tuna packed in water is a low-cost but still healthy and tasty choice. Eggs are another non-plant food that provides full flavor while being filling.

Plus, research now connects eggs with weight loss. Though they were once frowned upon because they are high in cholesterol, eggs are back in favor and they make excellent substitutes for sugar-sweetened cereals, pancakes with syrup, or bacon and sausage. Plain low-fat yogurt, with or without fruit, can be a healthy, filling, and flavorful choice for breakfast or a snack. *But buyer beware:* Many fat-free yogurts include more added sugar than some ice creams. I bought a popular brand that on the container advertised "25% less sugar," but the six-ounce cup actually contained 70 percent of a day's healthy allotment of sugar! Fortunately, starting in 2017, food labels will break down the amount of added sugar versus naturally found sugar.

The top priority for public health is to help people get free from sugar-sweetened beverages (SSB) like soda and even healthy sounding sports drinks like Gatorade. These SSBs account for about half the sugar that has been added to the food supply. Not only do the SSBs add unhealthy calories, they do not satisfy appetites—so people pour down the extra sugar and calories without reducing how much they eat and how much weight they gain.

There is evidence that the more healthy and helpful foods you eat, the less you need to count calories. The only way you will know is to adopt some of these healthy substitutes and see how much weight you lose each week.

Make Healthy Foods Taste Better

We talked earlier about how the food industry has reengineered so many foods by adding sugar. By associating or pairing sugar with a processed food, they can produce a *conditioned* taste for their less tasty and less healthy product. They have followed a similar process with salt.

Your challenge is to reengineer your food supply to make healthy foods taste better. For example, Jan pairs tasty and healthy berries with no-fat and low-sugar plain yogurt, which she would not eat on its own. Over time, she has made this healthy source of protein appealing and a stable part of her diet. For me, greens were too dry even though I knew I could consume almost unlimited lettuce and other leafy vegetables without gaining weight. Pairing tomatoes and avocado, which are tasty and juicy, helped change my appetite for a growing range of greens.

The following exercise presents some healthy food that people often avoid for a variety of reasons.

Reengineering Your Food

Think about which of these foods you might reengineer either by pairing them with foods you prefer or by preparing them differently.

HEALTHY FOOD	WHAT YOU WOULD LIKE TO REENGINEER	HOW YOU MIGHT PAIR IT OR PREPARE IT DIFFERENTLY
Fish	Dry or little flavor	Pair with grapes, grapefruit, or spices, and don't overcook.
Greens	Dry or little flavor	Add some olive or canola oil, juicy vegetables you like, onions, or spices.
Lean meats	Too tough, little flavor, or dry	Don't overcook; pair with onions, mushrooms, or spices.
Water	No taste, no color	Add slice of lemon or lime and ice.
Beans	Little flavor, chewy	Pair with spices or healthy oil, and prepare with grains.
Raw carrots, broccoli, and other vegetables	Little flavor, dry	Include in broth-based soup with seasonings and veggie or chicken pot stickers.

Pair Mental and Emotional Associations to
Promote Healthy Foods

When Jan and I first met with a consultant who had owned an advertising firm in Atlanta, he asked us what academic discipline we thought was responsible for changing the most behaviors of the greatest number of people. Of course we wanted to say psychology or behavioral science, since those drive our mission, but given his expertise, I guessed economics. He said, "Good guess, but wrong. It's marketing. Look what masters of marketing have done in the past to promote high-risk products like cigarettes, alcohol, soda, and candy. Look at the images and messages they associated with their products."

There's a saying in psychology that constructs (ideas) drive behavior. What were the constructs and images that made the Virginia Slims cigarette slogan "You've come a long way, baby" so popular with women? *Slim* to enhance appearance, reduce or prevent weight gain, celebrate increased freedom (to smoke)—paired with tennis tournaments that brought to mind women's heroes like Billie Jean King. Marlboro cigarettes were pitched to men who pictured themselves as the independent and masculine cowboy featured in the ad, a man who rode his horse across the rugged Western landscape. I was "branded" by Marlboros myself as an urban teen who longed to be in the open spaces riding horses like my father did as a kid. There was also the cigarette cartoon character Joe Camel that especially appealed to kids who learned to associate Joe the camel with the coolest cigarettes (Camels, of course) at a very young age. And don't forget about the beer slogan "Weekends were made for Michelob," with the ad showing young men and women partying and having fun fueled by drinking. A society like ours that considers weekends to be the happiest days of the week quickly learned from these ads that if you want to be happier, you know which brand of beer you should drink.

At the time of this writing, Coke has taken over the happiness franchise, replacing alcohol with sugary beverages that produce a sugar high. In the past, Coke was the "Real Thing," playing on the desire of people who longed to be "authentic" individuals. Later, Coke promoted campaigns to reclaim creeks and make them clear for fish to thrive—which positioned their products with environmental causes and also hearkened back to those images of the West once featured in the Marlboro ads. I wonder if Coke can "hook" young people with these lines.

So here is a challenge for you. How can you "market" positive messages to yourself and give yourself images that can *counter* the powerful desire to eat too much sugar, salt, unhealthy oils, and other high-risk foods that is triggered by ads like the ones just described? What kind of compelling messages and images will "sell" you on the goal of reducing your calories in order to lose weight or prevent weight gain?

Here is a dramatic example of what we mean by a counter ad that was developed by Dr. Cati Brown Johnson, a postdoctoral student at Stanford. The ad showed a teen pouring nine packets of sugar down his throat and said, "You wouldn't let your child pour nine packets of sugar down his throat. But that is what he is doing when he drinks a twenty-ounce soda."

When they were filming this ad, the boy pouring sugar down his throat vomited! They didn't use this unexpected reaction on film, but you could create your own image of that ad if you are craving a sweet but toxic soda.

Slow Down to Stop Your Stomach from Screaming

Since it takes our stomachs twenty minutes to sense they are full, we need to slow down before we get stuffed. Mindful eating includes slowly savoring the flavors of food.[53] Many people worry that a healthy diet means eating tasteless food. But we often miss many flavors when we sprint through a meal rather than eating it slowly and smelling the roses—or the aromas of the fruit. Smell makes up about 90 percent of taste, so just smelling an apple can reduce your appetite and fool your stomach into thinking you have tasted it. Do yourself a favor and appreciate the flavor.

Chewing your food more and putting your fork down after each bite also contributes to mindful eating, as does not watching TV or reading. This also helps you avoid ads that might tempt you to eat mindlessly and less healthfully.

Also do yourself a favor and keep from getting stuffed. Read through the following messages and then check those your stomach and your senses have sent you when you have really stuffed yourself.

☐ My stomach is going to burst.

☐ I feel like a glutton.

☐ I should not have eaten the whole thing.

☐ I feel fat.

☐ I lost control.

☐ My digestive system is going to be upset with me.

☐ What was I thinking (or not thinking)?

☐ Why did I eat so much so fast?

☐ Too much food is going down and my weight is going up.

☐ I ate to reduce my stress and now I am feeling distressed.

Here is a message that comes from the French who have managed to avoid the growing rates of overweight and obesity that plague the United States. One of their smart goals is to eat until they are about 80 percent full. They are mindful that their slow and savory eating is satisfying their hunger without stretching their stomachs. Think in terms of the 80-20 rule: For example, most people wear 20 percent of their clothes 80 percent of the time (which is a good reason to clean out our closets); about 20 percent of scientists account for about 80 percent of the discoveries; and 20 percent of the computer programmers produce about 80 percent of the software. With eating, a rule of thumb could be that the extra 20 percent you eat may account for 80 percent of a weight problem. Eating just 20 percent less could decrease calories by about 500 per day. So, no more stuffed closets or stuffed stomachs!

Use Portion Control to Enhance Your Self-Control

Research shows that the more food that is put on a plate, the more people eat; the bigger the plate, the more people eat; the more food available to eat (like at a buffet restaurant), the more food is eaten; and the more food there is in serving dishes on the table, the more you eat. The simple message is this: Put about 20 percent less in your bowl or on your plate; use a smaller dish, like an eight-inch salad plate instead of a ten-inch dinner plate; and avoid having seconds to prevent getting stuffed.

Most people eat significantly less at home than they do at restaurants. This is largely because at restaurants we are under *decisional* control, which as you have learned, is a much weaker form of behavior control. And so much of decision making around food is emotional rather than rational. One way to avoid overeating at a restaurant is to make it a rule to tell the waiter you aren't terribly hungry, so please just bring a half order and put the other in a box you can take home for tomorrow. My eighty-year-old Aunt Helen, having been a waitress herself, would joke with the waiter, "I could have three dinners with your generous servings, so just bring me a third of my order. Then I will think about you for days!"

Use Social Liberation to Notice Social Trends That Help Make Healthy Eating More Mindful

To help people be more mindful, the Food and Drug Administration (FDA) requires food companies to include nutritional labels on almost all foods so we know what we are eating and how many calories we are eating. But not enough people take advantage of this regulation designed to enhance social liberation. Too many people feel overwhelmed by all the information found on food labels—but remember, if you don't read the label, you can be misled by the ads on the containers. If you are not already being more mindful in your food shopping, you can start by looking at the riskiest label ingredients, such as sugar. Keep these "cons" in mind: Low-risk eating equals twenty-five grams (or one ounce) of sugar, but doubling your daily increase in sugar increases your risk of diabetes by ten times. Eating two and a half times more sugar than the public health recommendations can increase your risk of diabetes by twenty-seven times.

Your next step could be to check the amount of high-risk fats in the product. Trans fats are found in processed foods and should not be a part of healthy eating. Saturated fats are found mostly in red meats and should be limited to twelve grams or half an ounce per day. Then you can start to count calories if you need to. Hopefully you have already learned how relatively few calories there are in carrots compared to cookies. For example, two and a half cups of carrots equals the same number of calories found in just one-eighth cup of most cookies.

Increasingly restaurants are offering healthier alternatives identified with heart health icons, and more restaurants are starting to show how many calories there are in each entrée. Many are offering small plates for portion control. And friendly restaurants welcome requests to bring customers just half portions on a plate and the rest in a box for the next day.

"Check Out" What You Believe You Should "Check Out" in a Market

Here's a little quiz to keep in mind the next time you go grocery shopping. Mark the things you think you should check before you purchase a food item:

- ☐ Sugar content on the food label (Remember that 80 percent of sugar is added, usually to processed foods without natural sugars.)

- ☐ Types and amounts of healthy versus risky fat

- ☐ Amount of calories per serving or portion

- ☐ Amount of servings you would typically eat

- ☐ Type of carbohydrates per serving (This is tricky to find out: You can only determine this by the type of food you are checking out.)

- ☐ Amount of calories in alcohol drinks (This is also tricky—it's not required by the FDA to be on the packaging, but it can be a big source of calories.)

- ☐ Amount of cholesterol in a soda (Tricky ads sometimes claim they are fat free, which is true, but that doesn't mean the product is healthy.)

Seek Out Supportive People to Help You Make Healthy Changes

Remember that social networks—even from across a continent—can be helpful and pull us in positive directions when we are trying to make healthy changes. Social networks near and far can also pull us in a less healthy direction, like friends who try to push junk food on us.

What we haven't discussed enough is the most important and influential social network of all: the family. Parents who smoke influence whether their children will smoke more than their peers do. Parents who misuse alcohol influence their children to start drinking at younger and riskier ages. And remember our surprising discovery of how children can have a big influence on their family's diet. We'll now take a closer look at the vital role of family in the change process.

A Family That Cares

Given the challenge of overweight households, it can be particularly helpful if you try to get your family on board with the change process. Here is the good news! We provided an online computerized version of the TTM-tailored program you are using in this book to youth in ten middle schools to tackle their three risk factors for weight problems: unhealthy eating, inadequate exercise, and too much television or other screen time. Then we compared their outcomes to youth in ten middle schools who received programs aimed only at smoking and alcohol use. What we found was a significant improvement in diet, exercise, and screen habits in the ten middle schools treated for weight-related behaviors. But we were surprised to discover that in these schools, we also produced significantly less smoking and drinking than in the middle schools that addressed only these addictive behaviors.[54]

We encourage you to try to make yours a family that cares about healthy eating, moving, feeling, and helping. Here are some small steps you might take to start the family change process. Depending on the age of your children, you can tell them and others the good news you just learned about how the type of program you're learning about in this book had such a positive impact on the health and well-being of young people. You can teach them how children can help their parents develop healthier and happier habits and how parents can help their kids with this as well. But start by asking for their support in tackling what many experts believe is the toughest task today.

Explain that you want them to be a support for you, just as you are working to support yourself. Let them know they can be a really positive influence on your health and happiness, just as you want to be a more positive influence on their current and future well-being. Share what you have been learning about becoming freer to change your own behavior. Let them know you can all influence each other in positive ways whether you are ready, getting ready, or even if you're not yet ready to take action.

Consider letting their teacher or principal know about the programs available that can help students make these changes so they can be healthier and happier. (See the program at www.prochange.com/obesitydemo.)

Use Rewards to Reinforce Others to Reinforce You

Here is a creative approach that self-changers have appreciated as a way to encourage their families' participation as they move to healthier eating and happier weight management. This technique is based on our findings that children can be a negative influence on the family's diet. Instead of reinforcing only themselves, self-changers with children gave each child a small monetary reward for every pound the parent lost. Do you want social support? Do you want social monitoring? Kids love to "parent" their parents if given the chance—especially if they are getting paid to do so!

This approach can be extended to making a shopping list. Children can help identify foods that could be scratched from the list (such as potato chips and ice cream) to help the parent eat healthier. The same thing could be done with adding healthy snacks. This positive approach can help the family become a more positive social network that can pull together rather than pull apart.

In the same way, parents should try to be positive influences on their children's eating rather than being negative forces. Here's me trying to be a positive influence with our son Jason when he was three:

"Jason, I would really appreciate it if you ate your peas."

"I know, Dad, but I can't like it!"

"I know Jason, but it's important that you learn to like them."

"Give me a reason, Dad," said Jason, trying to be open to influence.

"So you can grow up to be healthy and strong," I said.

"That's no reason. I'm already healthy and strong!"

"Then you can't watch television!" I declared.

"Now that's a reason!" Jason said.

Although I got the result I sought, I was not happy with the process. Look at how quickly I shifted from influence to pressure without even being aware of it. Forcing children to eat particular fruits and vegetables they are not ready to eat can condition them to react negatively about foods associated with such coercion.

Remember Harry and the messages he got about eating as a child? Another mistake that parents often make with all good intentions is to force their children to eat everything on their plates. Here are some messages that are well meant but not well met:

"You cannot leave the table until you clean your plate," says Dad.

Child: "But Dad, I'm not hungry."

Dad: "Kids in Africa are starving and you are not going to waste food." (Coerce with guilt.)

Such scenarios are excellent ways to condition the "completion obsession," where people feel compelled to finish their food even though they are 80 percent full and don't need to stuff their stomachs. Such examples may also help explain why so many of our children are overweight.

A more positive approach is to have a family meeting about how meals can be healthier and happier. Consider asking your family how each of you can be a positive influence on the others rather than be individuals who argue over the fundamental life force of eating.

Here is a scenario in which a household works together to have a healthier diet and to prevent weight gain. A father and mother, their ten-year-old daughter, and their seven-year-old son hold a family meeting to talk about reducing their sugar intake to low-risk levels. First they talk about the benefits, or pros, of reducing sugar in their diet. They talk about how they might feel about themselves individually and collectively for pulling together rather than apart. They set goals of eating less sugar for three weeks and then checking in on how they felt. Would they have more energy and not feel sluggish? Would their brains work better? And how much would they miss the foods they were leaving behind? These included sodas and other sugar-sweetened beverages, cookies, cakes, and ice cream. Healthy snacks would be substituted. They discuss how they can support each other when struggling to stay essentially abstinent from sugar. As a result of their respectful process, they all feel proud of their experiment and are more hopeful about reaching their goals than when they each were trying to reduce their sugar intake individually in isolation.

Progressing from Action to Maintenance

Fortunately we are learning more about what helps people progress from action to maintenance. As we've mentioned, with alcohol, smoking, and weight-loss programs based on an action model, relapse typically begins soon after treatment ends. We call this pattern of relapse a *declining* trajectory, where the positive effects of treatment decline over time. As we've stressed throughout this book, TTM is different. As far as we have been able to tell, our controlled population trial is the only one that has produced an *increasing treatment trajectory,* where participants continue to lose weight well after treatment ends.

Why is this? Remember that action-oriented programs assume all participants are prepared to take immediate action on each of their multiple behaviors (eating, moving, and mindful eating rather than emotional eating) that are critical for long-term maintenance. However, in a Stages of Change program, the emphasis is on progress, and individuals are allowed and encouraged to progress at their own pace. As more participants progress to action after treatment ends, they would continue to lose weight.

Also, remember TTM emphasizes more than the goal of losing weight or preventing weight gain. Our goal is to help you appreciate the multiple pros, or benefits, that come with healthy eating, regular exercise, and mindful or non-emotional eating. As you have learned, these benefits include enhancing multiple areas of well-being or happiness. The more your changes affirm your physical, emotional, social, functional, financial, and purposeful domains of well-being, the more motivated you will be to continue to progress long after you have finished this book.[55]

There is a phenomenon called "post-dissertation depression," where PhD graduates feel depressed five to ten years after they complete their final project. Oh, they certainly enjoy a period of celebration, but then a gnawing question begins to eat away at them. "Is that all there is? I thought this long, arduous process was going to change my life." Disappointment and depression can begin to set in. Something similar can happen with people who achieved their weight goals but who were driven to change by too few pros. Changing the multiple behaviors that drive long-term weight loss can transform your life if you prepared for it by raising your pros and then by recognizing a new benefit each week. So let's practice those pros with stimulus control.

Use Stimulus Control to Manage Your Environment and Make Eating Healthier, Happier, and More Meaningful

To repeat what we stressed in earlier chapters, the strongest form of behavior control is stimulus control. What is the stimulus that can have the most control over what you eat? It is (or should be) your shopping list.

 **EXERCISE**

Shopping for Self-Control

On a separate paper or digital sheet make out a brief shopping list with twelve foods you typically buy. Include at least one or two foods that can tempt you to eat in a less healthy way. Here is an example from a list Jan and I prepared:

Shopping List

1. Greens
2. Skim milk
3. Spaghetti
4. Bread
5. Plain Greek yogurt
6. Berries
7. Ice cream
8. Fish
9. Bananas
10. Potato chips
11. Tomatoes
12. Toilet paper

Now, cross two unhealthy foods off your list.

We quickly identified the two foods we should delete to help set limits on what we eat. Of course, you know which two. It wasn't easy, but we worked up the confidence that we could cope with stress without counting on chips or ice cream. When I was shopping, I had to be mindful of not automatically being pulled to the ice cream cooler or the potato chip aisle.

At home it took time to keep from following my tracks to the fridge. Like Harry whose home was completely free of food, I would open the fridge and sigh. But then I would substitute the yogurt with fruit for ice cream and chips. Over time, I quit craving those comfort foods to feed my emotional needs.

I thought I had terminated that behavior pathway. But then we moved close to our five grandchildren. When making out our shopping list, we felt compelled to add chips and ice cream as treats for the kids. I'm certain this was a less-than-conscious emotional decision where we wanted to be "sweet" grandparents who treated our grandkids with some of their favorite foods.

What surprised me was how rapidly my craving for these foods came back in full force. The old hardwired habit was too strong to resist as long as my old favorites were in the freezer or cupboard. Here I am, a psychologist who helped discover how children can change their parents' eating patterns. I never thought the same pattern could skip a generation with my grandkids' desires triggering my desires. I still haven't decided the best way to be a "sweet" grandpa without offering sweets for treats. Imagine a smoker who is trying to progress through maintenance while keeping cigarettes in the house or a person with a severe alcohol problem storing liquor in the cabinet. What are the lessons learned here? Use stimulus control to clear your house of the comfort foods you crave the most. Substitute them with a healthy, tasty alternative. (And maybe find some other way to treat your kids or grandkids!)

Perhaps a more profound implication is that when it comes to healthy eating and healthy weight management, we may never reach the termination stage where we have zero temptations and total confidence that we will not return to foods that we have craved the most. With rare exceptions, healthy weight management is likely to be a lifetime of maintenance.

Learning from Long-Term Maintainers

Dr. Rena Wing and her colleagues at Brown University have done some wonderful work with individuals succeeding with long-term weight loss. Her National Weight Control Registry includes more than 10,000 people who participated in assessments over time. Similar to our research with 1,000 smokers who taught us so much about how people change, Dr. Wing is learning a lot from her participants. First, about half of the participants were successful as self-changers and about half made changes with expert guidance. These participants have lost, on average, more than seventy pounds and have been successful for five-plus years.

These lessons alone are inspiring, since too many professionals and the general public doubt their abilities to lose a significant amount of weight and keep it off. The fact that about half changed on their own matches our experience that most individuals have the potential to make major changes that can enhance their health and well-being. The challenge is how to best help them put their potential into practice. One of our mottos is "Working in harmony with how people change naturally."

Another striking discovery is that most of the individuals continue to lose weight long after their treatment has ended. This is like the increasing treatment trajectory that we just discussed with many of our participants losing more weight after treatment ends. Another message here is that many of Wing's successful participants do not sit back on their laurels—they are not content with their success. Instead, they continue to raise the bar by losing more weight over time.

The good news is that maintenance may get easier over time. Participants who joined the Wing Registry with two to five years of maintenance had a much greater chance of longer-term success. Although these individuals may not terminate, or lose, their temptations after five years, they seem to have turned healthy eating and regular exercise into positive habits and potentially permanent parts of their lifestyles.

Their healthy eating habits seem to be consistent across weekdays and weekends, suggesting that those strong habits have come under stimulus control. They consume relatively low-calorie and low-fat diets and eat breakfast daily. They also weigh themselves regularly as a form of stimulus control that can quickly signal if they are getting off track. This helps them keep a lapse from becoming a relapse. They follow the criteria we will discuss in the next chapter as they engage in one hour of exercise each day. With such inspiration from our peers, let's keep moving forward.

We urge you to consider the information presented in this chapter, think about what may work best for you and your overall well-being, and try some of our suggestions. We are convinced the higher and more holistic your goal is, the more likely you are to lose clinically significant weight while gaining health and happiness.

10

The Impact of Exercise
WELL-BEING AND HEALTHY WEIGHT MANAGEMENT

In the last chapter, you learned about the importance of mindful and healthy eating and how to use the Transtheoretical Model (TTM) to change your unhealthy eating habits. Now it's time to talk about exercise. Before we dig into this discussion, it is helpful to figure out which Stage of Change you are in when you begin your exercise program. To do that, let's look at the public health benchmarks for exercise. Here are the goals we recommend:

    1a. At least 150 minutes per week of moderate exercise—things like walking briskly, biking 10 miles per hour, or playing an active sport like doubles tennis—to prevent weight gain.

    1b. At least 300 minutes per week to lose weight.

OR

    2a. At least 75 minutes per week of vigorous exercise—things like running, hiking uphill, or playing an active sport like singles tennis—to prevent weight gain.

    2b. At least 150 minutes per week of vigorous exercise to lose weight.

Choose the option that is most appealing and doable for you. Then consider which stage of change you are currently in:

  1. Precontemplation: I do not exercise this much and do not intend to start in the next six months.

2. Contemplation: I do not exercise this much but intend to start in the next six months.

3. Preparation: I do not exercise this much but intend to start in the next month.

4. Action: I exercise this much and have been doing so for less than six months.

5. Maintenance: I exercise this much and have been doing so for more than six months.

Increase Your Pros to Move from Precontemplation

In earlier chapters, we talked about how moving beyond precontemplation requires motivation. As we all know, establishing and maintaining a regular exercise program requires major motivation, so we encourage you to assess yourself in this section even if you have already progressed past precontemplation in your journey of change. When it comes to exercise, the more pros you embrace, the faster and more effectively you can progress through the Stages of Change.

Here is a brainstorming exercise to help you begin moving toward a more active life. Think of this challenge as the mental equivalent of a five-minute mile, which is a really good time.

——————————————— **EXERCISE** ———————————————

The Pros of Regular Exercise—a Five-Minute Brainstorm

On a separate paper or digital sheet, write as many pros of regular exercise that you can name in five minutes. It can help to use your smartphone or watch as a timer.

———————————————————————————————————————

The average person in precontemplation can only identify four or five pros. How many did you come up with? Here are some typical responses that self-changers have given when we've asked them to list their exercise pros. They want to do the following:

1. Achieve a better weight

2. Improve their heart health

3. Have more energy

4. Get stronger

5. Reduce their stress

Are your initial pros similar to those of other precontemplators? Now, how long did you last before you dropped out of the "brainstorming race"? Most people drop out well before five minutes. If you did too, you probably are not yet mentally prepared to tackle the marathons required to sustain weight loss or prevent weight gain.

Contrast your list with what we find when we do this brainstorming exercise with a group. We start with the person in the first seat in front and then go around, asking each person to name a new pro, giving people the option to pass if they cannot come up with one. It is like they are in a relay race, passing a baton to their team members, and the pros fly rapidly through the audience. Here are the types of things they come up with:

1. Improved circulation

2. More alertness

3. Better balance

4. Feeling better

5. Better fitting clothes

6. Sleeping better

7. Being happier

8. Getting stronger bones

9. Having fewer colds

10. Better at work

11. Having more endurance

12. Better working brain

13. Better blood pressure

14. Healthier immune system

15. Better mood

16. Better sex

17. Improved memory

18. Can keep up with grandchildren

19. Can keep up with friends

20. Better self-esteem

. . . and the race goes on.

When we do this group exercise, we discover that audience members who hardly know each other begin to function like a social network that is positively pulling for one another. As they pass the baton, they are raising each other's behavior change IQ. They are also experiencing that the more they pull together, the "smarter" they can be. Now when someone asks me how smart I am, my answer is, "It depends on who I team up with." We're guessing that without the benefit of such a social network, very few readers could come close to listing twenty-five pros in five minutes. So if you weren't able to, don't worry—you're in the majority. Those who are able to rapidly brainstorm this list are probably speed writers or health coaches!

If exercise were a new medication, we'd probably see it advertised on TV and in magazines everywhere, like the multitude of medicines touted as cure-alls for whatever ails you. But it will be you, not some corporation, who will profit from this miracle behavior medicine—and it doesn't come with a long list of frightening side effects. We like to call exercise the "bargain basement" of behavior medicine, because you can do it for free. And all of us like a good bargain.

So let's make a bargain now. We bet that completing the next exercise will better prepare you for your lifelong race with weight. Has your weight already gained on you and caused you to slow down? Let's look at how you can begin to tackle your weight challenge.

In the last chapter, we found that the pros for multiple domains of well-being also predict long-term weight loss. Also, remember the goal is not just to lose weight or prevent weight gain. The bigger goal is to enhance your *overall well-being*. As your body, mind, spirit, and your relationships improve, your happiness grows. The following lists identify the many possible benefits from using the Transtheoretical Model with exercise. As in chapter 9, the pros are organized into areas of well-being, because these are among the best predictors of success.

—————————————————— **EXERCISE** ——————————————————

Pros of Regular Exercise for Healthy Weight Management

Look over these lists and check the benefits you would like to see from exercise. The more pros you have to gain, the more you are likely to progress toward action and beyond.

Physical Well-Being

- ☐ Reduce your risk of heart disease
- ☐ Reduce your risk of stroke
- ☐ Reduce your risk of colon cancer
- ☐ Reduce your risk of breast cancer
- ☐ Reduce your risk of esophageal cancer
- ☐ Reduce your risk of prostate cancer
- ☐ Reduce your risk of pancreatic cancer
- ☐ Reduce your risk of obesity
- ☐ Reduce your risk of arteriosclerosis
- ☐ Reduce your risk of kidney cancer
- ☐ Reduce your risk of diabetes
- ☐ Reduce your risk of endometrial cancer
- ☐ Reduce your risk of sleep apnea
- ☐ Reduce your body fat
- ☐ Reduce triglycerides
- ☐ May lower your blood pressure
- ☐ Improve your blood flow
- ☐ Decrease your risk of clogged blood vessels
- ☐ Decrease pressure in your joints
- ☐ Reduce risk of high blood sugar
- ☐ May improve your breathing
- ☐ Improve your sleep
- ☐ Reduce pain
- ☐ Lower your resting heart rate

☐ Decrease irregular heart rhythms

☐ Improve circulation

☐ Improve immune system function

☐ Help your body use insulin

☐ Improve bowel regularity

☐ Lower the risk of erectile dysfunction

☐ Reduce and prevent lower back pain

☐ Reduce muscle tension

☐ Prevent weight gain

☐ Decrease your risk for a fatal heart attack

☐ Lower your risk for hip fracture

☐ Lower your risk for lung cancer

☐ Lower your risk for gallstones

☐ Lower your risk for dementia

Functional Well-Being

☐ Have more energy

☐ Increase your endurance

☐ Promote effective problem solving

☐ Promote feelings of control

☐ Increase confidence

☐ Be more productive

☐ Increase stamina

☐ Be more alert

☐ Be more flexible

☐ Be better coordinated

☐ Reduce your risk of falling

☐ Have fewer illnesses and absences from work

☐ Improve your balance

☐ Control your appetite

☐ Make yourself stronger

Financial Well-Being

- ☐ May save money
- ☐ Lower health care costs
- ☐ Get a promotion or better paying job

Social Well-Being

- ☐ Improve your relationship with others
- ☐ Set an example about making healthy choices
- ☐ Be around longer for your family
- ☐ Gain pride from your friends
- ☐ Cause your loved ones to worry less about your health
- ☐ Feel happier around other people
- ☐ Improve your sex life

Appealing Well-Being

- ☐ Have better fitting clothes
- ☐ Improve your appearance
- ☐ Have a healthier image
- ☐ Look better
- ☐ Improve your posture

Emotional Well-Being

- ☐ Feel better about yourself
- ☐ Make your emotional life richer
- ☐ Learn new ways to cope with distress
- ☐ Manage your stress better
- ☐ Feel more relaxed and at ease
- ☐ Feel like you're taking the best possible care of yourself
- ☐ Enjoy life more
- ☐ Be happier
- ☐ Improve your mood
- ☐ Feel less nervous or anxious
- ☐ Manage your anger better

☐ Improve your quality of life

☐ Take your mind off other things for a while

Purposeful Well-Being

☐ Live longer

☐ Improve your quality of life

☐ Improve your self-worth

☐ Fulfill your passions

Increase Your Consciousness: Raise Your Behavior IQ by Learning More about Eating and Exercise

Here is a quiz to help increase your knowledge about diet and exercise habits in the United States.[56] Circle the letter of your best guess to the following questions.

---

1. What percentage of adults in the United States does not exercise at a healthy level?

   A. 35%   B. 45%   C. 55%   D. 65%   E. 75%

---

2. What percentage does not eat a healthy enough diet?

   A. 35%   B. 45%   C. 55%   D. 65%   E. 75%

---

3. What percentage is overweight or obese?

   A. 35%   B. 45%   C. 55%   D. 65%   E. 75%

The correct answer to the above is about 65% in all three cases.
Do you see a clear connection here?

---

4. What percentage of people in the U.S. Army is overweight or obese?

   A. 35%   B. 45%   C. 55%   D. 65%   E. 75%

The answer here is surprising: Almost two-thirds (65.5%) of people in the army are overweight or obese. No wonder the U.S. Army has made diet and exercise its top two priorities for military preparedness. Let's prepare you for the widely shared struggle with weight.

Our collective consciousness as behavior change scientists increased dramatically when we discovered positive behavior networks between changing diet and exercise. In our studies on multiple behavior changes, we had always assessed whether the treatments connected to our Stages of Change produced statistically and clinically significant changes in our total populations. We consistently found greater success in our treatment groups compared to the control groups (those not receiving treatment). So for years we assumed that our interventions worked the same for different pairs of behaviors, for example, diet and exercise, and diet and smoking. At the beginning of a project, we looked at each behavior separately, treated each separately, and analyzed each outcome separately. The hidden assumption was that each behavior changed independently. Based on that research, we had no reason to assume that pairs of behaviors affected each other positively *or* negatively.

Then we analyzed how different pairs of behaviors changed within individuals and we found different results. To our amazement, people who successfully changed their exercise habits were about twice as likely to change their diets as well, compared to those who did not change their exercise habits. This was also true in the untreated control groups, though the individuals in the control groups changed both behaviors significantly less than those in our intervention groups.[57] Those results indicate that diet and exercise are positively linked. These are like the social networks we mentioned earlier that positively influence each other to quit smoking.

This was the good news. The bad news was that other pairs of behaviors, like diet and smoking, seemed to be negatively linked. These pairs changed together about 50 percent less than we predicted would be the case if they just changed independently. So, why do you think pairs of behavior like diet and exercise appear to be positively linked but diet and smoking are negatively linked?

Some colleagues and students on our research teams made the case that most people are well aware that diet and exercise are intrinsically linked to weight. In other words, they argued that the public recognizes that losing weight requires changing *both* behaviors. But the public also knows that diet and smoking are critically linked to heart disease and heart attacks, so why wouldn't they be linked when it comes to changing behavior? Good question, but the truth is—at least for now—we just don't know the answer. But we can still apply the knowledge we do have.

Calories In and Calories Out

Our theory about the positive link between diet and exercise is based on the fact that these two behaviors are naturally related as "energy balance" behaviors. This means that our diet accounts for the amount of calories we take in. Exercise or physical activity plays a primary role in how many calories we burn up. Simply put:

- The calories we take in that exceed the calories we put out
  = weight gain.
- The calories we take in that are less than the calories we put out
  = weight loss.
- The calories we take in that equal the calories we put out
  = weight unchanged.

Eating moves calories in, and exercise moves calories out. When these behaviors are balanced, our weight stays the same. But for decades now, in many of the highly developed countries, our environments have changed, and we eat more calories while exercising less. Agriculture has been reengineered to make many unhealthy and fattening foods cheaper. Marketing of food has been reorganized to make those foods more widely and easily available. Restaurants (especially fast-food restaurants) and vending machines are seemingly everywhere. For the first time in history, people in the United States consume more of their food from restaurants than from a grocery store. As a result, the financial and time-consuming cons for eating comfort foods and other less healthy choices have decreased dramatically.

For even longer, our environments have changed in ways that dramatically reduce our physical activity. Automobiles replace walking and biking. Time-saving devices like vacuum cleaners, dishwashers, and power lawn mowers reduce physical exertion at home. Tractors, balers, and other machines make much of farming more sedentary. And these are just a few examples.

A recent study found that just ten minutes of vigorous exercise produced one thousand molecular changes in our bodies.[58] And we thought a list of one hundred pros was impressive! But what is the goal of this research? These researchers wanted to produce a drug that can generate the same one thousand molecular changes. They are medical engineers who want to eliminate our need to exercise at all. What this study suggests to us is that just ten minutes of exercise can change our bodies in dramatic ways. It is as if going from sitting to moving transforms us from being more like sedentary vegetables to being the active animals we were intended to be. As kids, we learn about animals who become so inactive for months that they totally stop eating. In preparing for such hibernation, they eat more and more calories to increase their weight so they can weather a winter when food is not available. They intentionally store calories that they can later burn to survive cold, dark, and barren winters.

It is a fact that the more weight we humans gain, the less we exercise. And the more sedentary we become, the more weight we gain. When this happens, these energy-related behaviors get out of balance. A major challenge for our times is to reengineer these behaviors to get back to a healthier and happier balance. Fortunately, we now know that diet and exercise are linked together in such a way that they can pull together rather than apart. This discovery did not come from what we know about multiple behavior change; it occurred in individuals with no help from behavior change experts like us. However, our increased awareness of how diet and exercise are linked greatly influenced how we now teach the Stages of Change to achieve healthy weight management.

This book reflects this new approach—an approach that will help you find a positive balance between diet and exercise by giving you ways to change both behaviors with less effort. You may have discovered, for example, how similar many of the pros of healthy eating and adequate exercise are. In this book, we are also emphasizing for the first time the multiple areas of well-being that are linked to both healthy eating and regular exercise. These areas of well-being are also among the best predictors for successful long-term weight loss.

―――――――――― **EXERCISE** ――――――――――

Dramatic Relief:
Being Moved by Emotions to Progress to Contemplation

Read the statement in the left column and imagine that situation. Then imagine the situation in the right column.

BEFORE CHANGE	AFTER CHANGE
Imagine your colon starting to develop cancer because you don't move enough.	Imagine the relief from knowing that exercise is one the best ways to help prevent cancer.
Imagine your arteries getting blocked because you don't exercise enough.	Imagine the relief from knowing that exercise is one of the best ways to help prevent a heart attack.
Imagine you're feeling too down to exercise.	Imagine the relief from knowing that exercise is as effective as the best medicines for depression.
Imagine you're feeling too busy and burdened to exercise.	Imagine relieving the burdens of living an unbalanced life by exercising for the biggest returns you can get for your time.
Imagine your weight getting more and more in the way of your health and happiness.	Imagine exercising as one of your two best ways to win with your weight.

This exercise demonstrates how regular exercise can help relieve the negative emotions, like fear and anxiety, that can develop when we don't exercise enough.

Progressing in Contemplation: Use Environmental Reevaluation to Notice Your Effects on Others

As you may recall, an important factor in moving in contemplation is to evaluate how your changing can help others. So far, we've learned an important lesson about losing weight. Change processes can have negative effects and end up reversing our progress. A friend and colleague named Bob had been obese since childhood, like his two sisters and parents. When he was once again struggling to lose weight, including developing an exercise program and cutting calories, he imagined that his success could have positive impacts on his social network, especially his family.

But remember what you learned about how social networks can influence each other to gain weight. There is more risk that social networks will work in reverse and help produce weight gain rather than loss. Why? Since most adults in this country are overweight and so few succeed in losing weight, the majority of overweight people are likely to have the greatest influence. Bob was doing remarkably well—exercising, losing over thirty-five pounds, and looking good. But he said that none of his four family members even spoke a word about his success. He believed his changing through weight loss somehow threatened their secure image of being part of a "fat family." Unfortunately, the family's majority influence eventually won. Bob's weight went into reverse: He stopped exercising and eating healthily, and he went back to being his old overweight self. Sadly, Bob later died from weight-related chronic heart disease.

In contrast, a client named Alice accepted my suggestion that she recruit supportive people from her social network to team up for regular walks around their neighborhood. She led the way and was the first to lose significant weight. Her teammates didn't pull her back, even though they had not yet lost any noticeable weight themselves. But Alice knew from our model that they were changing by progressing through their own Stages of Change. The lesson here is to be proactive about influencing your social network by recruiting some of them to join your team. You can support each other and share the joys that positive change can bring.

---------- **EXERCISE** ----------

Progress from Contemplation by Decreasing Your Cons

Here is a list of cons that can be barriers to regular exercise. Select the cons that are true for you and list them on a separate paper or digital sheet:

☐ I feel vain when I'm trying to improve my appearance.

☐ I think that changing habits is a hassle.

☐ I don't like the many decisions I would have to make.

☐ I could risk failing at losing weight.

☐ I think changing takes a lot of time.

☐ I feel demoralized about my ability to lose weight over the long term.

☐ My family and friends may not want me to change.

☐ I don't know the best ways to exercise.

☐ It think it's easier to not change.

Now add your own cons to the list.

Here are some suggestions for countering your cons. Read each con and then think about how the counter "pro" might spur you on to change.

CON	COUNTER
Changing takes a lot of time.	You are going to learn how to change multiple behaviors with less time and effort.
I would risk failing at losing weight.	If you don't lose weight, you risk losing your health and well-being.
I don't know the best ways to exercise.	You don't need the best ways—you just need to learn better ways that work for you.
It's easier to stay inactive.	I will remind myself that being inactive equals smoking a pack of cigarettes a day. Would changing that behavior be easier?

Progressing to Preparation

Harold's story is a good example of how a change process can work in reverse.

Harold was a huge guy in his mid-twenties who worked in a jewelry factory. At 6'4" and 360 pounds, he stood out in a crowd. His weight was handicapping his love life and was beginning to produce early signs of type II diabetes, so Harold began trying to lose weight in a big way, eating better and exercising regularly for the first time in years. Yet the more weight he lost, the more distressed he became. Then it struck him—he was no longer "Big Harry." He no longer stood out in a crowd. People didn't get out of his way as he walked through a crowd. He went in to "reverse," regaining weight faster than he had lost it.

Lesson learned here: Harry hadn't prepared himself by considering how his self-image and social image would change with the remarkable changes in his body's appearance. Fortunately, Harry relapsed only back to the preparation stage and then struggled successfully to shed his old self-image before taking action and gradually shedding significant weight.

Using Self-Reevaluation to Create a New Self-Image

Remember our discovery that long-term weight loss was driven, in part, by the pros of pride that family, friends, and self could take in a leaner image. So lean on your self-image to be sure that you are prepared for your new way of being. Here is an exercise to help you change your image for physical exercise.

───────────── **EXERCISE** ─────────────

Changing Your Self-Image

If you were someone who doesn't exercise regularly, how would you view yourself? Take this opportunity to take a hard and honest look at yourself. Select the descriptive terms that apply from the list on the next page and write these down on a separate paper or digital sheet. Feel free to add your own ideas to your list.

**HOW WOULD YOU VIEW YOURSELF AS AN INACTIVE PERSON?
CHECK THOSE THAT ARE TRUE FOR YOU.**

I am . . .

- ☐ overweight
- ☐ active
- ☐ irresponsible
- ☐ responsible
- ☐ strong
- ☐ weak
- ☐ confident
- ☐ not confident
- ☐ energetic
- ☐ sluggish
- ☐ in shape
- ☐ out of shape

- ☐ a healthy weight
- ☐ passive
- ☐ proud
- ☐ dissatisfied
- ☐ healthy
- ☐ unhealthy
- ☐ successful
- ☐ regretful
- ☐ determined
- ☐ lazy
- ☐ like a smoker
- ☐ _____

**HOW WOULD YOU VIEW YOURSELF AS A REGULAR EXERCISER?
CHECK THOSE THAT ARE TRUE FOR YOU.**

I am . . .

- ☐ overweight
- ☐ active
- ☐ irresponsible
- ☐ responsible
- ☐ strong
- ☐ weak
- ☐ confident
- ☐ not confident
- ☐ energetic
- ☐ sluggish
- ☐ in shape
- ☐ out of shape

- ☐ a healthy weight
- ☐ passive
- ☐ proud
- ☐ dissatisfied
- ☐ healthy
- ☐ unhealthy
- ☐ successful
- ☐ regretful
- ☐ determined
- ☐ lazy
- ☐ like a smoker
- ☐ _____

Imagine progressing to a more positive image by moving more. The act of imagining how exercising regularly can change your image can actually help you take steps to get started.

Using Self-Liberation to Increase Your Commitment and Your Willpower

What are three good choices for exercise that can enhance your health and happiness while decreasing your weight? The path most self-changers, especially women, choose is walking. Today, men are still more likely to view themselves as athletes, and they are more likely to choose vigorous exercise, like running or biking. They are also more likely to choose resistance training to build their muscle mass. If time is your biggest barrier to regular exercise, then the vigorous choice may work well. But talk with your health care provider about the potential risks of such exercise, especially if you are managing a chronic condition.

Taking Action by Countering Sedentary Habits with Healthier Ones

You have already learned that you need to be prepared to counter overlearned or conditioned habits that control your lifestyle. The following chart presents some of the most common inactive habits and a series of healthier substitutions that can enhance your health and well-being.

COMMON INACTIVE HABITS	HEALTHIER ALTERNATIVES
Watching a sixty-minute television show	Record the show, take a twenty-minute walk, and watch the forty minutes without unhealthy commercials.
Watching a thirty-minute television show	Watch the show while walking on a treadmill or riding an exercise bike at the Y, health club, or at home. You can also walk in place.
Taking an elevator up four floors	Start by walking up the first floor and catching an elevator the rest of the way. Add a floor as your energy and confidence increase.
Riding up an escalator	Walk up the escalator and save time.
Driving around the parking lot looking for a closer spot to your destination	Park sooner and save some time while adding exercise.
Reading a favorite author or magazine	Read on an exercise bike and increase your benefits by multitasking.

COMMON INACTIVE HABITS	HEALTHIER ALTERNATIVES
Take a nap to relax	Do walking meditation and double your relaxation.
Playing games on your smartphone	Play real games like tennis or softball.
Spending time on your virtual online social network	Spend time walking with your real network; add the real people from your virtual network.
Spending time talking with your partner	Spend time talking and walking and holding hands like you did in the old days.

Use Social Liberation to Notice Social Trends

Reports from the World Health Organization (WHO) and the U.S. Surgeon General's report on physical activity and exercise are having big impacts on exercise, just as previous WHO reports affected smoking rates. Public health efforts are spreading across communities, companies, and countries.

Jan has long been an advocate for the process of social liberation by developing exercise facilities to serve a broad range of populations. She especially worked for groups that are often outside of the mainstream, like skate boarders, who only had high-risk sidewalks and streets for their favorite physical activity. I am proud to report that she was recognized by the town council in South Kingstown, Rhode Island, for her twenty-three years of leadership on the Parks and Recreation Commission. She also served on the board of the National Parks and Recreation Association.

You can get involved in your community as well and help create opportunities and environments that encourage physical activity.

Notice Public Health Efforts to Help Maintain Movement

Take a moment to think about how society is changing to make it easier to exercise. Have you spotted a new bike or walking path in your town? Have you noticed campaigns for increasing physical activity? Here is a slogan we liked from a local church bulletin: "Exercise your soul: Walk to church!"

Check off which of the following public changes you think can help you make a commitment to regular exercise:

☐ Free or low-cost exercise programs and fitness classes offered through communities or employers

☐ Increased ways to exercise at home, such as fitness DVDs, streaming exercise classes online, active video games like *Dance, Dance Revolution, Wii Sports,* and *Wii Fit*

☐ Mobile wireless technology that makes it easier to track physical activity

☐ More articles, news stories, and books on the benefits of physical activity available to read

☐ Artwork in stairwells to encourage people to take the stairs

The more social trends you recognize, the easier it will be to move to action.

Get Support through Helping Relationships

Given the time and effort it takes for effective exercise, it is important to have helping relationships that support you. This is especially true in times when you are feeling distressed by being too busy, too tired, too down, bored, or too demoralized by the slow progress you are making in losing weight or increasing endurance. Research demonstrates that having at least one supportive teammate to walk and talk with can help get you through the times when you are tempted to abandon your efforts and return to your comfortable couch.

For years Jan was a member of a wonderful tennis team in a small club with just three courts. They grew older together but better together as well. Over the years, they made it to the New England sectionals numerous times and to the nationals five times. Last year they amazed others and themselves by winning the national championship for women over sixty-five. They had to win over teams from large clubs and large warm weather states like Florida, California, South Carolina, and the home team in Surprize, Arizona. What a surprise! And an inspiration that you can get better as you get older.

With my positive attitude toward golf, I am reminded of my alcoholic uncle George, who said he "only drinks alone or with someone."

Alone I play fast-paced golf, walking a hilly nine holes in sixty-three to seventy-two minutes. With my good friend Joel, we walk a good pace and talk at an even faster pace. I was particularly good at getting him out when the weather was cool and threatening. He was really good at getting me out when I was too busy. I waited a long time to join a team with Joel as my partner. The players ranged in age from twenty to ninety-three—so represented by Chuck, a man who had landed on D-Day in 1944 and who was a past president of the National Association for Veterans of Foreign Wars. What an inspiration he is for a golfer two decades his junior.

The following is a list of possibilities you might consider when teaming up for physical activity and social support. Check the ones that could be of help to you. Keep in mind the example of Alice who started her own neighborhood walking group.

Team or Support Groups:

☐ Neighbors walking

☐ Silver Sneakers (free for seniors at YMCAs via Medicare)

☐ Pickup tennis at town or school courts

☐ Free online social networks for health (such as MeYou Health)

☐ Church groups

☐ Town recreation programs (check catalogs and schedules for activities, such as Pickleball—an alternative to tennis for all levels)

☐ Employer programs, including gym memberships and team sports like softball

☐ Volunteering to coach a youth team

Use Rewards to Reinforce Increasing Your Activity

Check off ways to reinforce yourself that can help keep you moving:

☐ Call on your good inner coach: Tell yourself, "Attagirl, attaboy, you are moving now. Keep it up—you're getting stronger."

☐ Call on your good inner health provider: Feel your heart pumping to get stronger and your lungs breathing harder so you can breathe better.

☐ Call on your good inner scientist: Imagine one thousand healthy molecular changes occurring after ten minutes of vigorous exercise.

☐ Call on your good inner parent: Tell yourself, "How proud I am of you taking more control of your health."

☐ Call on your good inner preacher: Managing with such a healthy spirit.

☐ Call on your good team: Tell yourself, "Thanks for telling us about the progress you are making."

☐ Call on the good child within: Exercising to be getting a fresh start.

☐ Call on your good inner autobiographer: Tell yourself, "What a special story you are telling!"

Moving in Maintenance: Use Stimulus Control to Manage Your Environment

Given how much natural activity we lose out on because of the changes to our physical environments that we discussed earlier, it is essential that we reengineer our personal environments by developing ways to stimulate us to exercise more. Check off which changes you could make in your environment to help you get moving:

☐ Schedule time on your smartphone or calendar for walking, golfing, biking, tennis, or dancing. While your work and other obligations will still consume more than their fair share of your life, this will help you achieve a better balance.

☐ Keep exercise gear—like shoes and shorts, rackets, and gloves— always available in your car, workplace, or home.

☐ Bring more of your favorite exercise under "stimulus control"— exercise in the same place, for a set amount of time, with the same people, and at the same time.

☐ Develop new active habits to enhance your health and happiness: Increase the time you engage in such activities; increase variations of your favorite activities; expand your exercise to include additional environments like walking in a park as well as in a mall.

☐ Share your accomplishments soon after you achieve them to stimulate your social network's positive support.

☐ Pay ahead at the Y, health club, or team activity as a stimulus to keep you participating in these activities.

While this chapter focused principally on progressing through the Stages of Change with the single behavior of exercise, it also touched on how multiple behaviors of diet and exercise can change together. In the following chapters, you will discover more ways to combine the strategies we have introduced so you can change more behaviors with less effort.

11

Using Less Energy to Change Multiple Behaviors

In the last chapter, we discussed how the "energy balance" behaviors of diet and exercise are positively linked—diet accounts for the amount of calories we take in, and exercise accounts for the amount of calories we burn. You learned that when you change one of those behaviors, you at least double the chances that you'll succeed in changing the other. This combined effect is called "synergy." Here are some simple strategies that self-changers can adopt for increasing synergy as they apply the Stages of Change to multiple behaviors:

1. Simultaneously change multiple behaviors, but do not make the common mistake of trying to take action at the same time on each behavior. Recall the story of David in chapter 8, who came to me for guidance on changing his alcohol, smoking, weight, and exercise habits. If you are like David (and most other people), you aren't in the same Stage of Change for each behavior you want to change. Remember that making simultaneous change means you are making progress on each behavior you seek to change. For example, more women than men are likely to take action sooner on healthy eating, while men are likely to take action sooner on exercise. But *all* men and women can make progress on both behaviors. We don't know how much the synergy comes from the action stage behavior pushing along the earlier stage behavior or if progressing from precontemplation prevents the earlier stage behavior from pulling the reins on moving to action. We do know that making progress on both behaviors stimulates them to pull together rather than apart.

2. Drive both behavior changes with the same pros. Review the pros you listed for healthy eating compared with those for healthy exercise, and see how closely and positively linked they are. Working for the same prize produces more collaboration than competition for your time and effort.

3. If possible, positively pair with at least one supportive member from one of your social networks, including your family. This doesn't mean you have to always exercise together or progress at the same pace. It does mean that you can be pulling for each other, being positive influences that help you progress together rather than pull you apart. Remember that you are on the same team. This is not like a reality show where people compete to be the first to take action or lose the most weight. This is a journey that you both (or all) can win even when you progress at a different pace.

4. Apply the same simple techniques "above the surface" to stimulate complex change processes "below the surface." For example, with medications you have complex biochemical formulas below the surface and very simple techniques above the surface, such as taking two different pills each day. Compile a to-do list on your smartphone or calendar. Here's a sample list:

   ☐ This week: Progress on eating and moving for my weight. Check it off each day as I do it and share my progress with my social network

   ☐ Next week: Progress on eating and moving for my emotional life

   ☐ Next week: Progress on eating and moving for my self-esteem

   ☐ Next week: Progress on eating and moving for my heart, my brain, my friends, or family's pride

   ☐ Next week: Progress on eating and moving for my health and happiness

As you progress through the Stages of Change, give yourself credit for the complex multiple change processes you are applying to complex multiple behaviors. You are accomplishing the following:

1. Activating the many pros of changing for both behaviors

2. Strengthening your commitment as you lengthen your to-do list over time

3. Reinforcing your progress on both behaviors as you check off your repeated accomplishments

4. Reminding yourself of your commitment as you review your list

5. Influencing your social network to progress rather than regress as you share your pros, commitments, reinforcements, and reminders

One single, simple technique like creating a to-do list can stimulate at least five complex change processes and lead to progress on at least two of the behaviors that threaten your health and happiness. No number of medications can do that.

Changing a New Behavior: Sleeping Better by Breathing, Drinking, Eating, Moving, and Feeling Better

When I was writing this section, I received an invitation from David Katz, a renowned physician and scientist from Yale, to be part of a team that was applying for an international grant to advance the "True Health Initiative." This is a plan to better the health of individuals and groups of people as well as the health of the environment. David sought my input for using the Stages of Change for the initiative.

Katz identified six behaviors that can account for 80 percent of chronic diseases. In addition to the ones we've discussed so far, he also includes sleep—a fundamental process of life. When we don't get a healthy amount of sleep, we can experience major threats to our health and happiness.

Although we don't specifically include it as one of the major health threats in the introduction to this book, Jan and I think it is very important that self-changers treat sleep more seriously. Changing the multiple behaviors we have targeted thus far can also result in healthy sleep. By healthy sleep, we mean at least seven hours of regular, uninterrupted sleep, which is the amount recommended by the National Sleep Foundation.[59] Some self-changers will be in precontemplation about their sleep habits because they don't know the guidelines, some because they don't believe the guidelines, and some because they are demoralized about their ability to make changes to live a life with more and better sleep.

Some of the major causes of sleep disorders are breathing problems, drinking alcohol, eating certain foods, inadequate exercise, and upsetting feelings (lack of well-being). Let's start with well-being first, since that is connected to all of the high-risk behaviors we've discussed.

Addressing Stress and Distress in Tandem with the Other Four Top Threats for Healthier Sleep

Stress and distress may well be the most common disrupters of sleep. When we are stressed, depressed, anxious, or angry, it can be very difficult to relax enough to let go of the thoughts and worries, fears, and frustrations that can keep us awake. If we can just lie quietly in a bed, we can let our muscles go and drift off to sleep. We don't need them to hold us up; their work for the day is done.

In an earlier chapter, we talked about the three healthy choices ideal for managing stress and distress: relaxing, walking, and talking. Of course, you don't want to walk in your sleep. And you don't want to talk in your sleep. But sleep is all about relaxing, so the more progress you have made on being able to relax your muscles, mood, and mind, the more likely you are to sleep.

Having too many demands is another stress-related problem that can rob you of sleep. In an effort to accomplish all we want or need to do, we cut back more and more on the time we should be dedicated to sleep. We fool ourselves by telling ourselves we're working more for just a *short* time and we'll get back to a healthy sleep routine when the crisis is averted or the job is finished. Sure we will! How different are the excuses we use to justify our poor sleep habits from the ones we might use to rationalize other bad habits we embrace during times of high stress or distress: smoking more, drinking more alcohol, eating more junk food, or lying on the couch more?

It's all too easy for our particularly demanding times to become the norm rather than the exception, especially when we're connected to our work, family, and social circles 24/7 by the ever-present electronics in our lives today. To get more sleep, you may need to make your smartphone "dumb"—mute your cell phone as you prepare for bed. While you're at it, if you still have a landline phone, take it off the hook too. This change can be particularly difficult for those who are hooked on their digital technology. But try to remember that your mind was not made to work overtime during your sleeping hours. And there's a good reason we seek out a quiet dark place to sleep: to shut out the stimuli that keep the conscious parts of our brains awake.

Smoking at home during periods of high stress is another behavior that can interfere with sound sleep. With fewer and fewer places allowing people to smoke freely, most smokers compensate by significantly increasing their smoking at home—especially when they are stressed. One warning sign of a serious nicotine addiction is waking up during the night in need of a cigarette to prevent withdrawal symptoms—what used to be called a "nicotine fit."

People also often misuse alcohol to treat stress, depression, or anxiety. But any relief they might get from alcohol is temporary, and over time, the increased use of alcohol can produce more anxiety, depression, or other forms of emotional and psychological distress that may disrupt sleep. Binge drinking can interfere with normal sleep, too, when bingers drink late into the night then need to sleep far into the morning. The more severe the alcohol use disorder (AUD), the more biological and psychological systems are disrupted, including systems that govern sleep. An AUD can wreak havoc on a person's sleep patterns, no matter what time it is, how dark or quiet it may be, or how comfortable the bed (the usual conditions for sound sleep).

Unhealthy eating, especially in times of stress or distress, can also negatively impact our sleep, disrupting our digestive system and giving us heartburn, diarrhea, or gas. Too many people use late-night eating as a sedative to help them fall asleep. But, as is the case with alcohol, when people fall asleep after eating, it does not mean they will stay asleep. Eating until we are stuffed can also make us so uncomfortable that our sleep is impaired. And one of the most serious sleep disorders is "apnea," which is often related to obesity. Apnea is characterized by "stopped" breath, which often produces fear and sudden awakening. This condition typically requires medical attention and a prescription for using a breathing machine to keep airways open and functioning more effectively. However, many people with apnea have trouble using the machine because of the noise, which can disrupt their sleep, as well as their partner's sleep.

Finally, inadequate exercise—which can also result in the weight problems discussed earlier—is also related to sleep problems. As we have said, regular exercise helps us manage stress, depression, and other forms of distress in a healthy and, it follows, sleep-inducing way.

Applying the Change Processes to Improve Sleep

So, in the process of removing the five biggest threats to your health and happiness, you are also treating major contributors to sleep disorders. There are specific ways to apply change processes to develop healthy sleep habits. For example, stimulus control can be used by going to bed at the same time in your usual "sleep environment," where there is adequate darkness and quiet. In addition, we also recommend using your bed just for sleep and love making so that sleep doesn't compete with other habits that might keep you awake, like watching television, eating, or using your laptop, tablet, or smartphone in bed.

The more progress you make with changing your poor sleep habits, the more you should be reinforced by the energy and refreshment that comes with a good night's sleep. For the most part, healthy sleep can benefit from the synergy of other healthy behaviors pulling your life together rather than pulling your life apart.

Using Coaction to Change Multiple Habits

Remember that the TTM principles and processes of change, such as increasing the pros and decreasing the cons to progress to effective action, can be applied to at least fifty unhealthy behaviors. You have been raising your behavior change IQ and by now should be prepared to tackle most any bad habit you choose to change. "Coaction" is a new principle that can dramatically reduce the time and effort it can take to successfully change your habit of choice. First, you can apply the principle of coaction—in which changing one behavior, like being sedentary, can significantly increase the likelihood of changing a second risk behavior, like unhealthy eating.

We have found that when applying the coaction principle, self-changers can have success when they apply each of the change principles and processes to a primary behavior. Then with one or more secondary behaviors, they can have similar outcomes when they apply a single process at each Stage of Change. This type of synergy can reduce the time and effort self-changers need to dedicate to changing multiple behaviors. For example, they would apply all the change principles and processes toward becoming regular exercisers, then apply the process that would work the best to another behavior like healthy eating.

We'll now take a look at the principles and processes that can have the biggest impact at each Stage of Change.

Increasing Your Pros to Move beyond Precontemplation

You probably won't be surprised that increasing your pros for changing an added behavior is the most effective way to move beyond precontemplation to contemplation. Take procrastination, for example. If you keep procrastinating on changing one of your top threats, it certainly can hurt your health. But you've already learned what to do: Generate as full a list of the pros, or benefits, that will come from getting free from procrastinating. Don't limit your list to your imagination. Google "procrastination," and you can find more pros that you can add to your list. Or ask some of your friends for ideas.

Moving from Contemplation to Preparation Using Self-Reevaluation

The best process for moving from contemplation to preparation is self-reevaluation (creating a new self-image). So, model some of the change exercises you have practiced to date. Ask yourself how you think and feel about yourself when doing your unhealthy habit and how you would think and feel about yourself if you were instead doing the healthy behavior.

Here is an example:

How do I see myself as a procrastinator?	How would I see myself when free from procrastinating?

Moving from Preparation to Action Using Self-Liberation

The most effective way to move from preparation to action is by using self-liberation (making a commitment). The more people you tell about your plan to get free from procrastination, the more you strengthen your willpower. So, make a list like the one below, on a separate paper or electronic sheet, of who you will tell about your intentions to change an unhealthy behavior.

My List of People to Tell about My Upcoming Change:

1. _____

2. _____

3. _____

4. _____

5. _____

Try to add to your list as you progress.

Next, give yourself three choices for how you will start to change your procrastination, such as

1. Responding to communications in a timely fashion

2. Handling your finances on time

3. Starting to work on one of your top unhealthy behaviors

Strengthen your commitment by making your choice and practicing it.

Progressing from Action to Maintenance Using Counter Conditioning

Counter conditioning (substituting healthy behaviors and thoughts for unhealthy ones) is a major way to move from action to maintenance. What is it that you have to counter to free yourself from procrastination? The bad news is you need to use one of the most powerful laws of human behavior, one of Parkinson's Laws, which states: "Work expands so as to fill the time available for its completion." This means it will take you as long to complete a task as the time you allot to it. How can you counter this tendency? Set reasonable time limits.

One of Parkinson's principles states that Parkinson's Law will control your behavior unless you control his law.[60]

So, for you to complete tasks in a timely fashion, you will need to condition yourself to set reasonable time limits on tasks at both work and home. Even when there is a set deadline for a task, you can put yourself (and others) under increasing stress and distress as the time limit approaches and you feel like you're running out of time. So it's important to condition yourself to set your own reasonable time limits that help you manage stress, as well as time, more effectively.

Start with some small steps. On your lists of people you are going to tell about your new commitment to change, add a reasonable time limit for when you will do it. When deciding which area to tackle first—like communications, finances, or working on your other top threats—set a time limit. When you make a to-do list, put a time limit after each task. Make it *your* time limit, not someone else's (like your boss's), otherwise you can be controlled by deadlines that will only add stress and distress.

Remember that the more progress you make on each of the top threats to your health and happiness, the more you will enhance multiple areas of well-being. In the next chapter, you will learn how removing each threat also enhances multiple areas of well-being. You will discover how the improvements you are making can allow you to function better at home and at work. These elements of well-being can help you be more productive by tackling your procrastination and other threats to your well-being, allowing you to move in a positive direction.

12

Reducing Multiple High-Risk Behaviors

TO INCREASE MULTIPLE AREAS OF WELL-BEING

As we've shown in previous chapters, the Principles of Progress can be applied to a single behavior, like stress or smoking, or to multiple behaviors, like diet and exercise for healthy weight management, or as we learned in the last chapter, other behavioral threats to your health, such as sleep deprivation. Building on these common elements of change, we then added strategies to deal with multiple high-risk behaviors by increasing areas of physical, emotional, and social well-being.

Now we will add strategies to further help you as you continue to change and thrive. You will be driving change on two fronts: As you reduce your negative behaviors or unhealthy habits, you will increase your positive and healthy behaviors, with the added benefit of increasing your overall health and happiness.

Improving Your Physical Well-Being

Here is a winning formula to enhance your physical health: 0, 1, 2, 5, 10, and 20. Smoke 0 cigarettes, and drink 0 alcohol if you are recovering from alcohol addiction (a moderate to severe alcohol use disorder). If you aren't addicted, but your drinking has caused you problems, drink a maximum of 1 alcoholic beverage per day if you are a woman or if you are a man over sixty and drink a maximum of 2 alcoholic beverages per day if you are a man under sixty. Eat 5 cups of fruits and vegetables a day (for example, 2 cups of fruit and 3 cups of vegetables). Walk at least 10 thousand steps per day. Do deep relaxation exercises for at least

20 minutes per day. Think of 0, 1, 2, 5, 10, and 20 as a winning lottery ticket for a longer life. Research shows that if you "bet" on this set of numbers every day, you can be in the group that has the best health.

Unfortunately, less than 5 percent of the adults in the United States are in this group and practice this winning health formula. To see where you currently stand with your health habits, in the Health row of the following table, put a check mark under the rating that best reflects your physical health. You may want to recreate this table on a digital or paper sheet to have the results in your journal for future review.

Then, under your rating, write how many of the five big unhealthy habits you still have. Remember, these habits include smoking, alcohol abuse, unhealthy eating, sedentary behavior, and ineffective stress management.

	EXCELLENT	GOOD	FAIR	POOR
Health				
Number of High-Risk Behaviors (1–5)				

Now compare your ratings of the big five high-risk behaviors to averages from a broad range of people who have participated in our programs.

	EXCELLENT	GOOD	FAIR	POOR
Number of High-Risk Behaviors	0–1 unhealthy habits	2 unhealthy habits	3–4 unhealthy habits	5 unhealthy habits

You may have rated your current physical health as excellent yet still have three or four of the big five health risks discussed in this book. If so, it is excellent if you are continuing to invest your time and effort to progress toward getting free from these threats to your health and happiness. However, if you've already given up on your ability to change these behaviors, you are at risk of losing the healthy "lottery" and facing declining health and happiness in the future.

You may have noticed that individuals with only one of the big five threats can still be in the group with excellent health. But you should be aware that people who smoke almost never have just one single risky behaviors. The same is true for people who abuse alcohol. The general rule of thumb is the more severe your habit (like being quite sedentary or severely overweight because of a poor diet), the more likely you are to have more than one of these threats.

The message here is keep on progressing through the Stages of Change. This includes moving into long-term maintenance and ideally to termination to achieve or sustain excellent health. Also, remember that if you have a chronic condition that you manage well, you can still attain or maintain a life that is essentially healthy and happy. And in the case of some chronic conditions like heart disease, you may well be able to substantially reduce the problem or reverse the condition altogether.

Improving Your Emotional Well-Being

Psychologists long assumed that if we decreased negatives like depression or marital stress, positive behaviors would take their place. But this thinking has changed over the years as more studies find that reducing depression does not automatically increase happiness, just as reducing marital distress does not automatically increase marital happiness. Unlike the positive linking of diet and exercise, where changes in one behavior increase changes in the second behavior, behaviors like depression and marital stress appear to change independently.

Studies show that when depression is reduced by at least 50 percent, the emotions remaining are not particularly positive.[61] We have emphasized how important it is to manage stress and distress in healthy ways rather than falling into risky habits like smoking, drinking too much alcohol, eating unhealthily, or not getting enough exercise. Here are some more evidence-based strategies you can use to increase your positives and thereby your happiness and overall well-being.

Increase Your Positive Emotions to Achieve Happiness and Well-Being

Based on our experience with most self-changers who practice TTM, we are assuming that at this point most of you have progressed to the action or maintenance stage regarding stress or distress reduction. If you are not in action yet, this chapter can provide a boost. Think of these strategies as happiness exercises that can not only help you reduce negatives like stress, distress, depression, or anxiety but can also help you to increase multiple positive emotions that are essential for happiness.

In her 2009 award-winning book *Positivity,* University of North Carolina professor Barbara Frederickson writes that a major goal when working with people with depression is to focus on positives.[62] Rather than "happiness," she prefers the term "positivity" because she is concerned that the concept of happiness is overused and unclear. Jan and I agree that the term "happiness" is overused, such as in popular TV advertisements for sodas that would have us believe happiness can be found in a bottle of what is basically sugar water.

Because we believe happiness is a much more profound and meaningful phenomenon that, for us, is best represented by multiple areas of well-being, we find Frederickson's formula for emotional happiness extremely useful. Fredrickson found that having three times more positive emotions than negative ones is the most reliable road to emotional happiness. This formula indicates that emotional happiness does not require the complete absence of negative emotions and experiences. That is a fantasy life. But a happier life clearly calls for more positives than negatives. Her conclusions parallel what we learned decades ago: When self-changers find twice as many pros (or positives) than they have reasons for not changing (cons), the negatives for changing decrease accordingly. But it should be clear that your pros should include a full range of areas of well-being and not just *emotional* well-being. In her book, Frederickson identifies ten positive emotions, which we believe will increase a self-changer's well-being:

1. "Serenity" is the end result of reducing negative stress and distress by countering them with positive alternatives, like deep relaxation. Frederickson prefers meditation to help your mind and body feel completely relaxed. Studies show that just twenty minutes of deep relaxation each day in a safe and secure environment can benefit both mind and body. Hopefully you already have developed your own relaxation techniques for letting go of the stress and other negative emotions and experiences in your daily life. If not, please revisit the relevant sections in chapter 4.

2. "Interest" means finding something new or different that captures your attention, filling you with a sense of possibility. Interest builds heavily on the change processes of consciousness raising and counter conditioning, discussed in chapters 4 and 5. When you encounter a new set of challenges, you face an opportunity to build new skills. Hopefully, the increasing challenges in this book can capture your attention, such as synergistic strategies and skills for changing multiple behaviors.

3. "Hope" reflects the yearning for things to be better: better solutions to unhealthy habits, better emotions to counter distress and depression. In earlier chapters, we talked about how important hope is for people who are demoralized about their ability to lose weight, quit smoking, or stop abusing alcohol. Focusing on the positives (the pros) provides hope for not only reducing problems like depression but hope for replacing depression with a life filled by mostly positive emotions.

4. "Inspiration" involves witnessing human nature at its best. Such inspirational stories can uplift us, warm our hearts, and draw us in. Inspiration represents the positive side of the process of dramatic relief, where dramatic success stories elicit positive feelings. Jan loves the *CBS News Sunday Morning* television show and begins most days by watching a recorded segment of it. I love when she shares one of the program's many positive stories that show someone doing or experiencing something new to us. Similarly, we are inspired when our young grandchildren teach

us things we never knew before. In this book, we tried to share the extraordinary inspiration we experienced from those who taught us so much about the Stages of Change. Their generosity in sharing their experiences added greatly to what we learned from studying multiple theories of psychotherapy and behavior change. Their personal stories revealed the Stages of Change and made them real.

5. "Awe" is the feeling of being overwhelmed by amazing beauty, like a sunset that fills almost the entire sky, or the sensation of the extraordinary goodness in the world that can sometimes fill our hearts. Jan and I often experience this as we see the world through the innocent eyes of our grandchildren who regularly find things that we take for granted—it's "awesome!"

6. "Amusement" is the gift of laughter. What makes you laugh? Who makes you laugh? Do you seek out those experiences and people? I don't see my two best lifelong friends often enough but when I do, our time together is filled with joyful laughter. Laughter can be such a dramatic relief for times when we face too many demands and not enough resources to cope with those demands. Jan and I always laughed together when we watched a favorite television comedy show, *Everybody Loves Raymond*. We have a special attachment to that show, since we are friends of Steve Skrovan, one of the show's top writers. Among the other things he does, Steve serves as auctioneer every summer for a fund-raiser on Star Island, a place we've gone to for years with family and friends. On one occasion, he used his spontaneous wit and good humor to get his wife and sister-in-law to bid against each other for a week at a condo they were going to share anyway. Do you have favorite funny TV shows or movies? Who's your favorite funny person, whether a comedian or a friend with a great sense of humor? Do you make seeing it or them a priority?

7. "Gratitude" is the feeling of appreciation we have when something good comes our way or just for the everyday gifts that life brings. It opens our hearts with the urge to give back. When was the last time you felt grateful or thankful, when you felt deep appreciation for something, no matter how big or small? For example, Jan and I feel such gratitude when a friend spontaneously expresses affection or appreciation for our friendship. It's important for us that we let the person know how moved we were by this message. Gratitude is a key component in forming helping relationships.

8. "Joy" can be like a bright light bursting out of the darkness. There is a movie and a book called *The Unbearable Lightness of Being*. For us, joy represents the *bearable lightness of well-being*. In these times that all too often seem troubled, it can be hard to find time or room for joy. As you've probably gathered by now, our grandchildren are a constant source of joy for Jan and me. We love cooking with twelve-year-old Zach and ten-year-old Lila. I tell people the stereotype has it all wrong: Grandparents don't spoil grandchildren; grandchildren spoil us. What brings you joy? Can you relive times of joy through warm memories? Our hope is you will also feel the joy of changing.

9. "Pride" is the feeling that can be generated by succeeding in an effort that we are heavily invested in. We hope that each successful step you take in progressing against the biggest threats to your health and happiness generates a sense of pride. Feeling pride is one of the ways to reinforce your progress: progress generates pride, which generates more progress. We have already shared with you the pride that several self-changers had in succeeding against one of the toughest challenges in their life, like quitting smoking or drinking, after years of trying. Remember the story of our friend Don, the owner of the shoeshine stand, and the pride that all of us felt when he and his wife both had such success with the Stages of Change?

10. "Love" reflects the deep attachment and attraction we have for the special people, activities, ideas, experiences, and things in our lives. Select the forms that love has taken in your life from the list below and write them on a separate electronic or digital sheet. Add more things you love to your list as you think of them.

☐ love of a parent

☐ love of a child

☐ love of a spouse or partner

☐ love of a friend

☐ love of pets and other animals

☐ love of learning

☐ love of music

☐ love of a Higher Being

☐ love of travel

☐ love of nature

☐ love of our culture

☐ love of cooking and good food

☐ love of country

☐ love of freedom

☐ love of life itself

☐ more things that you love (list on a separate sheet)

Somehow love seems like the most positive force in life. But as the title of a great book by Bruno Bettelheim says, *Love Is Not Enough*—it takes more positives than love to experience lasting change. But love is certainly an essential ingredient for change and an effective emotion to embrace that can help you affirm all the ways you are changing to thrive.

Jan has found that practicing the ten positives has been very helpful to her health and well-being. When she has trouble sleeping from too much stress, she doesn't count sheep; she recalls the ways she experienced each of the ten positive emotions that day. The joy of having won a tennis match; the gratitude for the help she received from an employee at work; the hope for an even better life in our move to California; the serenity of the quiet living in the woods; the love of me (I hope!); the pride in how she helped an ex-prisoner to thrive; the interest she gets from reading a new book each week; the amusement of joking with a grandchild; the awe of driving over a beautiful bridge; the inspiration of seeing a *CBS News Sunday Morning* artist creating incredible sculptures from sand. If Jan finds she is "missing" one of the ten positives on a given day, she makes a point of taking time the next day to make room for the missing emotion. She would, for example, go out of her way on her drive to work to stop and look at a beautiful island in the middle of the bay.

These are just a few examples of some simple but effective ways to incorporate these positive emotions into our everyday lives. As we've stressed, practicing such positives helps to decrease the negatives that get in the way of long-lasting change and well-being.

Improving Your Social Well-Being by Sharing Your Changes

In the spirit of synergy, we will now build on these ten strategies for emotional well-being to enhance social networks. As you may have experienced, social networks can pull you in the wrong direction—even from a distance. Remember our earlier discussion of weight in which we explained how individuals who gained weight on one side of the continent influenced friends and family on the other side to also gain weight? To prevent this from happening, we want to help you be proactive and reach out to your social networks to influence them to support you in a *positive direction*. One way to do that is by sharing your happiness exercises with them.

1. *Serenity.* Most people choose to do serenity exercises like meditation in silent solitude to remove distractions (like a ringing cell phone). But after you emerge from deep relaxation or meditation, consider sharing with others what you have experienced, like peace and centeredness, and wish them the same well-being. When you share in such a way, they may give you positive reinforcement after seeing how important such practices are to you

and you encourage them to try some serenity exercises of their own.

2. *Interest.* When something new captures your attention, it is almost impossible not to share your enthusiasm with others. Hopefully you have been sharing each new challenge you have been tackling with the help of this book. We also expect that your sharing will be sensitive to the fact that some of your friends and family will not be prepared to take action on multiple behaviors or multiple areas of well-being. Just increasing their awareness of what is possible can have very positive impacts. Such sharing can also affect you in positive ways by strengthening your change process of commitment by going public with more people.

3. *Hope.* Sharing your hopes for a better life through a better way of changing has the potential to help those who may be demoralized from failed past attempts to change. In addition, it can be a way for them to support you positively because they see how important this is to you. You may want to give them a copy of this book so they'll have a better idea of what you're doing—and why you're doing it.

4. *Inspiration.* Just as Jan's sharing of inspiring stories adds to my own inspiration, your inspiration can benefit others while reinforcing your own positive emotion. Jan and I love to hear the stories self-changers share with us, and we invite you to also share your stories about the progress you are making with the Stages of Change so we can, in turn, inspire others by telling them about your success. Also remember that inspiration is a positive form of dramatic relief that can dramatically increase positive emotions and produce progress.

5. *Awe.* It is almost impossible not to share awesome experiences with others. Millions of photos of gorgeous sunsets, huge waves, crazy pet tricks, and works of art fly through cyberspace from friends to friends every day when they post the photos on Facebook or Instagram or describe them in a phone call or text. One of my favorite mottos is "Art is the source of my inspiration and science is the source of my validation."

6. *Amusement.* Laughter is often too spontaneous to share with others, but funny stories can help our family and friends "lighten up" a bit—especially when we tell funny stories where we laugh at ourselves and invite others to do the same. You can also watch your favorite comedians with others, either live or on TV, or go to funny movies together. Remember the story about my client with the severe inferiority complex who shared his belief that he was progressing by saying, "You know, Doc, I think I *am* getting better. Now I feel inferior to everybody but you."

7. *Gratitude.* This is also one of the emotions that is better shared. But too often we take for granted that our friends or family know we are grateful for something they have done. Remember that expressing our gratitude can add to our happiness as well as the happiness of others. If you haven't already, you may want to express your gratitude to family or friends who learned to be helpful by not pressuring you to take action when you were not yet prepared or who consistently support you in your efforts to change.

8. *Joy.* Like gratitude, joy is another positive emotion worth sharing. It gives Jan and me great joy to feel like we play a part in helping people lead happier, healthier lives by teaching them about the Stages of Change. We're hoping that you will also feel joy as you change and thrive and that when others witness how joyful you are, they will want to help you maintain your new healthy lifestyle.

9. *Pride.* Do not be humble when it comes to telling others about the monumental changes you have made with smoking, drinking, eating, moving, stress, or any other risky behaviors you've learned to manage. For so many of us, our history of change is like the "Myth of Mount Sisyphus." We roll a boulder or burden of our behavior farther and farther up Mount Change, only to have our powerful habits come rolling back over us. Sharing your pride of extraordinary accomplishments changing all-too-ordinary habits is a special way of rewarding yourself for a job well done.

10. *Love.* We are sure that your friends and family would love for you to share your list of the multiple forms that love has taken in your life. Invite others to make and share their own lists, so you can discover other ways you might bond and support each other.

Improving Your Purposeful Well-Being

Until recently, we called this area of well-being "work well-being" or "career well-being" because so many people define their purpose by their work. "What do you do?" is one of the first questions we are usually asked by someone new. "I'm a psychologist," I used to say. Often, they would then say, "Oh I better watch what I say!" So now I answer, "I am a professor." Oh, that's interesting. In what field?" "Psychology," I say. "Oh, I better watch what I say!" So not only does our job define our identity for us—it often defines it for others too.

Until recently, Jan would answer the what-do-you-do question by saying, "I am the president and CEO of Pro-Change Behavior Systems." Then she'd often get the reply, "Oh, that's interesting. But what do you do?" "We develop high-impact digital behavior change programs, like smoking cessation, stress management, or losing weight." Now she might answer, "I was the president and CEO of Pro-Change." Sometimes the current response is, "So you're retired?" When that happens, she says, "No, I'm 'repurposing' in order to have more focus to write, read, and help my family, friends, and community to thrive." Older people especially like her response.

Realizing that work is so connected to our sense of purpose, let's start by reflecting on ways that work can improve your well-being.

Review the following list and check ways that work currently enhances your well-being.

☐ Money

☐ Friends

☐ Sense of accomplishment

☐ Learning new things

☐ Respect from others

☐ Structuring my time

☐ Helping others

☐ Pride

☐ Being a role model for my kids or others

☐ Investments for retirement

☐ Feeling part of a team

☐ Feeling appreciated

☐ Creating a better future

☐ Making contacts

☐ Chances to advance

Total the number of items you checked (0–15): _____

Now, check all of the ways that your work detracts from your well-being.

☐ Not enough money

☐ A negative or problem employee at work

☐ Boring tasks

☐ Not enough respect from my boss or supervisor

☐ Not enough respect from other employees

☐ My commute

☐ Anxiety about the future of my job

☐ Anxiety about the future of my company or organization

☐ Not enough resources to do my job well

☐ Not enough time to do my job

☐ Too much stress

☐ Takes too much time away from what I like most to do

☐ No chance to advance

☐ Emails, texts, and phone messages at home

☐ What we do doesn't really help people

Total the number of items you checked (0–15): _____

For your work to best enhance your overall well-being, your total on the first set of positive items should be 10 or above. Also, your total on the first list should be at least four points higher than your total on the second list of negative things attached to your work experience.

In our experience working with self-changers who do this exercise, money matters the most for most employees. Earning enough money makes a big difference for them. Likewise, they tell us that not earning enough money makes their job less fulfilling. Besides money, here's what matters most for those who work at jobs that require greater education or more technical skills, using the numbers from the positive list: (3) A sense of accomplishment, (4) Learning new things, and (15) Chances to advance. For "support positions" that require less education or skill, what matters most are these positive numbers: (2) Friends, (5) Respect from others, (7) Helping others, and (12) Feeling appreciated. Here are the negative items that hurt well-being the most for people in most types of jobs: (2) A negative or problem employee at work, (6) Commute time, and (9) and (10) Not enough resources or time to do a job.

Many jobs—even high-salaried ones—involve highly repetitive tasks that can deaden spirits. At my university, for example, pharmacy students graduate with positions that have high prestige and one of the highest starting salaries around. But many pharmacists end up disliking their jobs. They quickly tire of filling prescription after prescription, day after day.

So what's a person with a boring job to do? One of the few most promising options is to have an "avocation"—a passion or hobby outside of their regular job that provides a sense of fulfillment or happiness and well-being. Let me share with pride what I witnessed as a kid growing up in a neighborhood surrounded by factories—Chrysler factories across one street, a huge Desoto factory across another, and a huge Dodge plant just a few blocks in a third direction. Many of the men and a few of the women could walk to work, so they at least did not suffer from a long commute. And many of the employees, like my father, had avocations that were more fulfilling than their jobs.

My dad's job was to attach bolts to a universal joint for Chrysler trucks. Minute after minute, day after day, and year after year, he attached his designated three bolts. There is no question this incredibly boring and alienating work did a job on my father's mood, mind, and future well-being. But some of his saving graces were his avocations. He was well known for his fishing expertise. He would take his small boat far out on Lake Superior on weekends when the wind was blowing in the right direction. And he would always catch his limit of seventy-five perch, each weighing a pound or two. Because Dad could only fit a small portion in our freezer, he would give fresh fish to our neighbors, friends, and relatives. Sometimes my sisters and I would get to go with him, even in the winter when he would drive out on the frozen lake to ice fish. More often, my father would fish alone and would enjoy many of the ten positive emotions we discussed earlier: the serenity away from a family of six as he patiently waited for the fish to bite; the awe and amusement when a three-foot pike or a five-foot sturgeon occasionally swallowed his bait; and the joy of giving to others.

Improving Your Financial Well-Being

As you might expect, there is a clear relationship between income and level of emotional well-being. The good news is that a 2010 study showed money and happiness part company at a certain salary level, which differs according to the size of the family.[63] In other words, money really can't buy more happiness—money beyond the level that meets basic financial needs does not lead to more and more happiness. This should not be too surprising considering what we know about people who have won big lotteries. Indeed, studies show how short-lived a lottery winner's happiness is after the initial shock and awe of suddenly being a millionaire wears off. When they get used to their new money, their happiness "relapses" back to what it was before they became rich; they usually seem more content because it's what they were used to.

That is not to say that you should not improve your financial well-being. Just be cautious about viewing money as a happiness solution. If you and your family are already earning a salary that easily provides for your financial security but you are not as happy as you would like to be, perhaps you should be spending more time and effort on increasing the ten positive emotions through personal and shared exercises to increase your happiness and social well-being.

That being said, there are healthy ways you can increase your financial well-being when it is necessary to do so. What distresses people most about their financial well-being is debt. And, as you may know, the most common distress is with credit card debt. Jan and I had the opportunity to work with Jean Chatzky, the author of *Pay It Down!*, in the development of a stage-based, TTM online "Debt Diet" program with Pro-Change Behavior Systems, Inc.[64] Users are staged on their readiness to start saving ten dollars a day and then given stage-matched activities to help them move through the Stages of Change. The goal of the program is to save $10 a day to get out of debt. If this is an unrealistic goal for those who are deeply in debt, it is suggested they save a lesser amount—whatever they think is doable. Self-changers who follow the TTM approach may be already saving money without realizing it. If they quit smoking or are progressing toward quitting, they can save an average of $4 to $8 a day, depending on their nicotine habit and the tobacco taxes in their state. Such savings can be used as a down payment on the $10-a-day plan; plus the savings on their health and well-being are even bigger bonuses. If self-changers quit drinking or reduce their alcohol habit significantly, they can save varying amounts, depending on how much they drink, what they drink, and where they drink. That amount can also be a decent down payment on their debt diet. Here again, the savings on their health and well-being are added pluses.

If self-changers cut back on the amount they spend on junk food, they can reduce their food budget by a comparable amount. Of course, how much they save also depends on how much they eat, what they eat, and where they eat. As we discussed in chapter 9, a recent report indicated that for the first time, people in the United States are consuming more food in restaurants than what they buy in grocery stores.[64] As a result, restaurant prices are increasing so customers are probably paying more. If you include the cost of traveling to restaurants, you could save even more by eating at home. An added bonus is that eating at home is often healthier.

One additional area where self-changers can save money is related to managing your stress and distress more effectively. As you know well by now, when stressed you are likely to smoke more, drink more, eat more, and take more drugs. You are more likely to go to the doctor, go shopping, and gamble more. Add in the costs of more illness and missing work, and you have more money for your debt diet.

For every $100 you pay down on your credit card debt, you are probably saving an additional $15 to $25 in interest that you would have paid the credit card company. These days, it's almost impossible to safely get a 15 to 25 percent return on your investment.

If debt is not a problem for you, what percent of your income do you save? The recommended goal these days is 15 percent. You may want to consider contributing some of your savings to your company's retirement plan, if they have one—especially if it includes an employer matching contribution. The average person in the United States saves only about 5 percent, so you will need to be above average to reach this suggested savings goal.

What we have seen in this chapter is that multiple healthy behaviors can indirectly enhance multiple areas of well-being. And one can go further and add strategies to directly increase different areas of well-being. We will close out our book by combining changes in each of the five major threats with multiple areas of well-being to show you how you can progress to a higher level of living—one where you can be thriving most of the time.

EPILOGUE

A Life of Well-Being

In the healthy eating chapter, we discussed how our stage-matched programs often produce increasing trajectories where people continue to progress long after our program has ended. With our healthy weight management project, for example, our participants continued to lose weight long after their treatment program ended. This pattern contrasts sharply with the decreasing trajectories typically found with other programs, where participants begin to gain weight soon after they complete them.

The message here is that you can continue to progress toward a healthier and happier life long after you finish this book. For now, let's chart your trajectory on each of the five biggest threats to your health and well-being covered in these pages. Look at figure 5 and first put an X on the line that represents the stage you were in with each of the five threats when you started this book. (The stages are abbreviated because of space limitations).

If you never acquired a high-risk habit, like smoking, put an X on the line under M for maintaining your status of being a nonsmoker.

FIGURE 5

Your Trajectory

PC – Precontemplation	PR – Preparation	M – Maintenance
C – Contemplation	A – Action	T – Termination

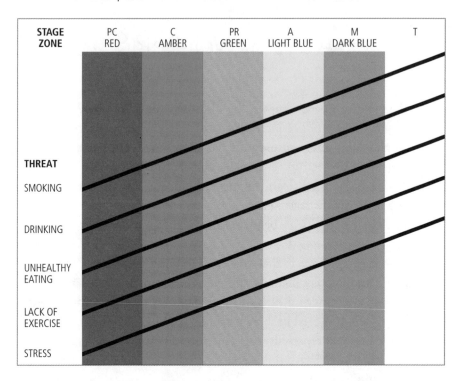

On figure 6 you will see my X under maintenance because I never identified as being a smoker. On figure 6, I also charted the stage I was in for the other four threats when I began to write the chapters on healthy eating and adequate exercise. I had relapsed back to the contemplation stage for eating and exercise because of the stress and distress I was experiencing from all the demanding transitions I was going through: trying to close out a long troubled project, moving across the country from Rhode Island to California, making hundreds of decisions related to the move, and having to stop progress on this book because of all the other demands. So, check my Xs under C for contemplation about eating, exercise, and healthy stress management. Fortunately, I did not relapse to risky drinking, so I put my X under maintenance in that risk category.

Next I put a circled X, under the stage that I am currently in for each of these three threats. You can see that, for each of these three threats, each circled X is in the A for action column. The arrows heading upwards on the lines indicate I am on an increasing trajectory because I am highly confident I will progress to maintenance soon after this book is completed.

FIGURE 6

Example: My Trajectory

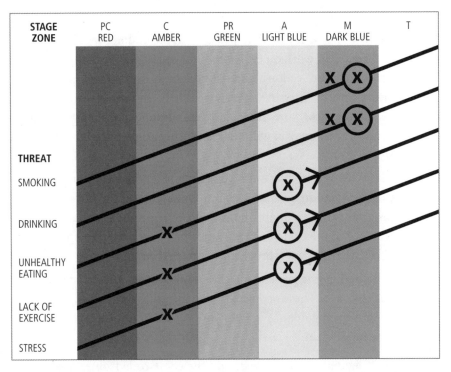

	PC – Precontemplation		**PR** – Preparation		**M** – Maintenance	
	C – Contemplation		**A** – Action		**T** – Termination	

Now it's your turn. Look at figure 5 again. For each of the five big threats you are dealing with, put a circled X under your current stage. For example, if you started in the precontemplation (PC) stage for smoking, you would place an X in the red zone. If you have now progressed to action, you would place a circled X under the A column in the light blue zone.

Here's what we want you to do next. For each risky behavior where you progressed one stage or more, congratulate yourself. You are on an increasing trajectory to become free from that health threat. For each threat where you placed a circled X in action or maintenance, give yourself even heartier congratulations. You are in a blue zone.

If your circled Xs are all in action or maintenance, you deserve an award. You are in rare company, since less than 5 percent of adults in the United States have none of the five big threats.

If you have not progressed on one or more of your biggest threats, know that we share your disappointment. But try not to get demoralized. Here are several strategies that could help you move onto an increasing trajectory:

1. Choose the behavior that you are furthest along in the stages and return to work on that section of the book, for example, the contemplation section about risky drinking in chapter 8. Put extra effort into progressing, such as by reducing the cons and re-evaluating how you think and feel about yourself as a risky drinker and how you will think and feel about yourself as a low-risk or nondrinker.

2. Access Pro-Change's online LifeStyle Management Suite that provides National Committee on Quality Assurance–accredited programs that are highly tailored to your personal needs. There is a fee, but the evidence clearly indicates these programs are cost effective. Go to www.prochange.com/myhealth

3. Talk to a helping professional, like your doctor, nurse, pastor, or a health coach. These people can provide more individualized and personalized guidance to help you to break out of the place you may be stuck in.

Look at figure 5 again and focus on the color-coded zones. The red zone represents precontemplation because this is the stage where most people get stopped or stuck. The amber zone represents contemplation, because of the ambivalence that can signal caution about going further. The green zone represents the preparation stage where you can get the green flag to move on full speed ahead.

Why do you think we use blue zones to represent the action and maintenance stages? We got the idea for blue zones from the name Dan Buettner used in his book *Blue Zones* to describe the rare places in the world where people live the healthiest and the longest.[66] In these blue zones, many more people live into their 90s and 100s than you find in almost all other places in the world. Not only do they have greater quantity of life, they also have better quality of life. In the United States, people on average spend their last four years on rapidly decreasing trajectories as their quality of life deteriorates. They experience more pain, more fatigue, more depression, poor functioning, more medications, and more surgery as the cons of living increase. As many studies have shown, by far and away more money is spent not on health care but on sick care during these deteriorating times of life.

If a fraction of those funds had been spent on health care, which includes helping people change the big five threats to their health and well-being, most of us could live healthier lives, longer lives, and happier lives for practically our whole lives. That's the lesson Buettner shares from what he learned about the blue zones. People who live in these zones don't deteriorate over four years due to chronic diseases. They die in a brief time, like six months, from what we learned as kids to call dying from old age—the time when our biological clocks run out.

In the blue zones, people are blessed not only with an absence of the biggest threats to our health, but also with purposeful lives that include high levels of social and emotional well-being. Most of the time, they feel at their best and they function at their best. They thrive for most of their lives.

So let's add the key indicators of well-being and thriving to our trajectories. Following are five critical questions that can help you assess whether you are likely to be thriving over extended periods of time.

Imagine a ladder with steps numbered from 0 at the bottom to 10 at the top. The top of the ladder represents the best possible life for you, and the bottom of the ladder represents the worst possible life for you.[67]

1. First, think of the most recent bad time in your life. With your best guess, circle which step you think you were standing on at that time.

WORST POSSIBLE LIFE   BEST POSSIBLE LIFE

| 1 | 2 | 3 | 4 | 5 | 7 | 8 | 9 | 10 |

2. Circle the step of the ladder that shows where you feel you personally stand at this time.

WORST   BEST

| 1 | 2 | 3 | 4 | 5 | 7 | 8 | 9 | 10 |

3. Make your best guess about which step you think you will stand on in the future—about five years from now.

WORST   BEST

| 1 | 2 | 3 | 4 | 5 | 7 | 8 | 9 | 10 |

Next are two key questions that can help you track how well you are thriving from day to day and week to week. Please circle the number that best represents the following:

1. How are you feeling today?

AT MY WORST   AT MY BEST

| 1 | 2 | 3 | 4 | 5 | 7 | 8 | 9 | 10 |

2. How are you functioning today?

WORST   BEST

| 1 | 2 | 3 | 4 | 5 | 7 | 8 | 9 | 10 |

Look at figure 7 to see how I've charted these answers on the color-coded trajectories. Now look at figure 8 and place an X on the number that represents your answer to each of the five questions above. For example, I put an X through 1 for how I think I would have evaluated my life during my most recent bad time. I put an X through 7 to reflect how I evaluate my current life. And I put an X through 9 to reflect how I imagine I'll feel about my life in the future. Then I put Xs through how I am feeling today (6) and functioning today (9). When I look at my life evaluation for past, present, and future, I see a pattern of an increasing trajectory. In a most recent bad time, I was in the red zone, which is a serious signal that I was suffering. In the present, however, I am flying high in the blue zone. Given my optimistic bias and where we now live, I imagine myself flying even higher.

FIGURE 7

Example: My Life Evaluation

PC – Precontemplation	**PR** – Preparation	**M** – Maintenance
C – Contemplation	**A** – Action	**T** – Termination

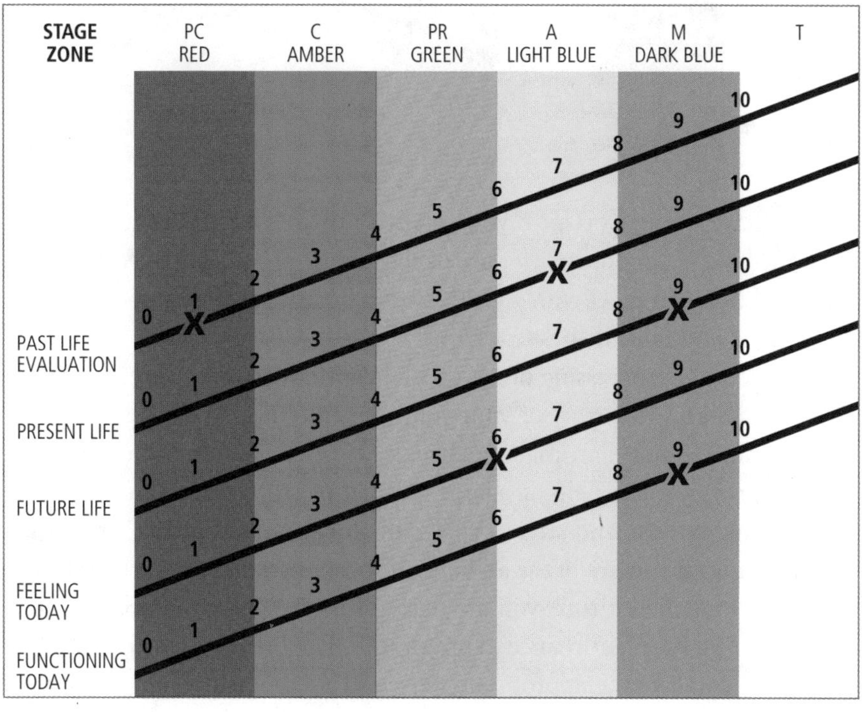

FIGURE 8

Your Life Evaluation

PC – Precontemplation	PR – Preparation	M – Maintenance
C – Contemplation	A – Action	T – Termination

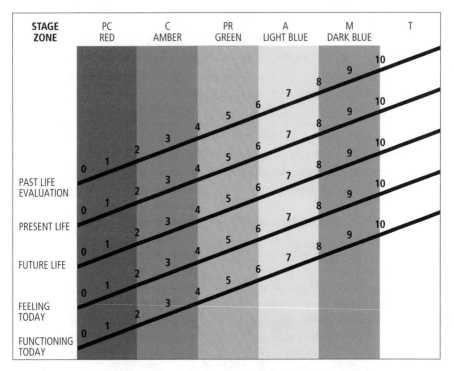

What zone are you in? If you are presently in the red zone and think you will be in the future, you are likely suffering. If this is the case, it is critical that you meet with your doctor to determine the causes of your suffering and find the best solutions.

If you are progressing on threats related to inadequate exercise and stress management, part of your solution should be to continue moving toward action and maintenance, if you can. Remember our well-being project where helping a large number of self-changers progress to action on exercise and stress management also helped people progress to thriving? If you are in the amber zone now and still see yourself there in your imagined future, you are likely to be struggling. However, you also have an excellent chance to progress to the blue zone where you can thrive if you take the appropriate steps and get the help you need now.

Our goal, of course, is to get to the blue zone. Hopefully you know that the freer you are from the biggest health threats addressed in this book, the more you are likely to live in the blue zone. What drives us to make such life-saving and life-enhancing changes? Progressing from one stage to the next by raising the benefits, or pros, of living in a blue zone and lowering the cons of not living in this reality of well-being and happiness. But remember, it's not just a matter of reducing bad habits, such as smoking and unhealthy eating. It is also a matter of enhancing the positive areas of well-being. As you track how well you are feeling and functioning from day to day, remember to use Barbara Fredrickson's positivity rule of 3 to 1. In an average week, if you spend five or six days in the blue zone, your happiness should be high. We know that not every day is going to be a blue-sky day emotionally and psychologically. But if you are spending too much time from day to day in the red or amber zone, we suggest returning to chapter 12 on well-being and focus more on increasing positivity for feeling at your best and prepare for functioning at your best.

When we build on the basic processes of life, we are freer to breathe the fresh air that often comes with the fresh blue skies of well-being. We discover that we don't need to drink or drug to get high on life. We do need to eat well to stay well. We need to move it, move it, move it. As we've emphasized, research shows that people who walk faster, live longer. So pick up the pace, so you can be more productive and purposeful. Unlike the fortunate people who were born into blue zones, the rest of us have to keep making the efforts to build and rebuild our own blue zones. Think of those who have been successful in maintaining significant weight loss. They do this by eating healthy, exercising healthily, and building healthy habits that can help them live happier lives. They have truly learned how to change to thrive.

Jan and I are grateful that you have let us into your lives even for a little while as you've read this book and used TTM in your own journey of change. We have tried to bring you the best of what behavior change science has to offer. We realize it isn't easy to make the significant life changes we've discussed in these pages. We know we've asked a lot of you, but we want you to experience the joy of well-being that so many other self-changers have gotten from our program.

It is our deep hope that you continue to progress long after we part company and that your future will be filled with good health and happiness and more days in which you thrive than you ever thought possible.

Acknowledgments

The continuing development of the Transtheoretical Model of Behavior Change has been a collaborative effort involving so many dedicated individuals who have made invaluable contributions. These include Drs. Wayne F. Velicer, Carlo C. DiClemente, Joseph S. Rossi, Colleen A. Redding, Sara S. Johnson, Kerry E. Evers, Bryan Blissmer, Andrea L. Paiva, Geoff Greene, Leanne Mauriello, Deborah A. Levesque, Carol O. Cummins, Seth Crothers, John C. Norcross, Patty H. Castle, Janet Johnson, Robert G. Laforge, Ben Leedle, James Pope, Crockett Dale, and Anne Marie Ludovici.

Others making special contributions include Kathryn S. Meier, Terri-Lyn Hodson, Tracey Barton, Valerie Hupf, and the entire staff and students at the Cancer Prevention Research Center and Pro-Change Behavior Systems, Inc. We also appreciate the expert feedback on healthy eating from Marily Ann Oppezzo, PhD, MS, RD.

Together we have had the privilege of publishing with more than 250 colleagues and students, simply too many to thank individually. Their numerous contributions have been so important to advancing the work we draw upon in this book.

We gratefully acknowledge the financial support we have received over decades from the National Institutes of Health, the American Cancer Society, the Robert Wood Johnson Foundation, Johnson & Johnson, Healthways, Healthstat, the University of Rhode Island, and Pro-Change Behavior Systems, Inc. Senior leaders at the University of Rhode Island, such as former president Robert Carothers, former dean Richard Gelles, current dean Winnie Brownell, and provost Donald DeHayes, have made extraordinary efforts to support our work. We cherish the sharing from thousands of participants in our research programs and interventions who have proven to be the ultimate teachers of how people change.

Sid Farrar and Cynthia Orange, our editors, committed their vitality to help transform our shared vision into a reality. The assistance of the staff at Hazelden Publishing is particularly appreciated given the special mission we share.

Our families and friends are the foundation for creative inspiration and personal support. Our children and their spouses, Jason and Gabrielle Prochaska, and Jodi and Mark Martini, are dedicated professionals, parents, and partners. Friends like Kathy and Hal DeHaven, Dorothy and Jim Youmans, Joel and Fran Cohen, Caroline Calia, Mary Ladiera, Vince Pope, and Jim Hadley are always present in our thoughts even from across the continent. We dedicate *Changing to Thrive* to our grandchildren who help us to thrive in so many ways.

Notes

1. Berrigan, D., Dodd, K., Troiano, R. P., Kerbs-Smith, S. M., & Barbash, R.B. (2003). Patterns of health behavior in U.S. adults. *Preventive Medicine, 26,* 615–623.

2. Connors, G. J., Walitzer, K. S., & Dermen, K. H. (2002). Preparing clients for alcoholism treatment: Effects on treatment participation and outcomes. *Journal of Consulting and Clinical Psychology, 70,* 1161–1169.

3. Prochaska, J. O., Norcross, J. C., Fowler, J. L., Follick, M. J., & Abrams, D. B. (1992). Attendance and outcome in a worksite weight control program: Processes and stages of change as process and predictor variables. *Additive Behaviors, 17,* 35–45.

4. Cohen, S., Lichtenstein, E., Prochaska, J. O., Rossi, J. S., Gritz, E. R., Carr, C. R., Orleans, C. T., Schoenbach, V. J., Biener, L., Abrams, D., DiClemente, C., Curry, S., Marlatt, G. A., Cummings, K. M., Emont, S. L., Giovino, G., & Ossip-Klein, D. (1989). Debunking myths about self-quitting: Evidence from ten prospective studies of persons quitting smoking by themselves. *American Psychologist, 44,* 1355–1365.

5. Beckie, T. M., Mendonca, M. A., Fletcher, G. F., Schocken, D. D., Evans, M. E., & Banks, S. M. (2009). Examining the challenges of recruiting women into a cardiac rehabilitation clinical trial. *Journal of Cardiopulmonary Rehabilitation and Prevention, 29* (1), 13–21. Quiz, 22–23.

6. Wallace, K. (2015, November 3). Teens spend a 'mind-boggling' 9 hours a day using media, report says. CNN. Retrieved from www.cnn.com/2015/11/03/health/teens-tweens-media-screen-use-report/

7. Brogan, M. M., Prochaska, J. O., & Prochaska, J. M. (1999). Predicting termination and continuation status in psychotherapy using the Transtheoretical Model. *Psychotherapy, 36,* 105–113.

8. Connors, et al. (2002).

9. Yang, G., Ma, J., Chen, A. (2001). Smoking cessation in China: Findings from the 1996 national prevalence survey. *Tobacco Control, 10* (2), 170–4.

10. The Health Consequences of Smoking—50 Years of progress. A Report of the Surgeon General 2014. www.surgeongeneral.gov.

11. Lichtenstein, E., & Hollis, J. (1992). Patient referral to a smoking cessation program: Who follows through? *Journal of Family Practice, 34* (6), 739–744.

12. Ibid.

13. Prochaska, J. O., DiClemente, C. C., Velicer, W. F., Ginpil, S., & Norcross, J. C. (1985). Predicting change in smoking status for self-changers. *Addictive Behaviors, 10* (4), 395–406.

14. Hunt, Barnett, & Branch. (1971). Relapse rates in addiction programs. *Journal of Clinical Psychology, 27,* 455–456; Hunt, W. A. (Ed.). (2007). *Learning Mechanisms in Smoking.* New Brunswick, NJ: Aldine Transaction.

15. Norcross, J. C., & Vangarelli, D. J. (1989). The resolution solution: Longitudinal examination of New Year's change attempts. *Journal of Substance Abuse, 1,* 127–134.

16. Duke Study: Exercise has long-lasting effect on Depression (2000). *Duke Today.* https://today.duke.edu/2000/09/exercise922.html.

17. McHugh, R. K., Whitten, S. W., Peckham, A. D., Welge, J. A., & Otto, M. W. (2013). Patient preference for psychological vs. pharmacologic treatment of psychiatric disorders: A meta-analytic review. *Journal of Clinical Psychiatry, 74* (6), 595–602.

18. Velicer, W. F., Prochaska, J. O., Rossi, J. S., & Snow, M. (1992). Assessing outcome in smoking cessation studies. *Psychological Bulletin, 11,* 23–41.

19. U.S. Department of Health and Human Services. (1990). The Health Benefits of Smoking Cessation. DHHS Publication No. (CDC) 90-8416. Retrieved from: https://profiles.nlm.nih.gov/ps/access/NNBBCT.pdf

20. Hunt (2007).

21. Janis, I. L., & Mann, L. (1977). *Decision Making.* London: Cassel and Collier Macmillan.

22. Hall, K. L., & Rossi, J. S. (2008). Meta-analytic examination of the strong and weak principles across 48 health behaviors. *Preventive Medicine, 46* (3), 266–274.

23. Freud, S. (1919). *Turnings in the ways of psychoanalytic therapy.* Collected Papers Vol. 2. London: Hogarth.

24. Perls, F. (1969). *Gestalt Therapy Verbatim.* Lafayette, CA: Real People Press.

25. May, R. (1958). *The origins and significance of the existential movement to psychology.* In R. May, E., Angel, & H. Ellengerger (Eds.), *Existence.* New York: Basic Books.

26. Wolpe, J. (1990). *The Practice of Behavior Therapy* (4th Ed.). Elmsford, NY: Pergamon.

27. Skinner, B. F. (1971). *Beyond Freedom and Dignity.* New York: Vintage.

28. Misleading claims about Safeway wellness incentives (2010). *The Seattle Times.* Retrieved from www.seattletimes.com/nation-world/misleading-claims-about-safeway-wellness-incentives

29. Curcio, V. (2013). *Henry Ford (Lines and Legacies Series).* New York: Oxford University Press.

30. Rogers, C. R. (1951). *Client centered therapy.* Boston: Houghton Mifflin.

31. Miller, W. R., & Rollnick, S. (2002). *Motivational Interviewing: Preparing People for Change.* New York: Guilford.

32. Kornblum, J. (2006, June 22). Study: 25% of Americans have no one to confide in. *USA Today.* Retrieved from http://usatoday30.usatoday.com/news/nation/2006-06-22-friendship_x.htm

33. Christakis, N. A., & Fowler, J. H. (2009). *Connected.* New York: Little, Brown and Company.

34. Luepker, R. V., Murray, D. M., Jacobs, D. R., Mittelmask, M. B., Bracht, N., Carlaw, R., Crow, R., Elmes, P., Finnegan, J., & Folsm, A. R. (1994). Community education for cardiovascular disease prevention: Risk factor changes in Minnesota Heart Health Program. *American Journal of Public Health, 84* (9), 1383–1393.

35. Blissmer, B., Prochaska, J. O., Velicer, W. F., Redding, C. A., Rossi, J. S., Greene, G. W., Paiva, A., & Robbins, M. (2010). Common factors predicting long-term changes in multiple health behaviors. *Journal of Health Psychology, 15,* 205–214.

36. Health Consequences of Smoking (2014).

37. Hunt, W. G. (Ed.). (2007). *Learning Mechanisms in Smoking.* New Brunswick, NJ: Aldine Transaction.

38. Jordan, P. J., Evers, K. E., Spira, J. L., King, L. A., & Lid, V. (2013). *Computerized, tailored interventions improve outcomes and reduce barriers to care.* Poster presented at the 17th Annual International meeting and Exposition of the American Telemedicine Association, Austin, TX.

39. Smith, B., Ryan, M. A., Wingard, D. L., Patterson, T. L., Slymen., D. J., & Macera, C. A. (2008). Cigarette smoking and military deployment: a prospective evaluation. *American Journal of Preventive Medicine, 35,* 339–546. http://dx.doi.org/10.1016/j.amepre.2008.07.009

40. Berrigan, D., Dodd, K., Troiano, R. P., Krebs-Smith, S. M., & Barbash, R. B. (2003). Patterns of health behavior in U.S. adults. *Preventive Medicine, 36* (5), 615–623.

41. Prochaska, J. J., Delucchi, K., & Hall, S. M. (2004). A meta-analysis of smoking cessation interventions with individuals in substance abuse treatment or recovery. *Journal of Consulting and Clinical Psychology, 72,* 1144–1156.

42. Hall, S. M., Tsoh, J. Y., Prochaska, J. J., Eisendroth, S., Rossi, J. S., Redding, C. A., Rosen, A. B., Meisner, M., Humfleet, G. L., & Gorecki, J. A. (2006). Treatment for cigarette smoking among depressed mental health outpatients: A randomized clinical trial. *American Journal of Public Health, 96,* 1808–1814.

43. National Institute on Alcohol Abuse and Alcoholism. Alcohol use disorder. Retrieved from www.niaaa.nih.gov/alcohol-health/overview-alcohol-consumption/alcohol-use-disorders.

44. Stahre, M., Roeber, J., Kanny, D., Brewer, R. D., & Zhang, X. (2014). Contribution of excessive alcohol consumption to deaths and years of potential life lost in the United States. *Preventing Chronic Disease, 11.*

45. Center for Disease Control and Prevention. Fact sheets: Alcohol use and your health. Last updated June 29, 2016. www.cdc.gov/alcohol/fact-sheets/alcohol-use.htm

46. Public Health England. (2014). UK & Ireland Prevalence and Trends. Retrieved from www.noo.org.uk/NOO_about_obesity/adult_obesity/UK_prevalence_and_trends

47. Luepker et al. (1994).

48. Johnson, S. S., Paiva, A. L., Mauriello, L., Prochaska, J. O., Redding, C., & Velicer, W. F. (2014). Coaction in multiple behavior change interventions: Consistency across multiple studies on weight management and obesity prevention. *Health Psychology, 33*(5), 475–80.

49. Prochaska et al. (1992).

50. Basu, S., Yaffe, P., Hills, N., & Lustig, R. H. (2013). The relationship of sugar to population-level diabetes prevalence: An econometric analysis of repeated cross-sectional data. *PLoS One. 8*(2):e57873. doi: 10.1371/journal.pone.0057873. Epub 2013 Feb 27.

51. Personal communication with Geoffrey Greene, professor of Nutrition at the University of Rhode Island.

52. Personal communication with Tony Buffington, professor of Veterinary Medicine, Ohio State University.

53. Wansink, B. (2006). *Mindless Eating.* New York: Random House.

54. Velicer, W. F., Redding, C. A., Paiva, A. L., Mauriello, L., Blissmer, B., Oatley, K., Meier K. S., Babbin S. F., McGee, H., Prochaska, J. O., Burditt, C. & Fernandez, A. C. (2013). Multiple behavior interventions to prevent substance abuse and increase energy balance behaviors in middle school students. *Translational Behavioral Medicine, 3*(1), 82–91.

55. Johnson, S. S., Paiva, A., Cummins, C. O., Johnson, J. L., Dyment, S. J., Wright, J. A., Prochaska, J. O., Prochaska, J. M., & Sherman, K. (2008). Transtheoretical Model-based multiple behavior intervention for weight management effectiveness on a population basis. *Preventive Medicine, 46,* 238–246.

56. Reyes-Guzman, C. M., Bray, R. M., Forman-Hoffman, V. L., & Williams, J. (2015). Overweight and obesity trends among active duty military personnel: A 13-year perspective. *American Journal of Preventive Medicine, 48* (2), 145–153.

57. Yin, H-Q, Prochaska, J. O., Rossi, J. S., Redding, C. A., Paiva, A. L., Blissmer, B., Velicer, W. F., Johnson, S. S. & Kobayashi, H. (2013). Treatment-enhanced paired action contributes substantially to change across multiple health behaviors: Secondary analysis of five randomized trials. *Translational Behavioral Medicine, 3*(1), 62–71. doi:10.1007/513142-013-0193-4

58. Goodchild, A. K., Bokiniec, P., Hassan, S. F., Haynes, P., Parker, L. M., VanderWall, R., Moghaddam, M., & Mirzaei, M. (2015). Molecular changes in the adrenal medulla and brain following glucoprivation. *Autonomic Neuroscience: Basic and Clinical, 192,* 45–46.

59. National Sleep Foundation. How much sleep do we really need? Retrieved from https://sleepfoundation.org/how-sleep-works/how-much-sleep-do-we-really-need

60. Parkinson, C. N. (1958). *Parkinson's Law.* London: John Murray.

61. Fredrickson, B. L. (2009). *Positivity.* New York: Random House.

62. Ibid.

63. Kahneman, D., & Deaton, A. (2010, September 1). High income improves evaluation of life but not emotional well-being. *Proceedings of the National Academy of Sciences of the United States of America 107*(38). doi: 10.1073/pnas.1011492107

64. Chatzky, J. (2004). *Pay It Down!* New York: Penguin Group.

65. Jamiesko, M. (2015, April 14). American spending on dining out overtook grocery sales for the first time ever. *Bloomberg Business.* Retrieved from www.bloomberg .com/news/articles/2015-04-14/americans-spending-on-dining-out-just-overtook -grocery-sales-for-the-first-time-ever.

66. Buettner, D. (2008). *The Blue Zones.* Washington, DC: National Geographic Society.

67. Cantril, H. (1965). *The Pattern of Human Concerns.* New Brunswick, NJ: Rutgers University Press.

About the Authors

James O. Prochaska, PhD, is one of the most preeminent clinical psychologists and was named one of the five most influential authors in psychology by the Institute for Scientific Information and the American Psychological Society. Dr. Prochaska is one of the originators of the Transtheoretical Model of Behavior Change and the author of more than 400 papers on behavior change for health promotion and disease prevention.

He has served as principal investigator on more than $80 million in research grants on the prevention of cancer and other chronic diseases and has received numerous honors, including major awards from the American Psychological Association, the Society for Prospective Medicine, and Harvard University.

The first psychologist to win a Medal of Honor for Clinical Research from the American Cancer Society, Dr. Prochaska has also received both an Innovators Award and an Innovators Combating Substance Abuse Award from the Robert Wood Johnson Foundation, as well as the Healthtrac Foundation Education Award.

He serves as director of the Cancer Prevention Research Center and professor of Psychology at the University of Rhode Island and is a consultant to Pro-Change Behavior Systems, Inc. which he cofounded in 1997. He is the author of *Systems of Psychotherapy, The Transtheoretical Approach: Crossing Traditional Boundaries of Therapy,* and *Changing for Good.*

Dr. Prochaska earned his PhD in clinical psychology at Wayne State University.

Janice M. Prochaska, PhD, is a cofounder and consultant to Pro-Change Behavior Systems, Inc. and holds an adjunct faculty position at the University of Rhode Island. She earned her master's degree in social work from Wayne State University and her PhD in social work administration and policy from Boston College, and she is one of the most widely published in her field. Her collaborations include applying the Transtheoretical Model to cutting-edge issues, such as simultaneously reducing multiple risk behaviors and enhancing multiple domains of well-being; promoting healthy weight management in children and adults; preventing bullying; keeping individuals out of trouble with the law; helping people be proactive in their health care; enhancing financial well-being; and advancing careers of women scientists.

James and Janice live among the redwoods in Mill Valley, California, near their children and grandchildren. They celebrated their fiftieth wedding anniversary in 2016. Readers can keep up with their events, presentations, and publications through their website www.jprochaska.com

About Hazelden Publishing

As part of the Hazelden Betty Ford Foundation, Hazelden Publishing offers both cutting-edge educational resources and inspirational books. Our print and digital works help guide individuals in treatment and recovery, and their loved ones. Professionals who work to prevent and treat addiction also turn to Hazelden Publishing for evidence-based curricula, digital content solutions, and videos for use in schools, treatment programs, correctional programs, and electronic health records systems. We also offer training for implementation of our curricula.

Through published and digital works, Hazelden Publishing extends the reach of healing and hope to individuals, families, and communities affected by addiction and related issues.

For more information about Hazelden publications,
please call **800-328-9000**
or visit us online at **hazelden.org/bookstore.**

OTHER TITLES THAT MAY INTEREST YOU

The Next Happy
Let Go of the Life You Planned and Find a New Way Forward
TRACEY CLEANTIS

When the best option is to let go of the life you planned for yourself and find a new path, a world of possibilities can surprisingly open up. Learn whether it is time to let go, and if so, how to move through your grief and find your way forward in *The Next Happy*.

Order No. 7768, also available as an e-book

The Gifts of Imperfection
Let Go of Who You Think You're Supposed to Be
and Embrace Who You Are
BRENÉ BROWN, PHD, LMSW

This New York Times best-seller by Brené Brown, a leading expert on shame, blends original research with honest storytelling and helps readers move from "What will people think?" to "I am enough."

Order No. 2545, also available as an e-book

Do You Really Get Me?
Finding Value in Yourself and Others through Empathy
and Connection
JOSEPH SHRAND, MD

Through his I-Maximum Approach, Dr. Shrand helps readers learn how to set aside self-doubt, show others they are valued, and make more meaningful connections.

Order No. 7408, also available as an e-book

For more information or to order these or other resources from Hazelden Publishing, call 800-328-9000 or visit hazelden.org/bookstore.